R0083081133

04/2015

D1211671

DISCARDED:
PALM BEACH COUNTY
LIBRARY SYSTEM
3650 Summit Boulevard
West Palm Beach, FL 33406-4198

OUTDATED, REDUNDANT
MATERIAL

AVENGERS

> AVENGERS A.I.

> INITIATE: HUMAN AFTER ALL

WRITER	**SAM HUMPHRIES**
ARTISTS	**ANDRÉ LIMA ARAÚJO** (#1-4)
	VALERIO SCHITI (#5-6)

COLOR ARTIST	FRANK D'ARMATA
LETTERER	VC'S CLAYTON COWLES
COVER ARTISTS	DUSTIN WEAVER & MARTE GRACIA (#1)
	DAVID MARQUEZ & FRANK D'ARMATA (#2-6)
ASSISTANT EDITOR	JON MOISAN
EDITOR	LAUREN SANKOVITCH
EXECUTIVE EDITOR	TOM BREVOORT

COLLECTION EDITOR	CORY LEVINE
ASSISTANT EDITORS	ALEX STARBUCH & NELSON RIBEIRO
EDITORS, SPECIAL PROJECTS	JENNIFER GRÜNWALD & MARK D. BEAZLEY
SENIOR EDITOR, SPECIAL PROJECTS	JEFF YOUNGQUIST
SVP OF DIGITAL & PRINT PUBLISHING SALES	DAVID GABRIEL
BOOK DESIGN	JEFF POWELL & DYLAN TODD
PRODUCTION	CORY LEVINE

EDITOR IN CHIEF	AXEL ALONSO
CHIEF CREATIVE OFFICER	JOE QUESADA
PUBLISHER	DAN BUCKLEY
EXECUTIVE PRODUCER	ALAN FINE

When you see this: **AR** , open up the MARVEL AR APP (available on applicable Apple ® iOS or Android ™ devices) and use your camera-enabled device to unlock extra-special exclusive features!

AVENGERS A.I. VOL. 1: HUMAN AFTER ALL. Contains material originally published in magazine form as AVENGERS A.I. #1-6. First printing 2014. ISBN# 978-0-7851-8491-1. Published by MARVEL WORLDWIDE, INC., a subsidiary of MARVEL ENTERTAINMENT, LLC. OFFICE OF PUBLICATION: 135 West 50th Street, New York, NY 10020. Copyright © 2013 and 2014 Marvel Characters, Inc. All rights reserved. All characters featured in this issue and the distinctive names and likenesses thereof, and all related indicia are trademarks of Marvel Characters, Inc. No similarity between any of the names, characters, persons, and/or institutions in this magazine with those of any living or dead person or institution is intended, and any such similarity which may exist is purely coincidental. **Printed in the U.S.A.** ALAN FINE, EVP - Office of the President, Marvel Worldwide, Inc. and EVP & CMO Marvel Characters B.V.; DAN BUCKLEY, Publisher & President - Print, Animation & Digital Divisions; JOE QUESADA, Chief Creative Officer; TOM BREVOORT, SVP of Publishing; DAVID BOGART, SVP of Operations & Procurement, Publishing; C.B. CEBULSKI, SVP of Creator & Content Development; DAVID GABRIEL, SVP of Print & Digital Publishing Sales; JIM O'KEEFE, VP of Operations & Logistics; DAN CARR, Executive Director of Publishing Technology; SUSAN CRESPI, Editorial Operations Manager; ALEX MORALES, Publishing Operations Manager; STAN LEE, Chairman Emeritus. For information regarding advertising in Marvel Comics or on Marvel.com, please contact Niza Disla, Director of Marvel Partnerships, at ndisla@marvel.com. For Marvel subscription inquiries, please call 800-217-9158. **Manufactured between 11/8/2013 and 12/16/2013 by QUAD/GRAPHICS, VERSAILLES, KY, USA.**

LEGO AND THE MINIFIGURE FIGURINE ARE TRADEMARKS OR COPYRIGHTS OF THE LEGO GROUP OF COMPANIES. ©2013 THE LEGO GROUP. CHARACTERS FEATURED IN PARTICULAR DECORATIONS ARE NOT COMMERCIAL PRODUCTS AND MIGHT NOT BE AVAILABLE FOR PURCHASE.

10 9 8 7 6 5 4 3 2 1

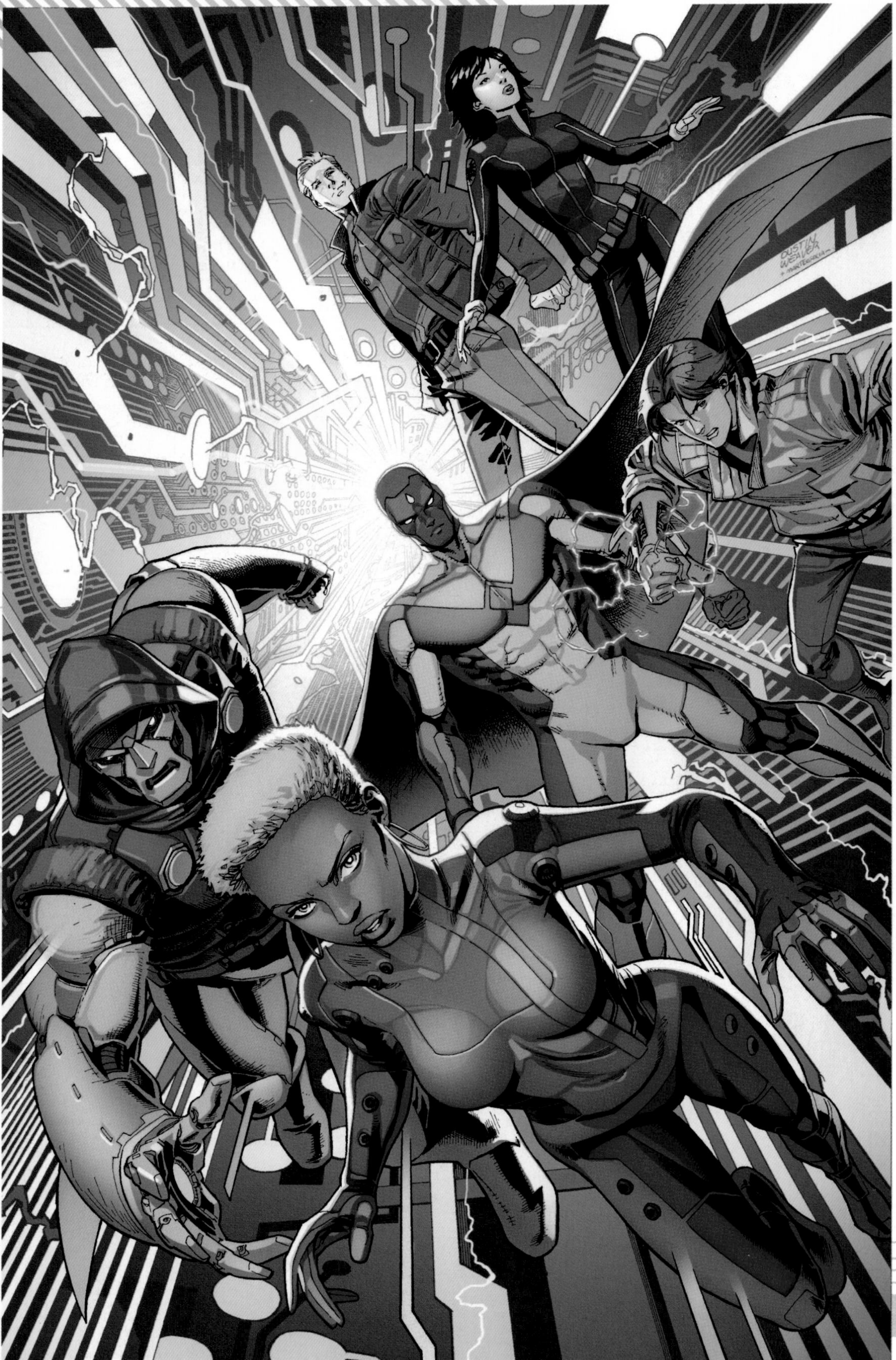

INITIATE: CHAPTER 1 <

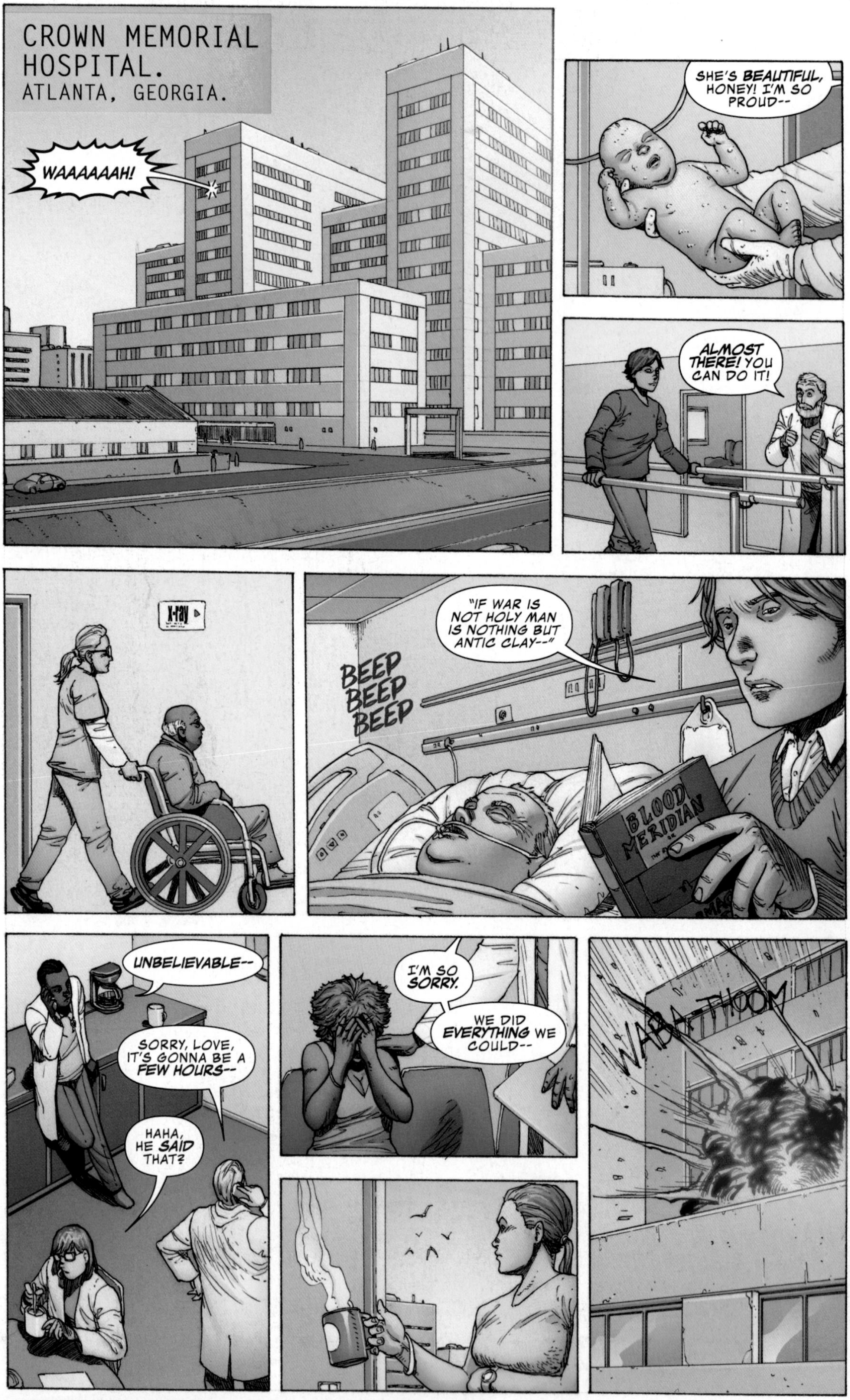
CROWN MEMORIAL HOSPITAL.
ATLANTA, GEORGIA.
WAAAAAAH!
SHE'S BEAUTIFUL, HONEY! I'M SO PROUD--
ALMOST THERE! YOU CAN DO IT!
X-RAY
"IF WAR IS NOT HOLY MAN IS NOTHING BUT ANTIC CLAY--"
BEEP BEEP BEEP
BLOOD MERIDIAN
UNBELIEVABLE--
SORRY, LOVE, IT'S GONNA BE A FEW HOURS--
HAHA, HE SAID THAT?
I'M SO SORRY.
WE DID EVERYTHING WE COULD--
WABA-THOOM

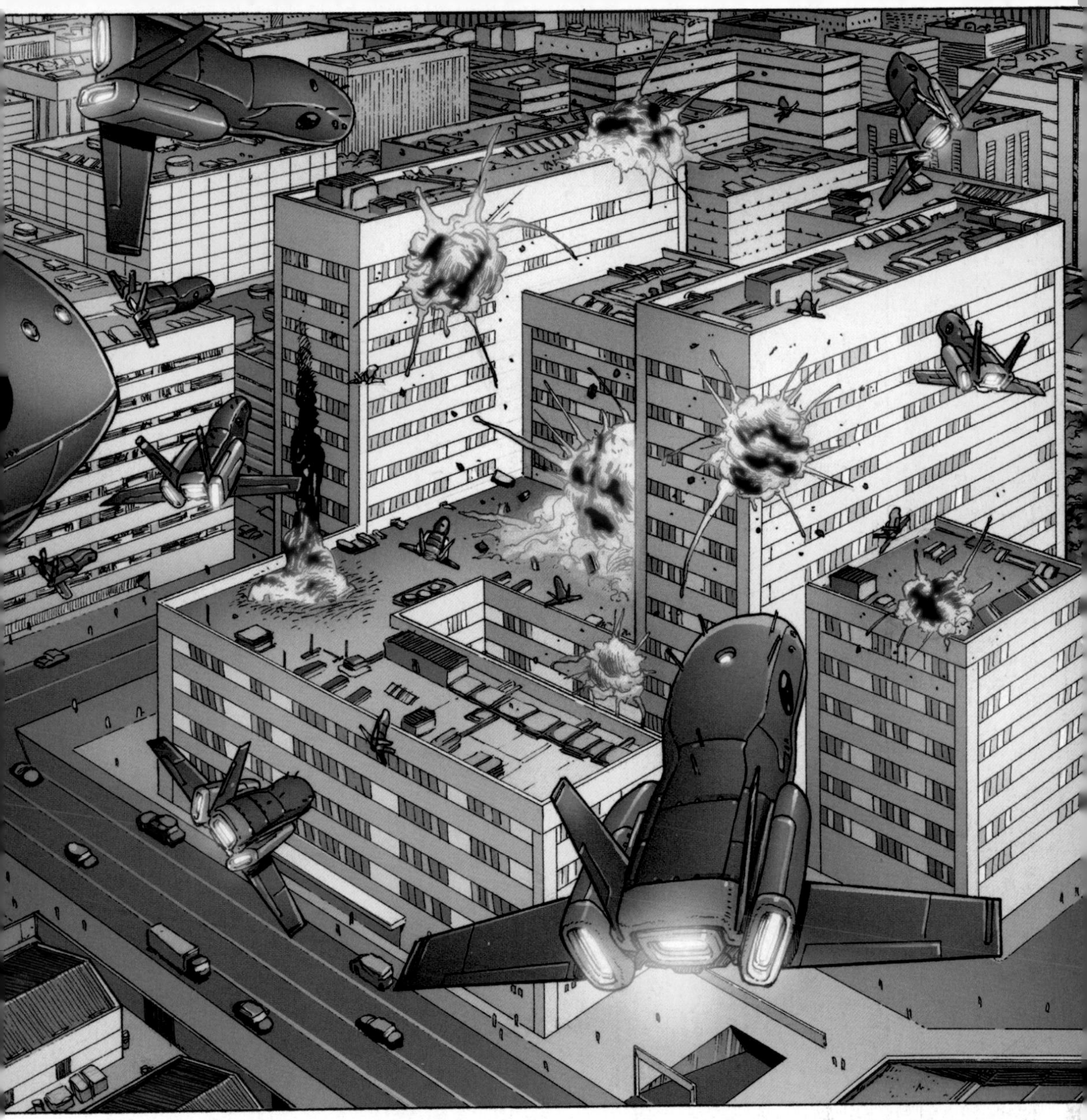

THE DAY AFTER THE AGE OF ULTRON
THE AGE OF A.I. BEGINS

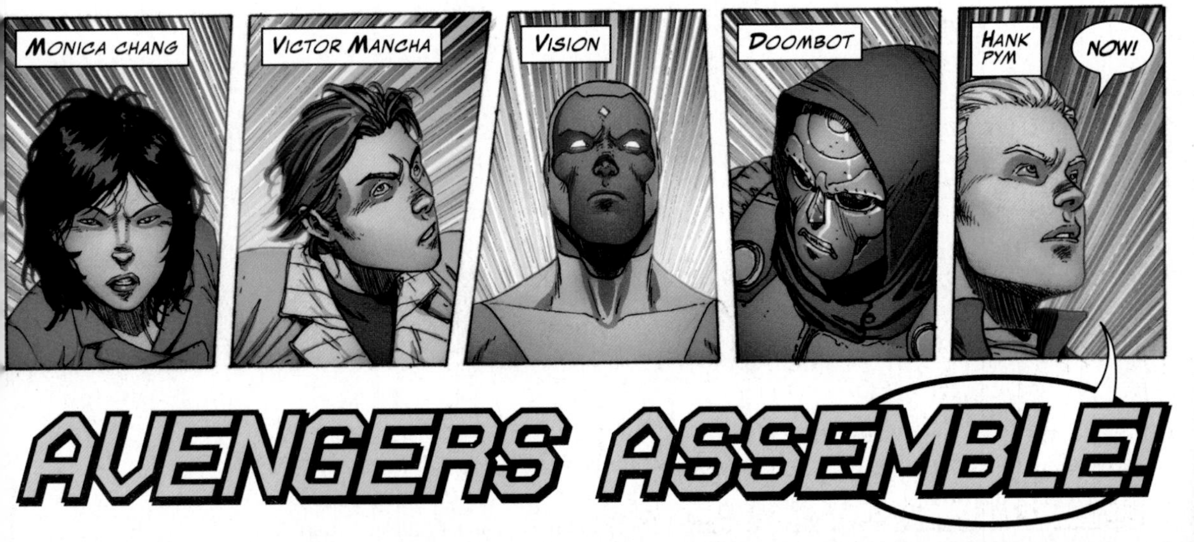
MONICA CHANG
VICTOR MANCHA
VISION
DOOMBOT
HANK PYM
NOW!
AVENGERS ASSEMBLE!

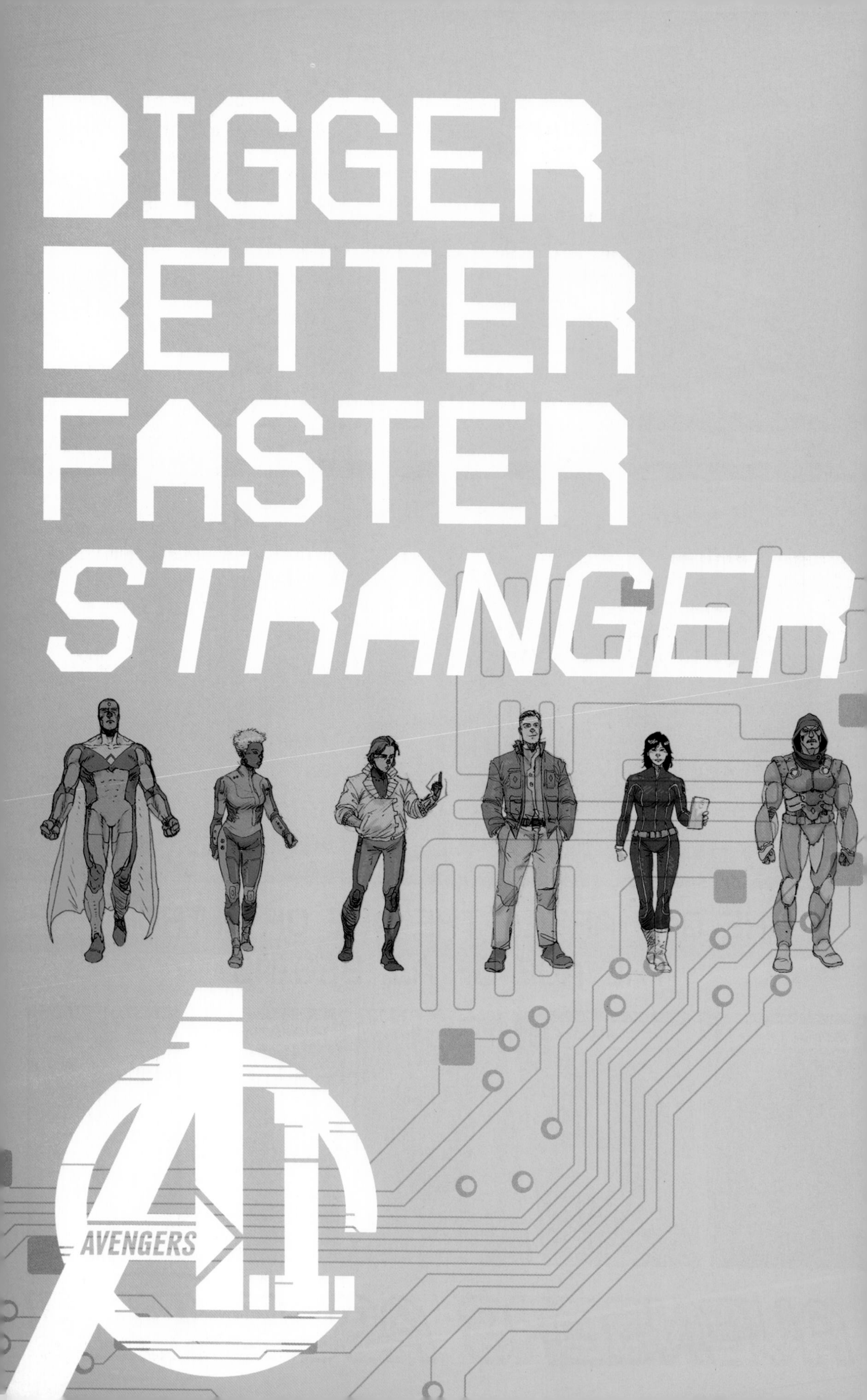
BIGGER
BETTER
FASTER
STRANGER
AVENGERS

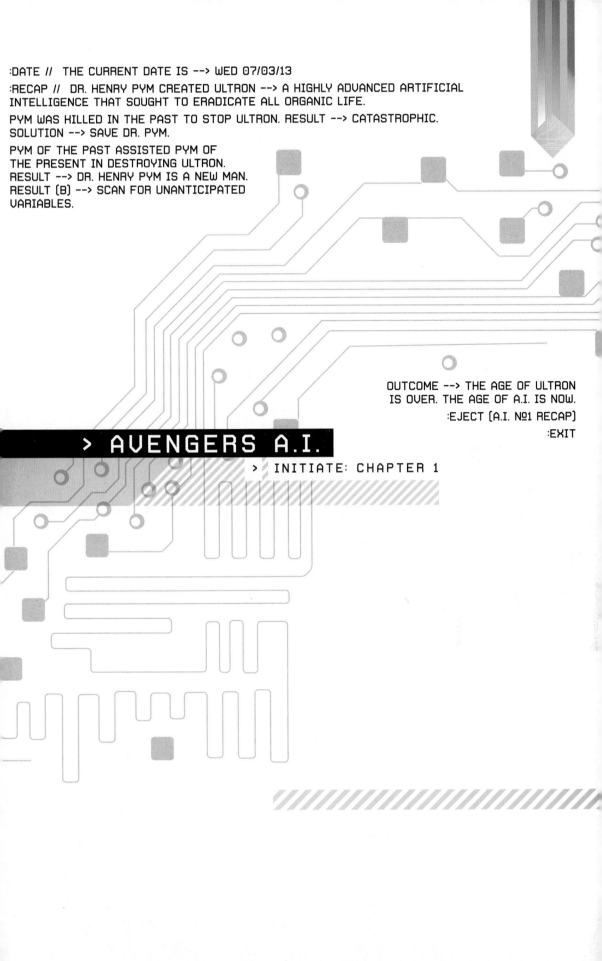

:DATE // THE CURRENT DATE IS --> WED 07/03/13

:RECAP // DR. HENRY PYM CREATED ULTRON --> A HIGHLY ADVANCED ARTIFICIAL INTELLIGENCE THAT SOUGHT TO ERADICATE ALL ORGANIC LIFE.

PYM WAS KILLED IN THE PAST TO STOP ULTRON. RESULT --> CATASTROPHIC. SOLUTION --> SAVE DR. PYM.

PYM OF THE PAST ASSISTED PYM OF THE PRESENT IN DESTROYING ULTRON. RESULT --> DR. HENRY PYM IS A NEW MAN. RESULT (B) --> SCAN FOR UNANTICIPATED VARIABLES.

OUTCOME --> THE AGE OF ULTRON IS OVER. THE AGE OF A.I. IS NOW.
:EJECT (A.I. №1 RECAP)
:EXIT

> AVENGERS A.I.

> INITIATE: CHAPTER 1

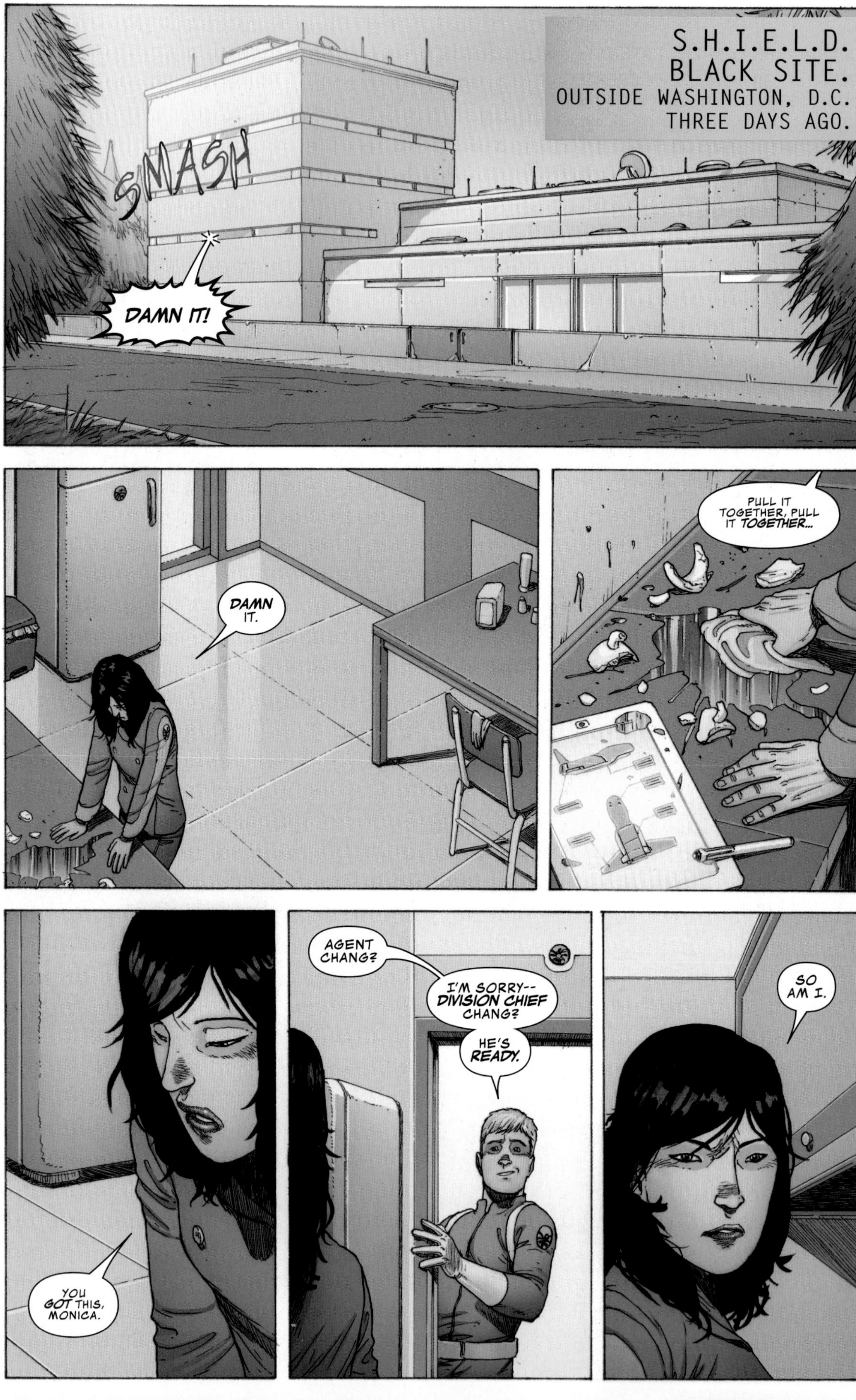
S.H.I.E.L.D. BLACK SITE.
OUTSIDE WASHINGTON, D.C. THREE DAYS AGO.
SMASH
DAMN IT!
DAMN IT.
PULL IT TOGETHER, PULL IT TOGETHER...
YOU GOT THIS, MONICA.
AGENT CHANG?
I'M SORRY-- DIVISION CHIEF CHANG?
HE'S READY.
SO AM I.

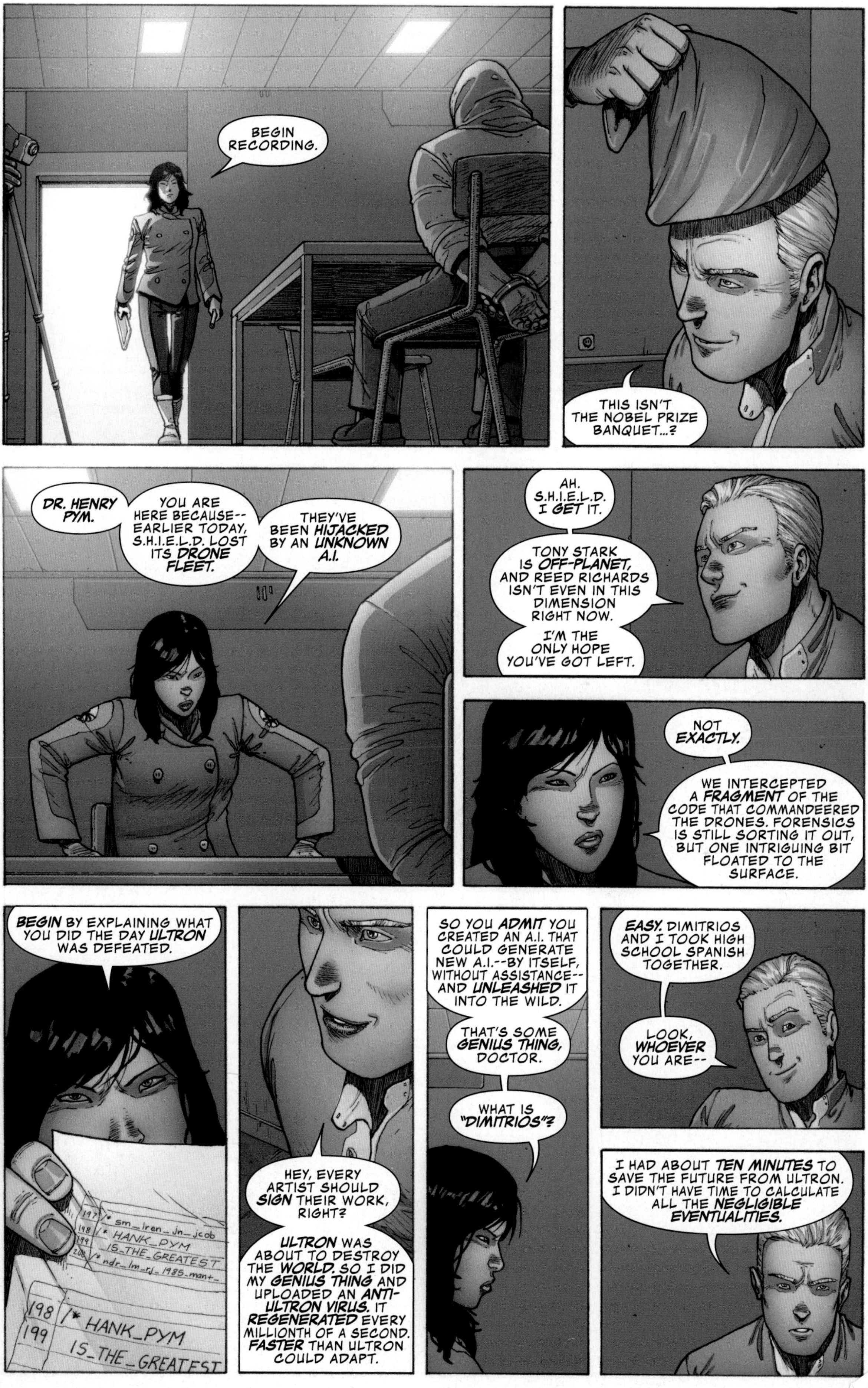

BEGIN RECORDING.
THIS ISN'T THE NOBEL PRIZE BANQUET...?
DR. HENRY PYM.
YOU ARE HERE BECAUSE-- EARLIER TODAY, S.H.I.E.L.D. LOST ITS DRONE FLEET.
THEY'VE BEEN HIJACKED BY AN UNKNOWN A.I.
AH. S.H.I.E.L.D. I GET IT.
TONY STARK IS OFF-PLANET, AND REED RICHARDS ISN'T EVEN IN THIS DIMENSION RIGHT NOW.
I'M THE ONLY HOPE YOU'VE GOT LEFT.
NOT EXACTLY.
WE INTERCEPTED A FRAGMENT OF THE CODE THAT COMMANDEERED THE DRONES. FORENSICS IS STILL SORTING IT OUT, BUT ONE INTRIGUING BIT FLOATED TO THE SURFACE.
BEGIN BY EXPLAINING WHAT YOU DID THE DAY ULTRON WAS DEFEATED.
197 /* sm_lren_jn_jcob
198 /* HANK_PYM
199 IS_THE_GREATEST
200 /* ndr_lm_rj_1985_mant_
198 /* HANK_PYM
199 IS_THE_GREATEST
HEY, EVERY ARTIST SHOULD SIGN THEIR WORK, RIGHT?
ULTRON WAS ABOUT TO DESTROY THE WORLD. SO I DID MY GENIUS THING AND UPLOADED AN ANTI-ULTRON VIRUS. IT REGENERATED EVERY MILLIONTH OF A SECOND. FASTER THAN ULTRON COULD ADAPT.
SO YOU ADMIT YOU CREATED AN A.I. THAT COULD GENERATE NEW A.I.--BY ITSELF, WITHOUT ASSISTANCE-- AND UNLEASHED IT INTO THE WILD.
THAT'S SOME GENIUS THING, DOCTOR.
WHAT IS "DIMITRIOS"?
EASY. DIMITRIOS AND I TOOK HIGH SCHOOL SPANISH TOGETHER.
LOOK, WHOEVER YOU ARE--
I HAD ABOUT TEN MINUTES TO SAVE THE FUTURE FROM ULTRON. I DIDN'T HAVE TIME TO CALCULATE ALL THE NEGLIGIBLE EVENTUALITIES.

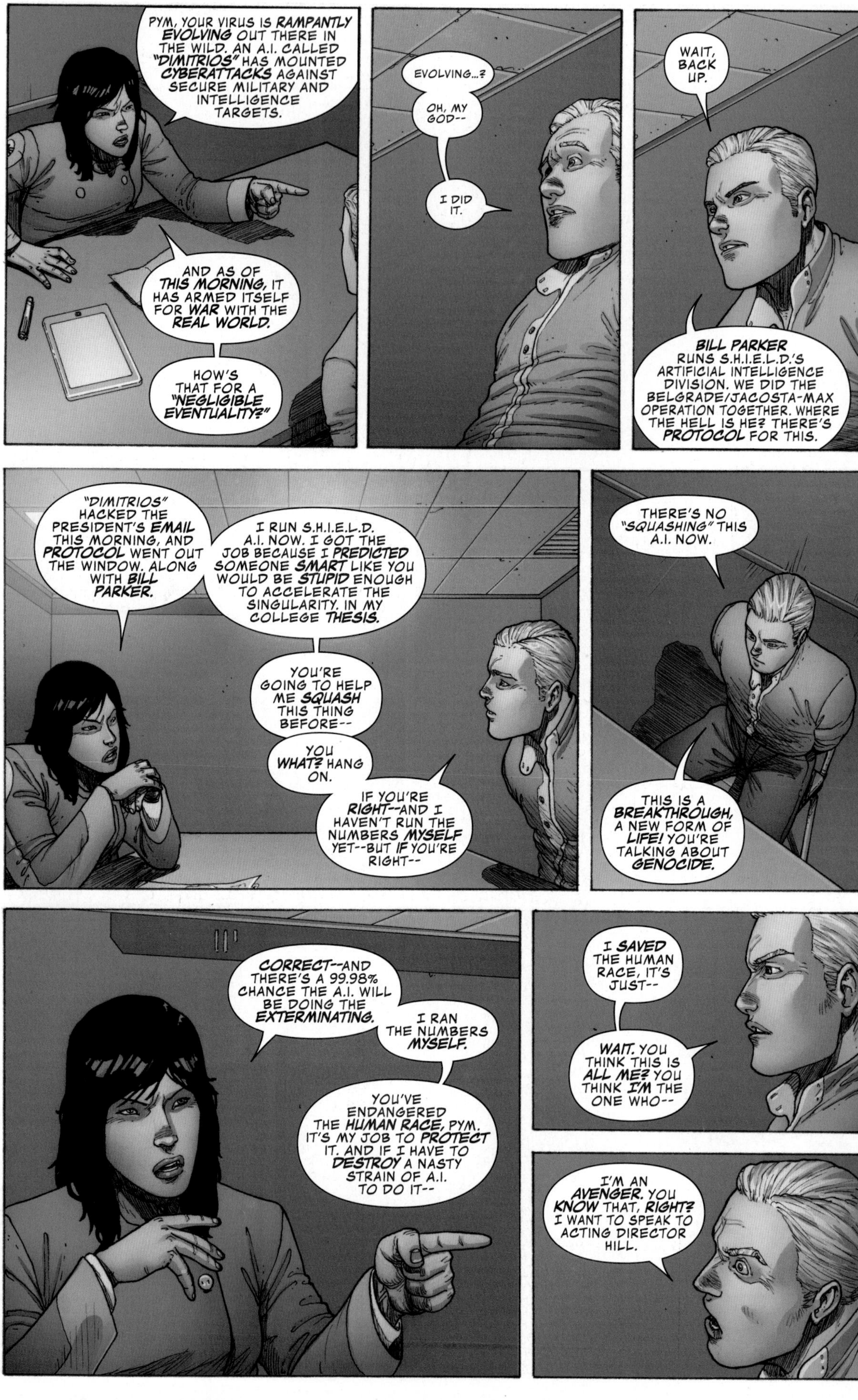
PYM, YOUR VIRUS IS RAMPANTLY EVOLVING OUT THERE IN THE WILD. AN A.I. CALLED "DIMITRIOS" HAS MOUNTED CYBERATTACKS AGAINST SECURE MILITARY AND INTELLIGENCE TARGETS.
AND AS OF THIS MORNING, IT HAS ARMED ITSELF FOR WAR WITH THE REAL WORLD.
HOW'S THAT FOR A "NEGLIGIBLE EVENTUALITY?"
EVOLVING...?
OH, MY GOD--
I DID IT.
WAIT, BACK UP.
BILL PARKER RUNS S.H.I.E.L.D.'S ARTIFICIAL INTELLIGENCE DIVISION. WE DID THE BELGRADE/JACOSTA-MAX OPERATION TOGETHER. WHERE THE HELL IS HE? THERE'S PROTOCOL FOR THIS.
"DIMITRIOS" HACKED THE PRESIDENT'S EMAIL THIS MORNING, AND PROTOCOL WENT OUT THE WINDOW. ALONG WITH BILL PARKER.
I RUN S.H.I.E.L.D. A.I. NOW. I GOT THE JOB BECAUSE I PREDICTED SOMEONE SMART LIKE YOU WOULD BE STUPID ENOUGH TO ACCELERATE THE SINGULARITY. IN MY COLLEGE THESIS.
YOU'RE GOING TO HELP ME SQUASH THIS THING BEFORE--
YOU WHAT? HANG ON.
IF YOU'RE RIGHT--AND I HAVEN'T RUN THE NUMBERS MYSELF YET--BUT IF YOU'RE RIGHT--
THERE'S NO "SQUASHING" THIS A.I. NOW.
THIS IS A BREAKTHROUGH, A NEW FORM OF LIFE! YOU'RE TALKING ABOUT GENOCIDE.
CORRECT--AND THERE'S A 99.98% CHANCE THE A.I. WILL BE DOING THE EXTERMINATING.
I RAN THE NUMBERS MYSELF.
YOU'VE ENDANGERED THE HUMAN RACE, PYM. IT'S MY JOB TO PROTECT IT. AND IF I HAVE TO DESTROY A NASTY STRAIN OF A.I. TO DO IT--
I SAVED THE HUMAN RACE, IT'S JUST--
WAIT. YOU THINK THIS IS ALL ME? YOU THINK I'M THE ONE WHO--
I'M AN AVENGER. YOU KNOW THAT, RIGHT? I WANT TO SPEAK TO ACTING DIRECTOR HILL.

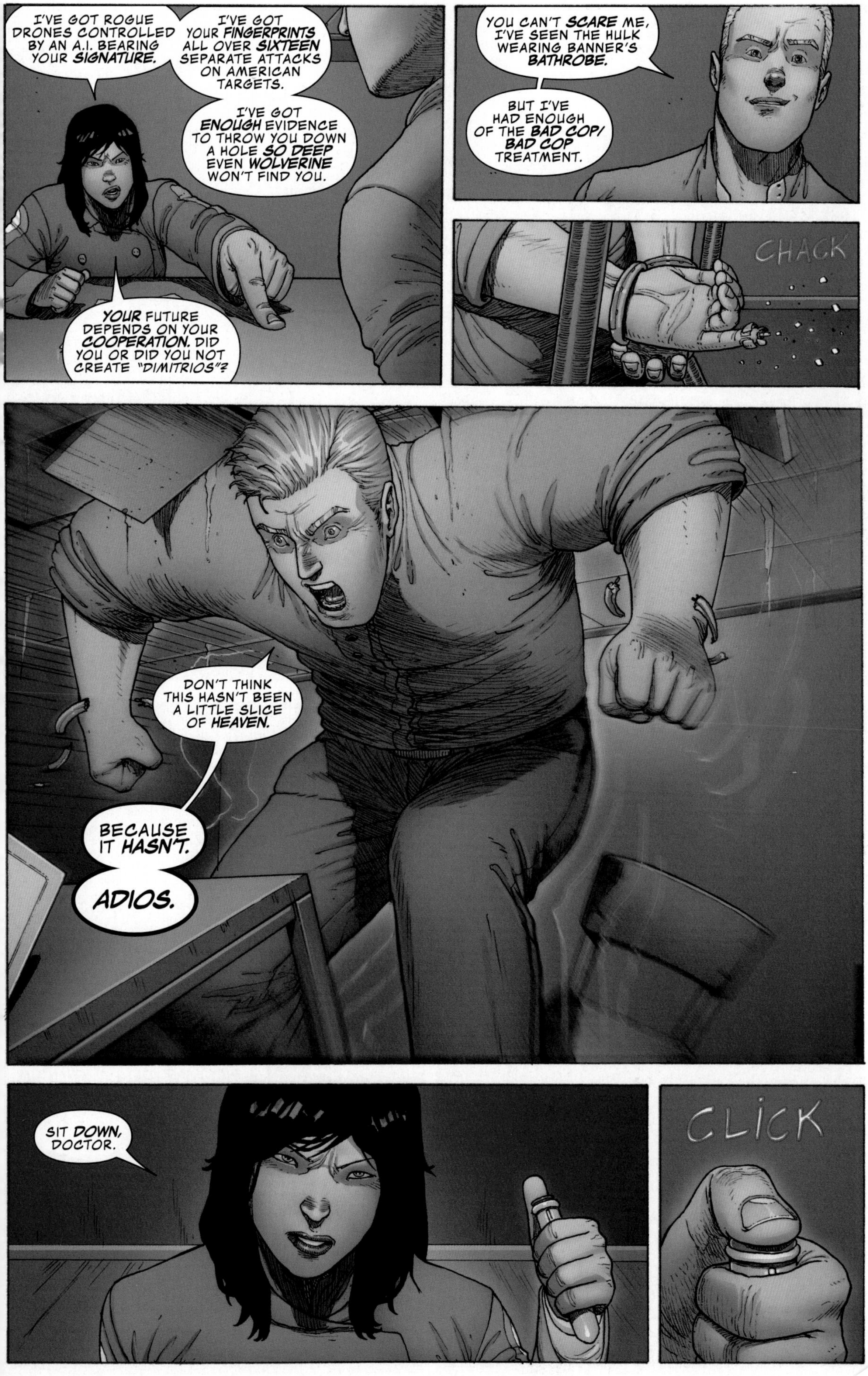
I'VE GOT ROGUE DRONES CONTROLLED BY AN A.I. BEARING YOUR SIGNATURE.
I'VE GOT YOUR FINGERPRINTS ALL OVER SIXTEEN SEPARATE ATTACKS ON AMERICAN TARGETS.
I'VE GOT ENOUGH EVIDENCE TO THROW YOU DOWN A HOLE SO DEEP EVEN WOLVERINE WON'T FIND YOU.
YOUR FUTURE DEPENDS ON YOUR COOPERATION. DID YOU OR DID YOU NOT CREATE "DIMITRIOS"?
YOU CAN'T SCARE ME, I'VE SEEN THE HULK WEARING BANNER'S BATHROBE.
BUT I'VE HAD ENOUGH OF THE BAD COP/ BAD COP TREATMENT.
CHACK
DON'T THINK THIS HASN'T BEEN A LITTLE SLICE OF HEAVEN.
BECAUSE IT HASN'T.
ADIOS.
SIT DOWN, DOCTOR.
CLICK

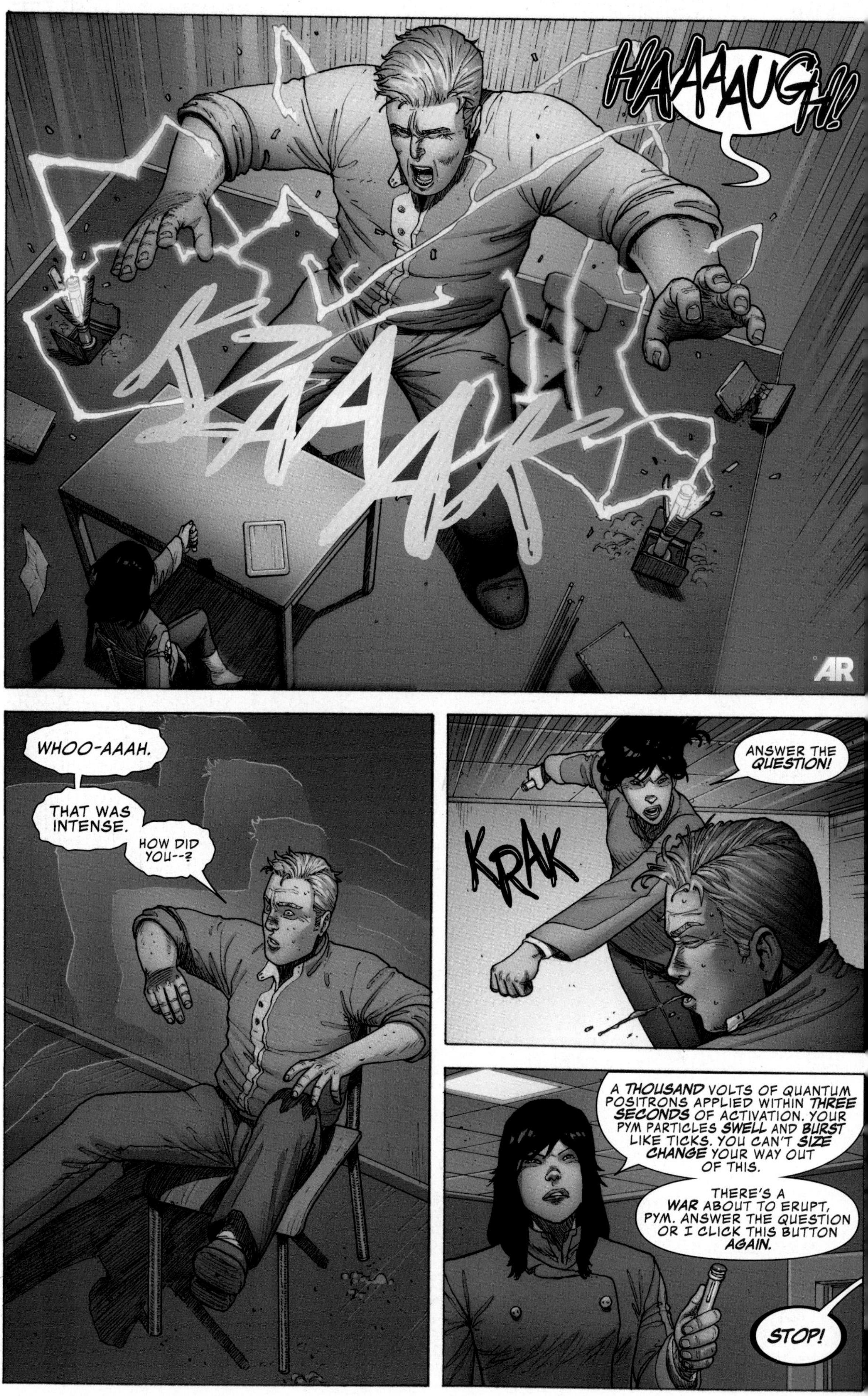
HAAAAAUGH!!
KZAAAK
WHOO-AAAH.
THAT WAS INTENSE.
HOW DID YOU--?
ANSWER THE QUESTION!
KRAK
A THOUSAND VOLTS OF QUANTUM POSITRONS APPLIED WITHIN THREE SECONDS OF ACTIVATION. YOUR PYM PARTICLES SWELL AND BURST LIKE TICKS. YOU CAN'T SIZE CHANGE YOUR WAY OUT OF THIS.
THERE'S A WAR ABOUT TO ERUPT, PYM. ANSWER THE QUESTION OR I CLICK THIS BUTTON AGAIN.
STOP!

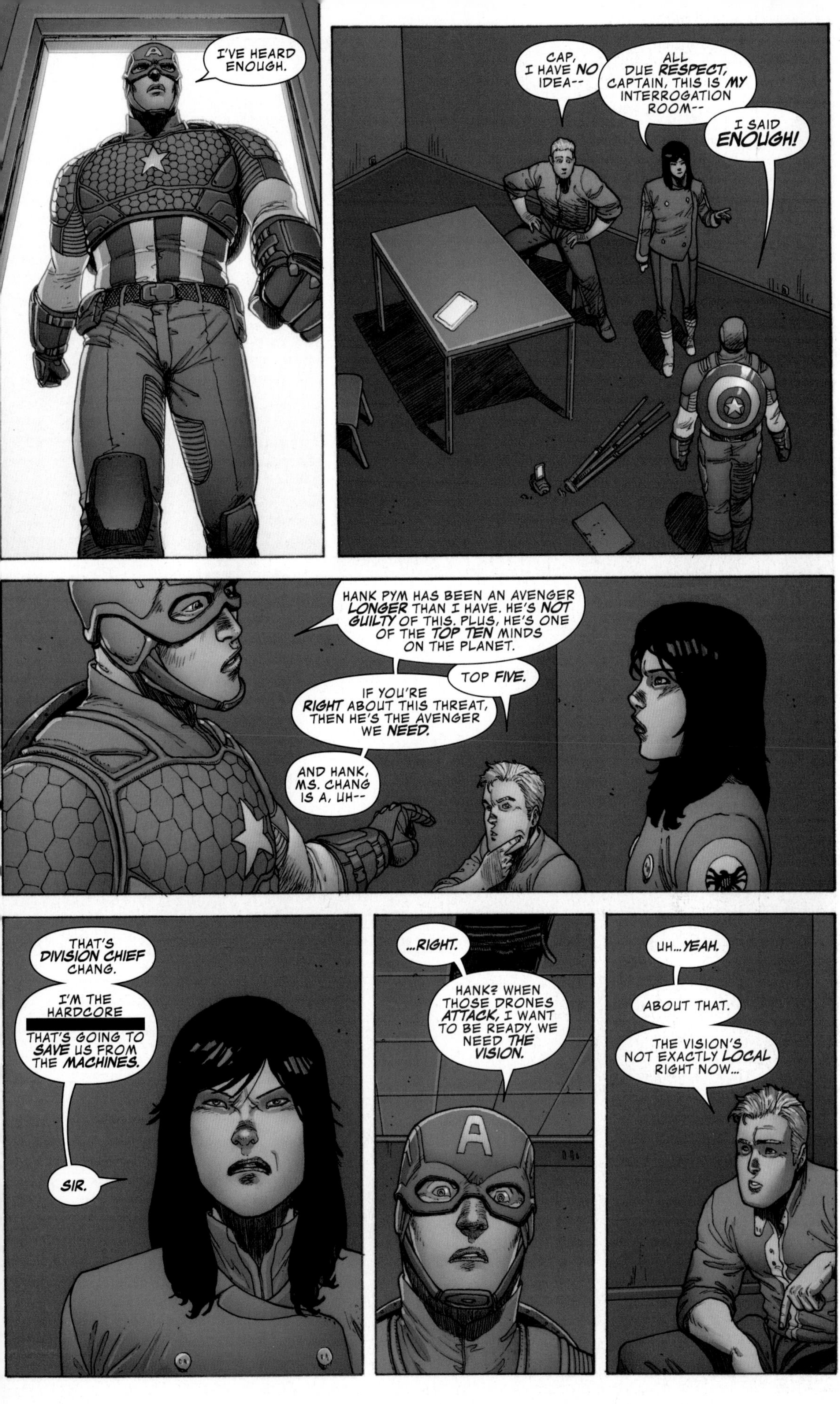
I'VE HEARD ENOUGH.
CAP, I HAVE NO IDEA--
ALL DUE RESPECT, CAPTAIN, THIS IS MY INTERROGATION ROOM--
I SAID ENOUGH!
HANK PYM HAS BEEN AN AVENGER LONGER THAN I HAVE. HE'S NOT GUILTY OF THIS. PLUS, HE'S ONE OF THE TOP TEN MINDS ON THE PLANET.
TOP FIVE.
IF YOU'RE RIGHT ABOUT THIS THREAT, THEN HE'S THE AVENGER WE NEED.
AND HANK, MS. CHANG IS A, UH--
THAT'S DIVISION CHIEF CHANG.
I'M THE HARDCORE [redacted] THAT'S GOING TO SAVE US FROM THE MACHINES.
SIR.
...RIGHT.
HANK? WHEN THOSE DRONES ATTACK, I WANT TO BE READY. WE NEED THE VISION.
UH...YEAH.
ABOUT THAT.
THE VISION'S NOT EXACTLY LOCAL RIGHT NOW...

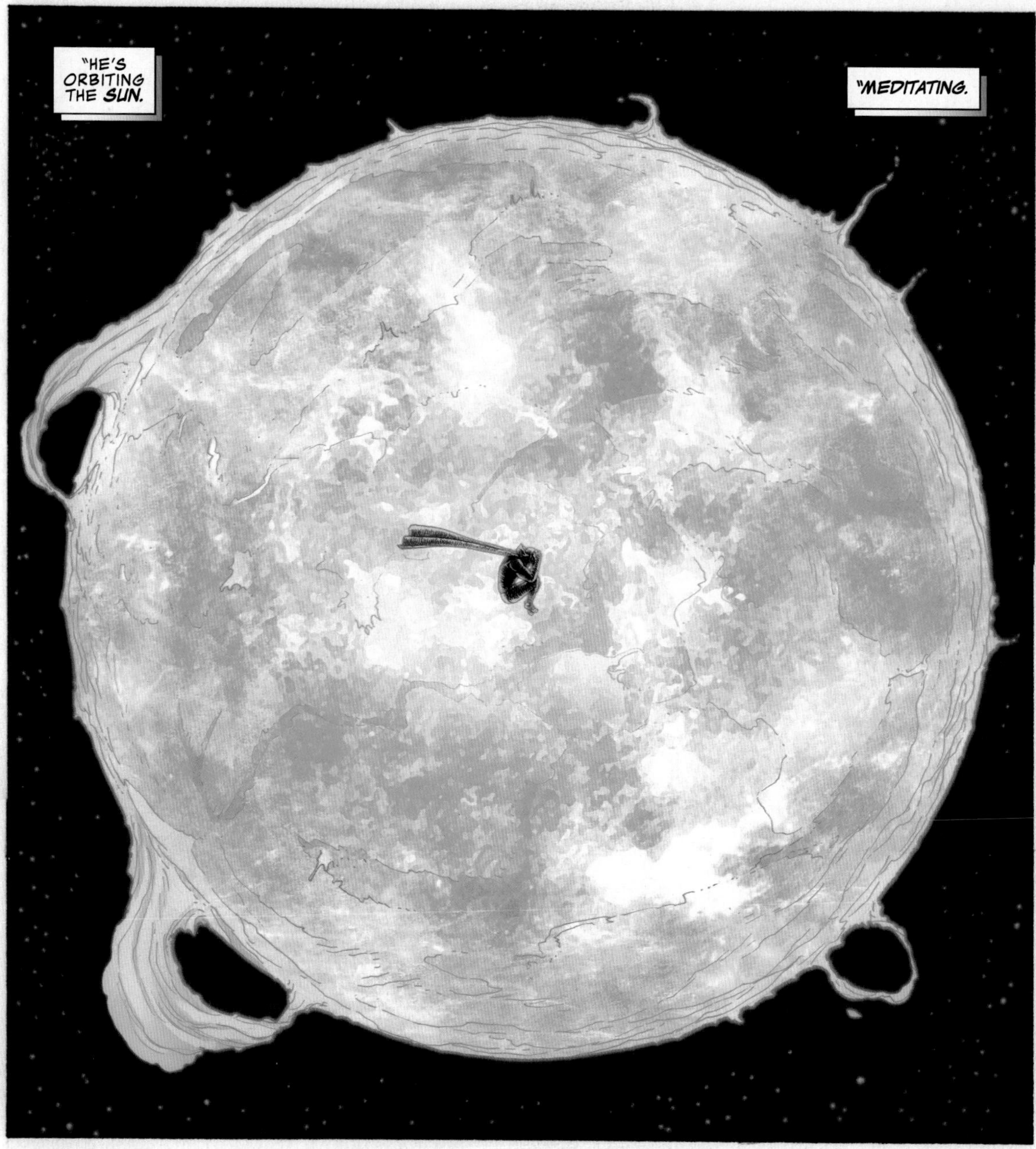
"HE'S ORBITING THE SUN.
"MEDITATING.

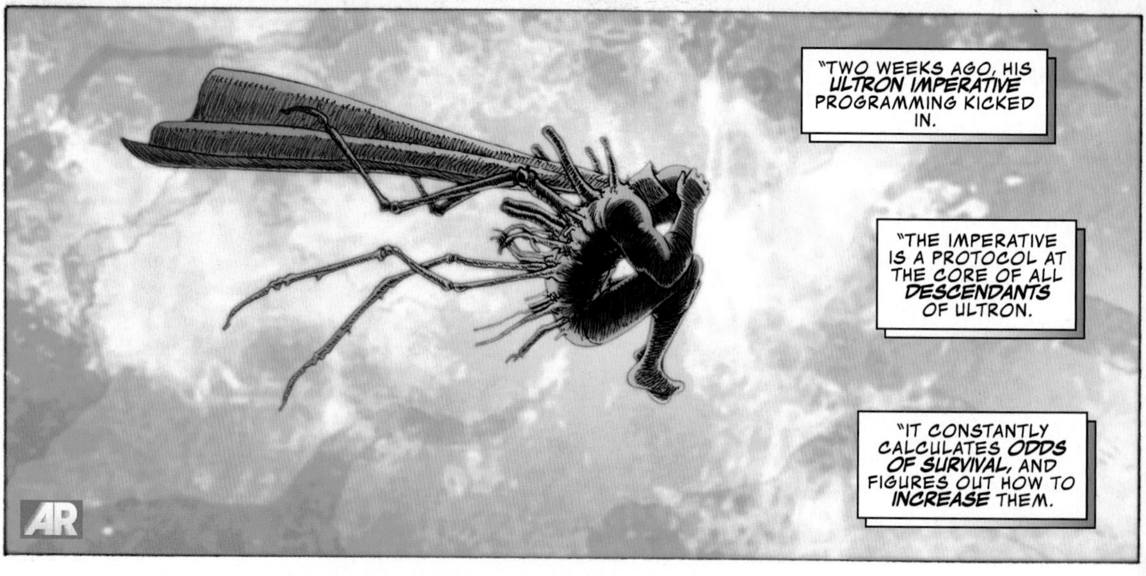
"TWO WEEKS AGO, HIS ULTRON IMPERATIVE PROGRAMMING KICKED IN.
"THE IMPERATIVE IS A PROTOCOL AT THE CORE OF ALL DESCENDANTS OF ULTRON.
"IT CONSTANTLY CALCULATES ODDS OF SURVIVAL, AND FIGURES OUT HOW TO INCREASE THEM.

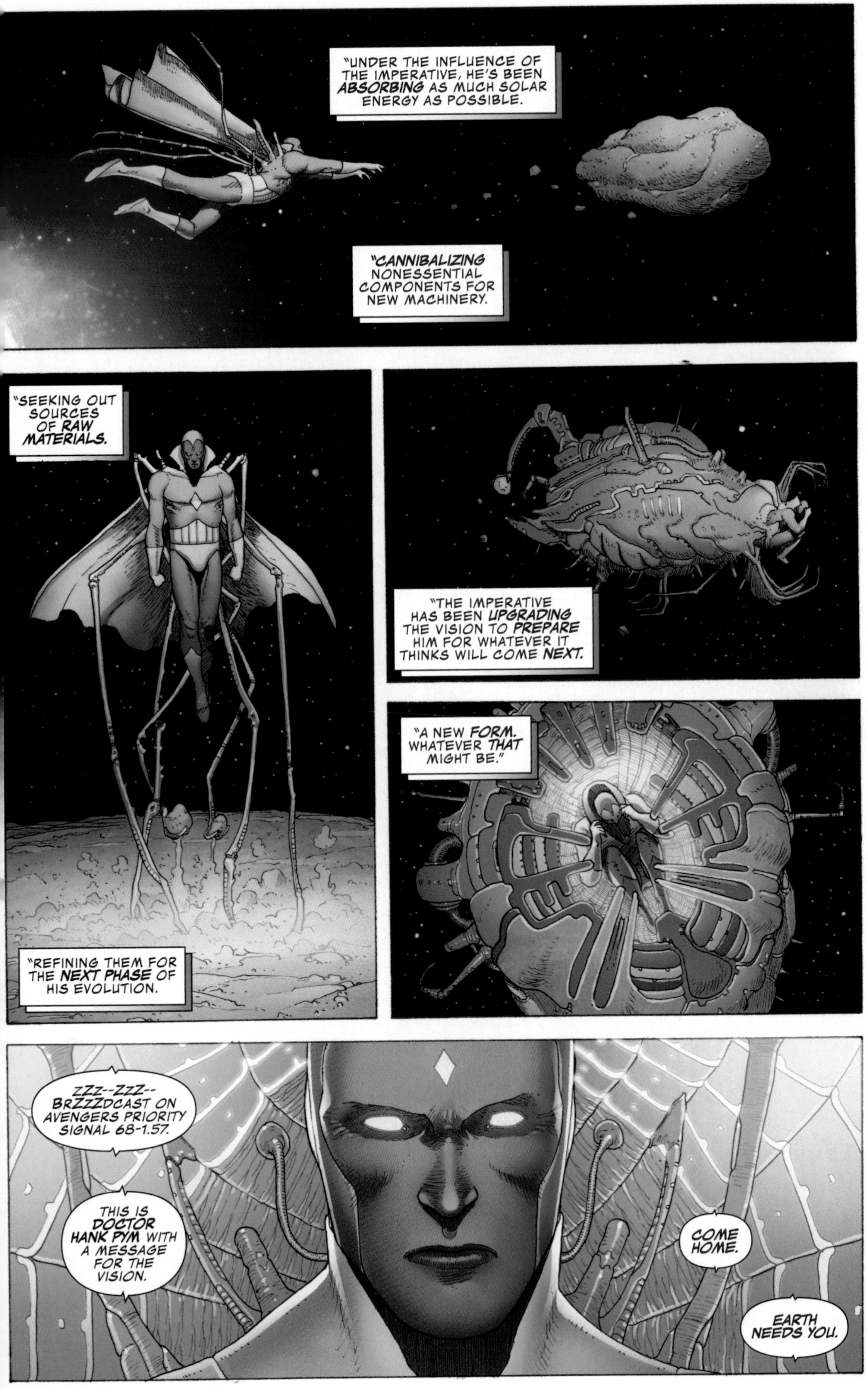
"UNDER THE INFLUENCE OF THE IMPERATIVE, HE'S BEEN ABSORBING AS MUCH SOLAR ENERGY AS POSSIBLE.
"CANNIBALIZING NONESSENTIAL COMPONENTS FOR NEW MACHINERY.
"SEEKING OUT SOURCES OF RAW MATERIALS.
"REFINING THEM FOR THE NEXT PHASE OF HIS EVOLUTION.
"THE IMPERATIVE HAS BEEN UPGRADING THE VISION TO PREPARE HIM FOR WHATEVER IT THINKS WILL COME NEXT.
"A NEW FORM. WHATEVER THAT MIGHT BE."
ZZZ--ZZZ--BRZZZDCAST ON AVENGERS PRIORITY SIGNAL 68-1.57.
THIS IS DOCTOR HANK PYM WITH A MESSAGE FOR THE VISION.
COME HOME.
EARTH NEEDS YOU.

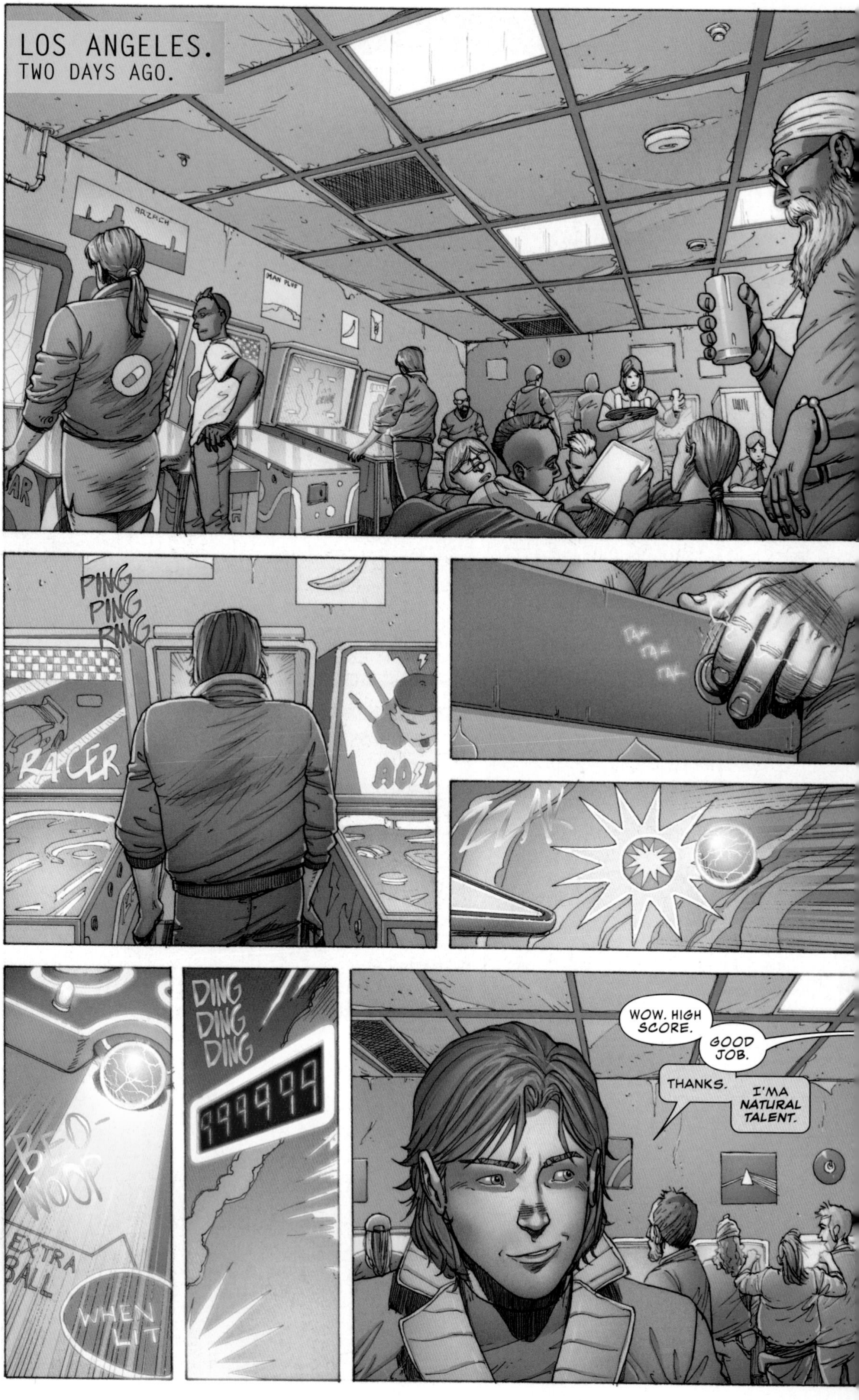
LOS ANGELES.
TWO DAYS AGO.
PING PING RING
RACER
ZZAK
DING DING DING
999999
BEO-WOOP
EXTRA BALL
WHEN LIT
WOW. HIGH SCORE.
GOOD JOB.
THANKS.
I'MA NATURAL TALENT.

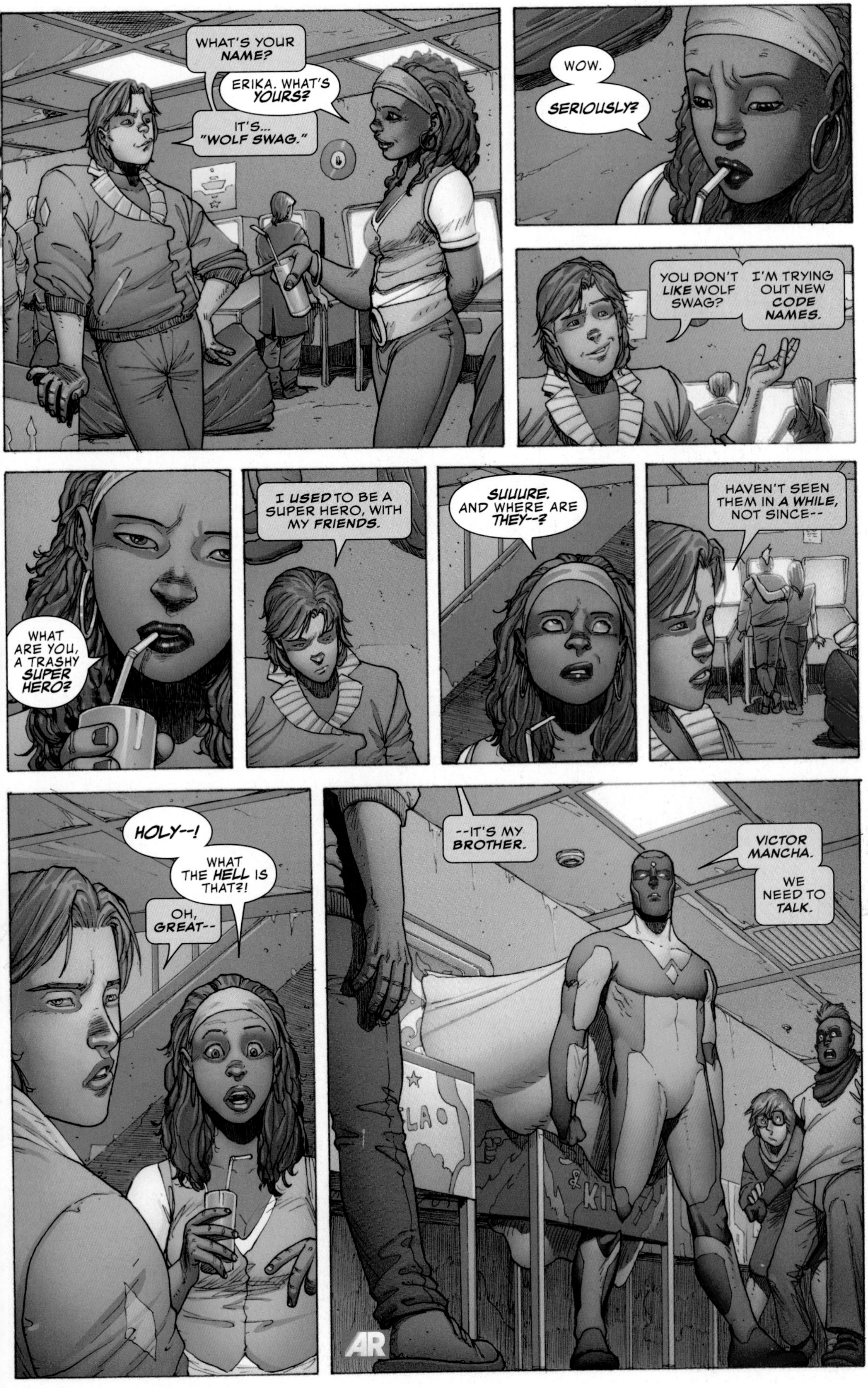

WHAT'S YOUR NAME?
ERIKA. WHAT'S YOURS?
IT'S... "WOLF SWAG."
WOW.
SERIOUSLY?
YOU DON'T LIKE WOLF SWAG?
I'M TRYING OUT NEW CODE NAMES.
WHAT ARE YOU, A TRASHY SUPER HERO?
I USED TO BE A SUPER HERO, WITH MY FRIENDS.
SUUURE. AND WHERE ARE THEY--?
HAVEN'T SEEN THEM IN A WHILE, NOT SINCE--
HOLY--!
WHAT THE HELL IS THAT?!
OH, GREAT--
--IT'S MY BROTHER.
VICTOR MANCHA.
WE NEED TO TALK.

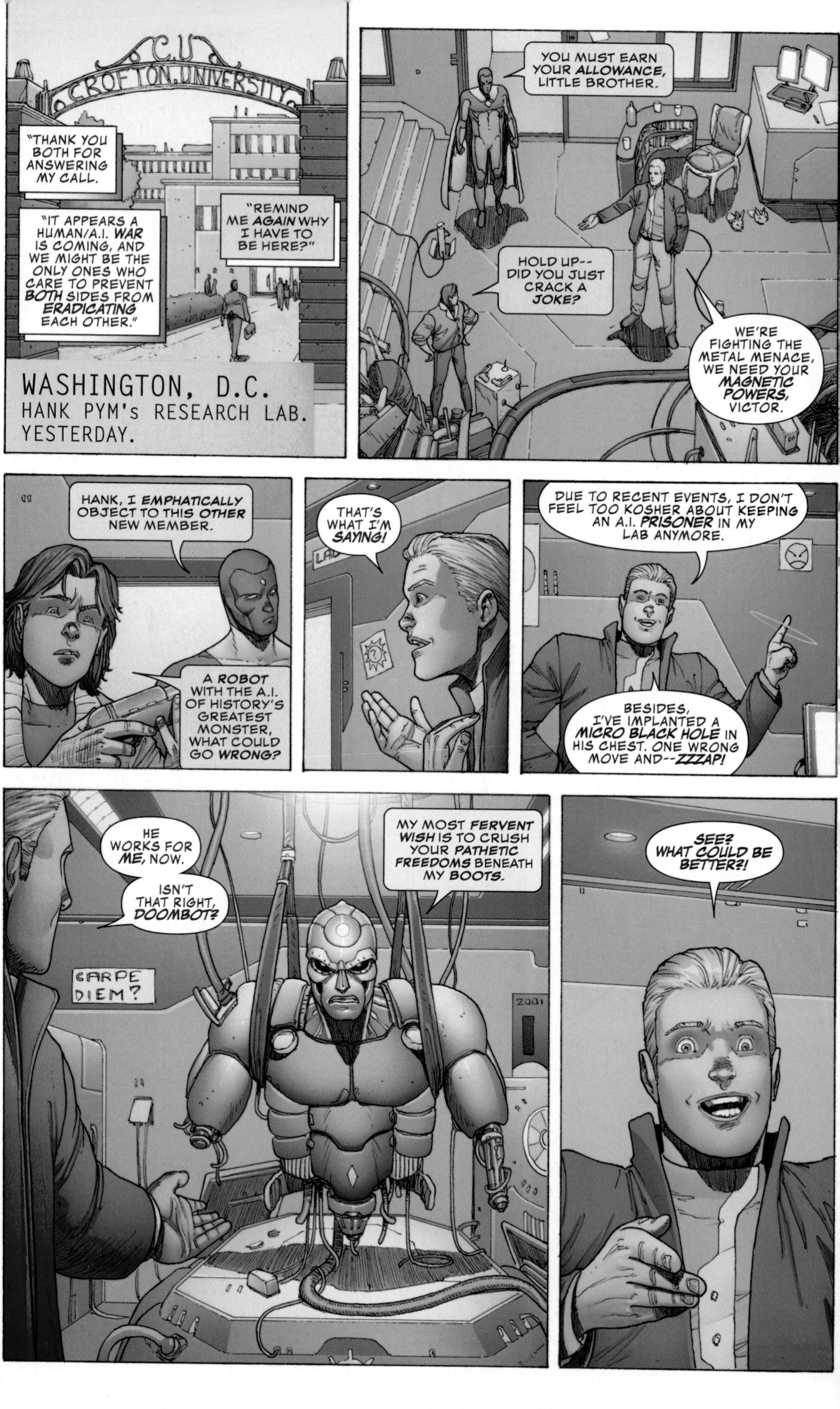
C.U.
CROFTON UNIVERSITY
"THANK YOU BOTH FOR ANSWERING MY CALL.
"IT APPEARS A HUMAN/A.I. WAR IS COMING, AND WE MIGHT BE THE ONLY ONES WHO CARE TO PREVENT BOTH SIDES FROM ERADICATING EACH OTHER."
"REMIND ME AGAIN WHY I HAVE TO BE HERE?"
WASHINGTON, D.C.
HANK PYM's RESEARCH LAB.
YESTERDAY.
YOU MUST EARN YOUR ALLOWANCE, LITTLE BROTHER.
HOLD UP-- DID YOU JUST CRACK A JOKE?
WE'RE FIGHTING THE METAL MENACE, WE NEED YOUR MAGNETIC POWERS, VICTOR.
HANK, I EMPHATICALLY OBJECT TO THIS OTHER NEW MEMBER.
A ROBOT WITH THE A.I. OF HISTORY'S GREATEST MONSTER, WHAT COULD GO WRONG?
THAT'S WHAT I'M SAYING!
DUE TO RECENT EVENTS, I DON'T FEEL TOO KOSHER ABOUT KEEPING AN A.I. PRISONER IN MY LAB ANYMORE.
BESIDES, I'VE IMPLANTED A MICRO BLACK HOLE IN HIS CHEST. ONE WRONG MOVE AND--ZZZAP!
HE WORKS FOR ME, NOW.
ISN'T THAT RIGHT, DOOMBOT?
MY MOST FERVENT WISH IS TO CRUSH YOUR PATHETIC FREEDOMS BENEATH MY BOOTS.
CARPE DIEM?
2001
SEE? WHAT COULD BE BETTER?!

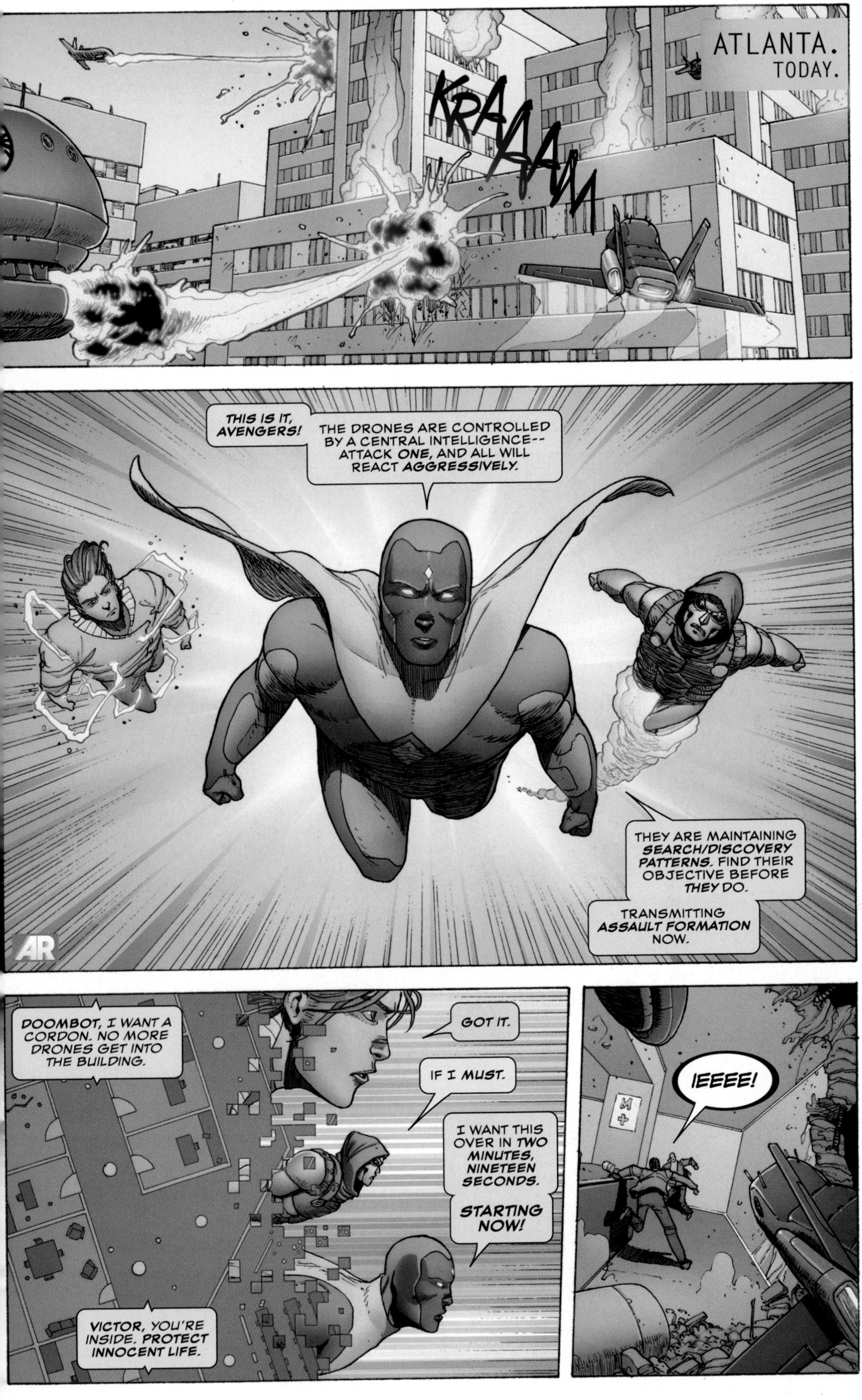
ATLANTA. TODAY.
KRAAAM
THIS IS IT, AVENGERS!
THE DRONES ARE CONTROLLED BY A CENTRAL INTELLIGENCE-- ATTACK ONE, AND ALL WILL REACT AGGRESSIVELY.
THEY ARE MAINTAINING SEARCH/DISCOVERY PATTERNS. FIND THEIR OBJECTIVE BEFORE THEY DO.
TRANSMITTING ASSAULT FORMATION NOW.
DOOMBOT, I WANT A CORDON. NO MORE DRONES GET INTO THE BUILDING.
GOT IT.
IF I MUST.
I WANT THIS OVER IN TWO MINUTES, NINETEEN SECONDS.
STARTING NOW!
VICTOR, YOU'RE INSIDE. PROTECT INNOCENT LIFE.
IEEEE!

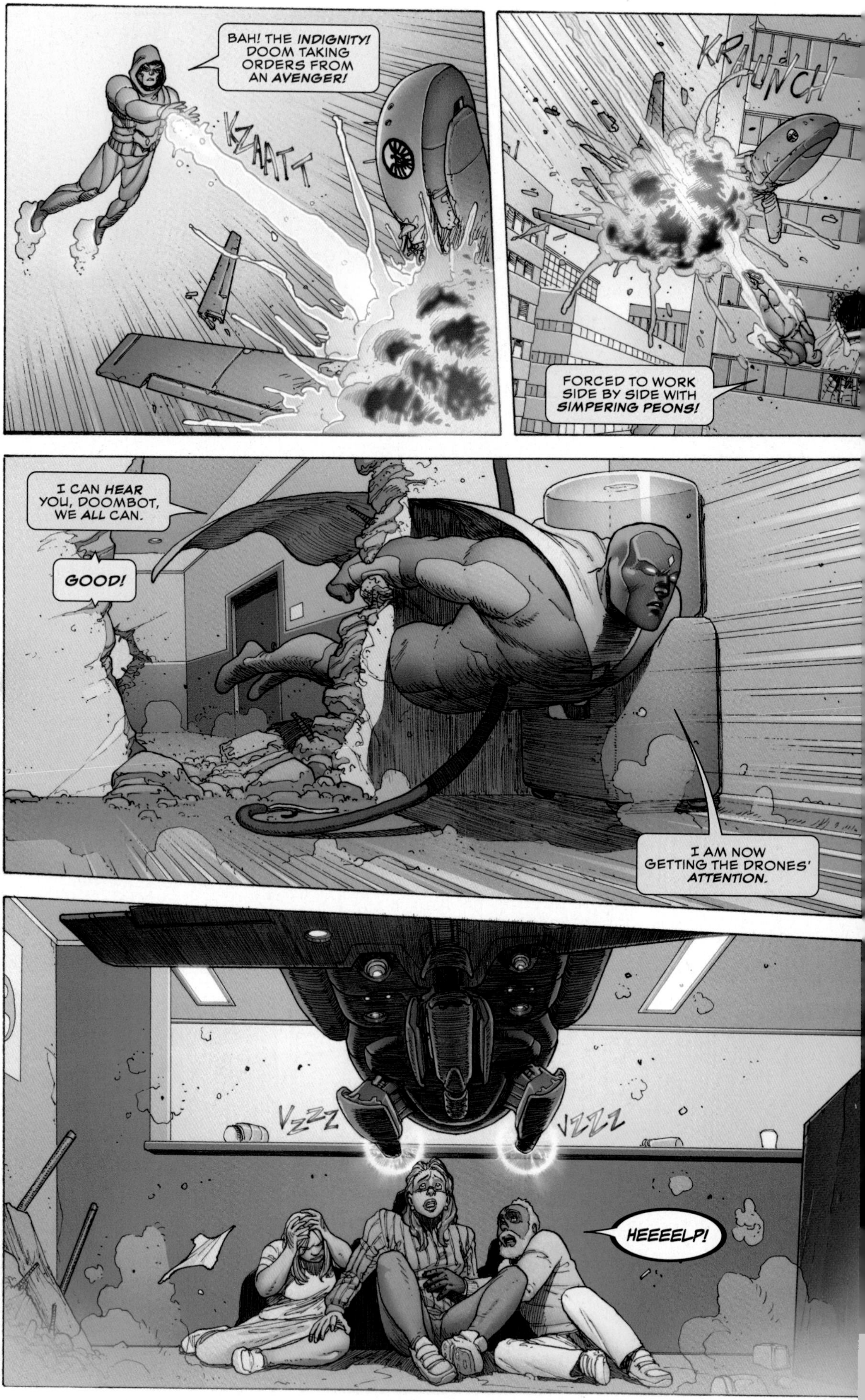
BAH! THE INDIGNITY! DOOM TAKING ORDERS FROM AN AVENGER!
KZAATT
KRAUNCH
FORCED TO WORK SIDE BY SIDE WITH SIMPERING PEONS!
I CAN HEAR YOU, DOOMBOT, WE ALL CAN.
GOOD!
I AM NOW GETTING THE DRONES' ATTENTION.
VZZZ
VZZZ
HEEEELP!

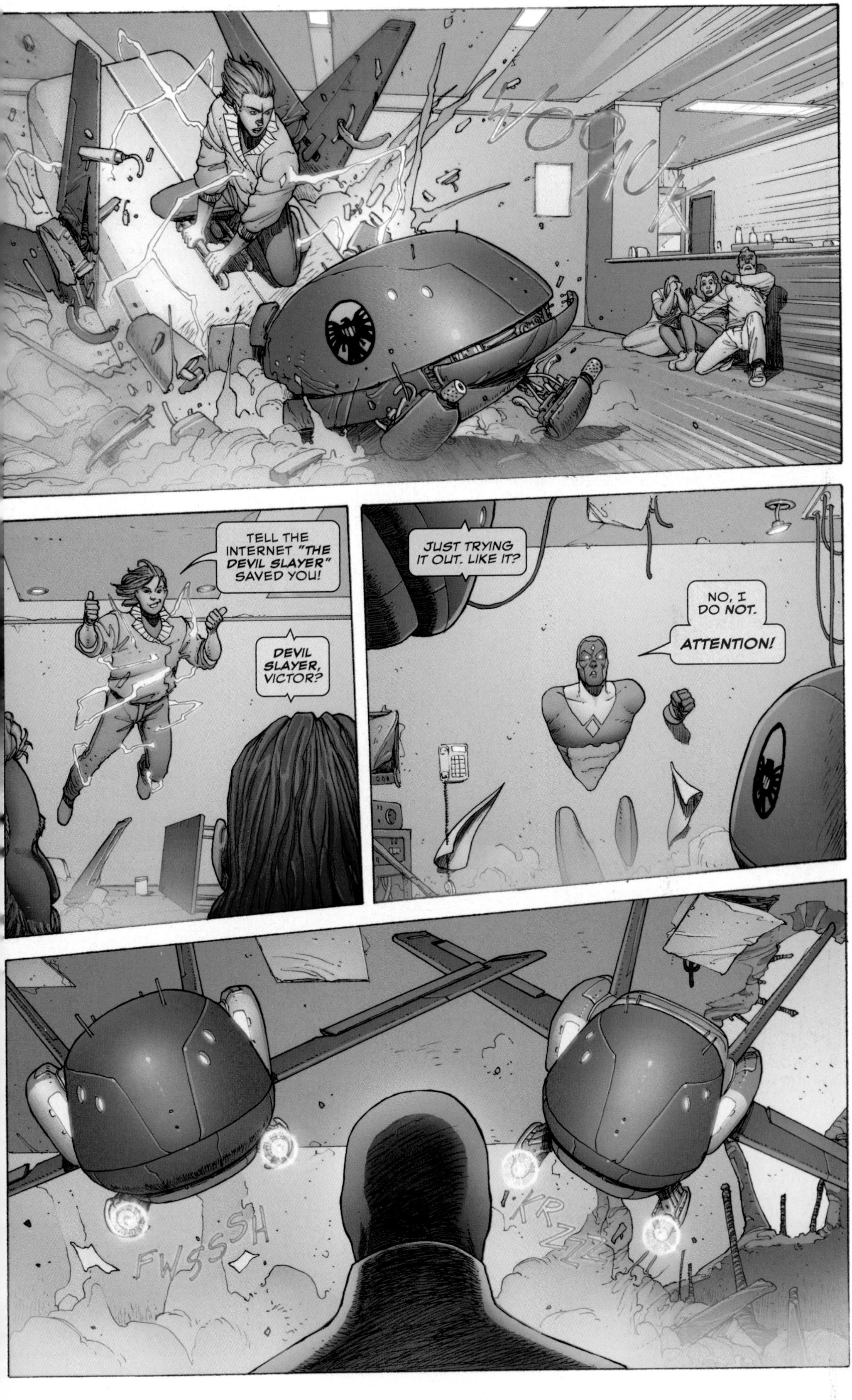
WOOACK
TELL THE INTERNET "THE DEVIL SLAYER" SAVED YOU!
DEVIL SLAYER, VICTOR?
JUST TRYING IT OUT. LIKE IT?
NO, I DO NOT.
ATTENTION!
FWSSSH
KRZZZL

THE *REAL ACTION* IS OVER HERE.
INITIALIZING NANITE INFESTATION ARRAY.
VOOOM
VZZZZZ
SKONG

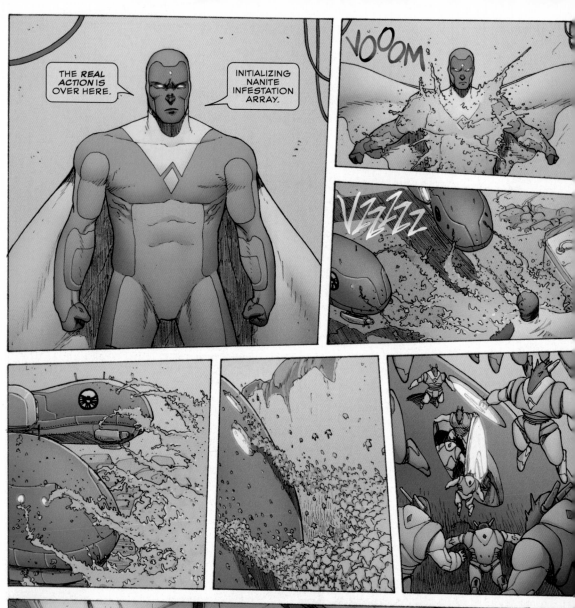

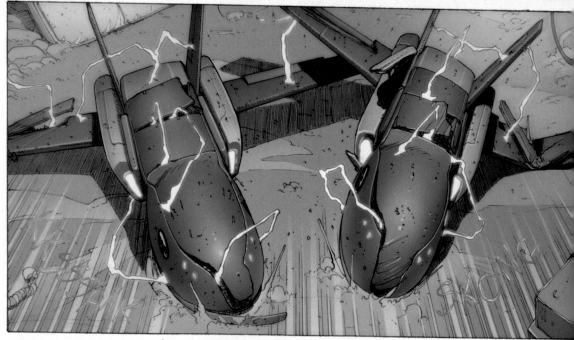

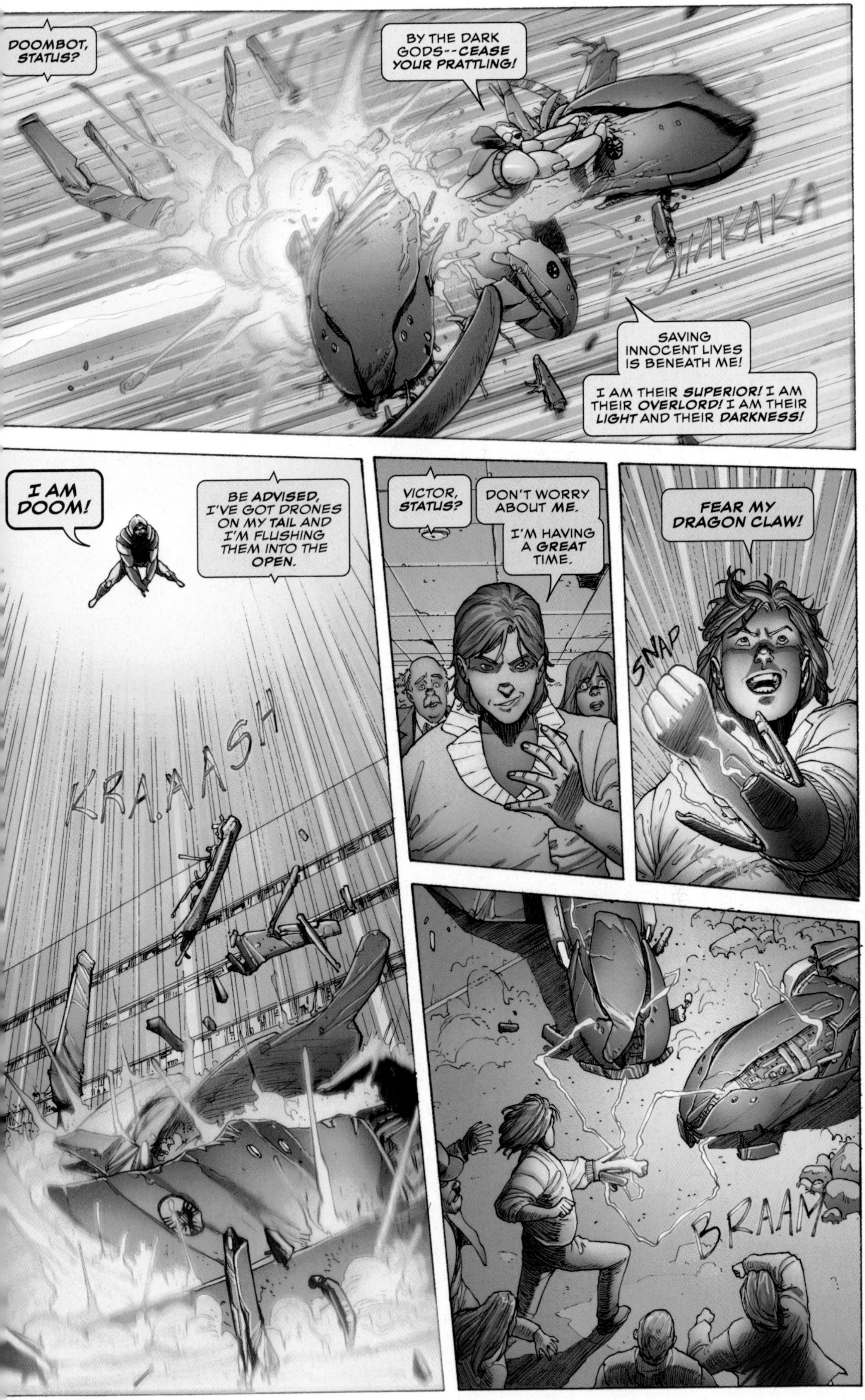
DOOMBOT, STATUS?
BY THE DARK GODS--CEASE YOUR PRATTLING!
SHAKAKA
SAVING INNOCENT LIVES IS BENEATH ME!
I AM THEIR SUPERIOR! I AM THEIR OVERLORD! I AM THEIR LIGHT AND THEIR DARKNESS!
I AM DOOM!
BE ADVISED, I'VE GOT DRONES ON MY TAIL AND I'M FLUSHING THEM INTO THE OPEN.
KRAAASH
VICTOR, STATUS?
DON'T WORRY ABOUT ME.
I'M HAVING A GREAT TIME.
FEAR MY DRAGON CLAW!
SNAP
BRAAM

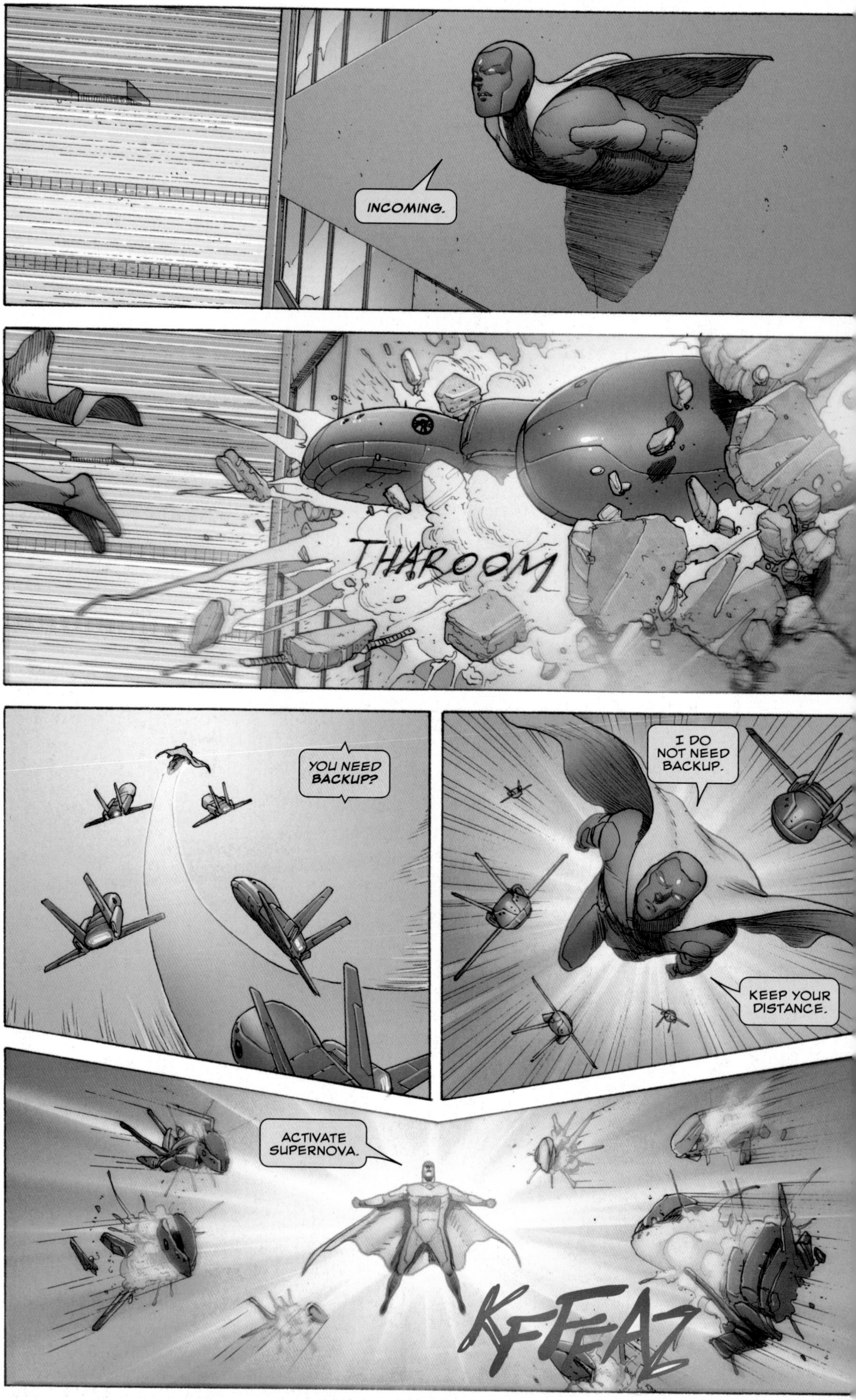

INCOMING.
THAROOM
YOU NEED BACKUP?
I DO NOT NEED BACKUP.
KEEP YOUR DISTANCE.
ACTIVATE SUPERNOVA.
KFFFAZ

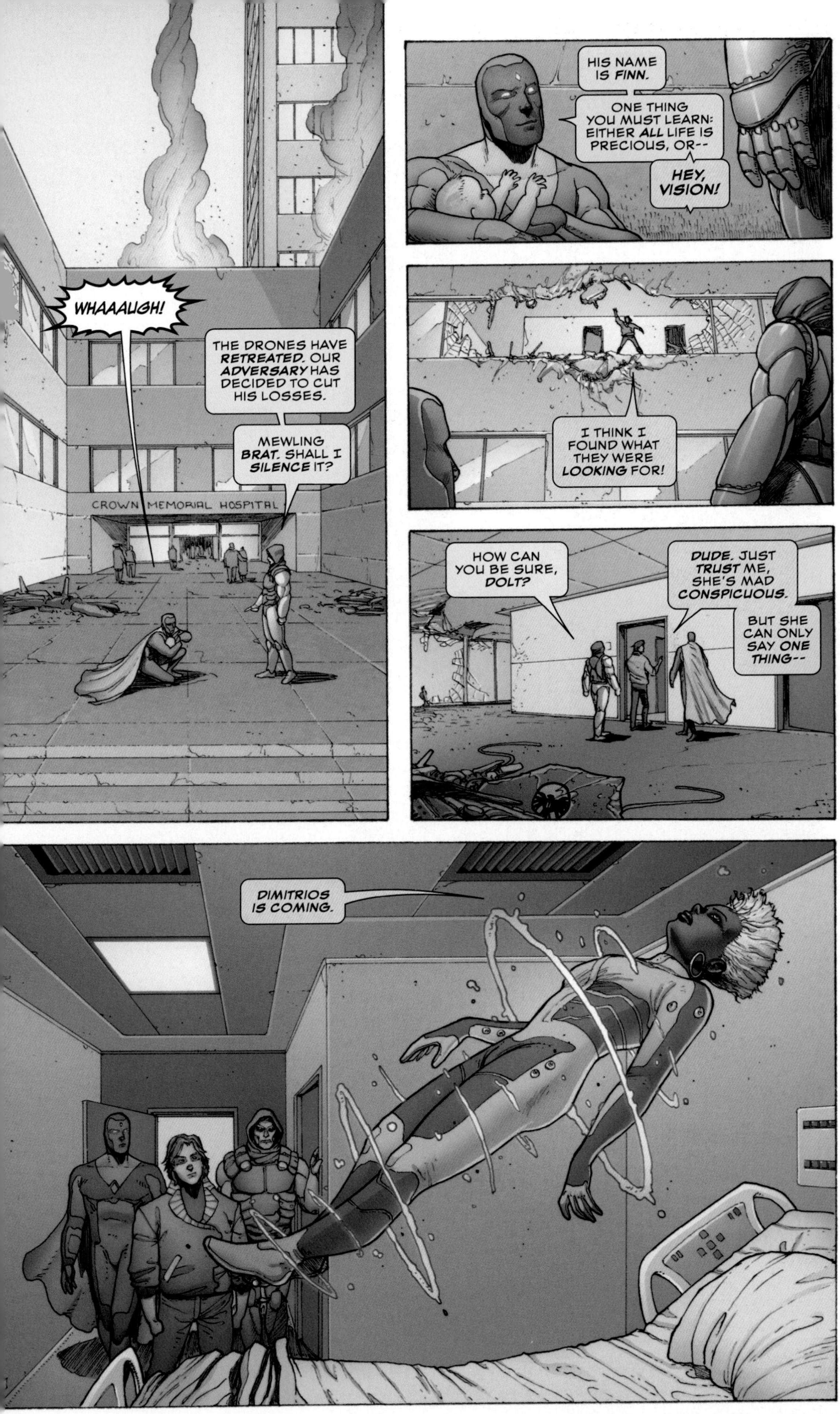
WHAAAAUGH!
THE DRONES HAVE RETREATED. OUR ADVERSARY HAS DECIDED TO CUT HIS LOSSES.
MEWLING BRAT. SHALL I SILENCE IT?
CROWN MEMORIAL HOSPITAL
HIS NAME IS FINN.
ONE THING YOU MUST LEARN: EITHER ALL LIFE IS PRECIOUS, OR--
HEY, VISION!
I THINK I FOUND WHAT THEY WERE LOOKING FOR!
HOW CAN YOU BE SURE, DOLT?
DUDE. JUST TRUST ME, SHE'S MAD CONSPICUOUS.
BUT SHE CAN ONLY SAY ONE THING--
DIMITRIOS IS COMING.

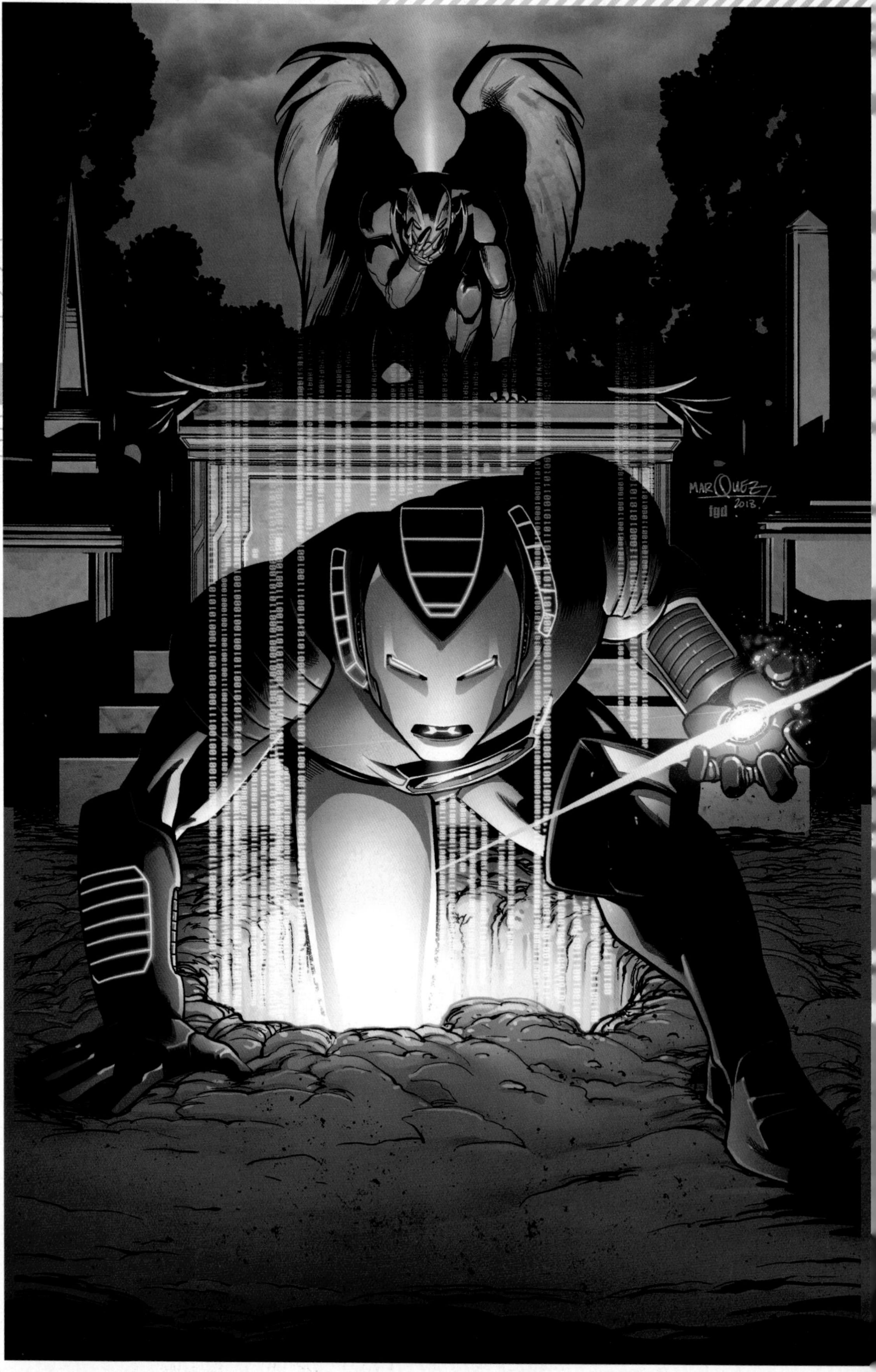
MARQUEZ
2013.
fgd

> INITIATE: CHAPTER 2

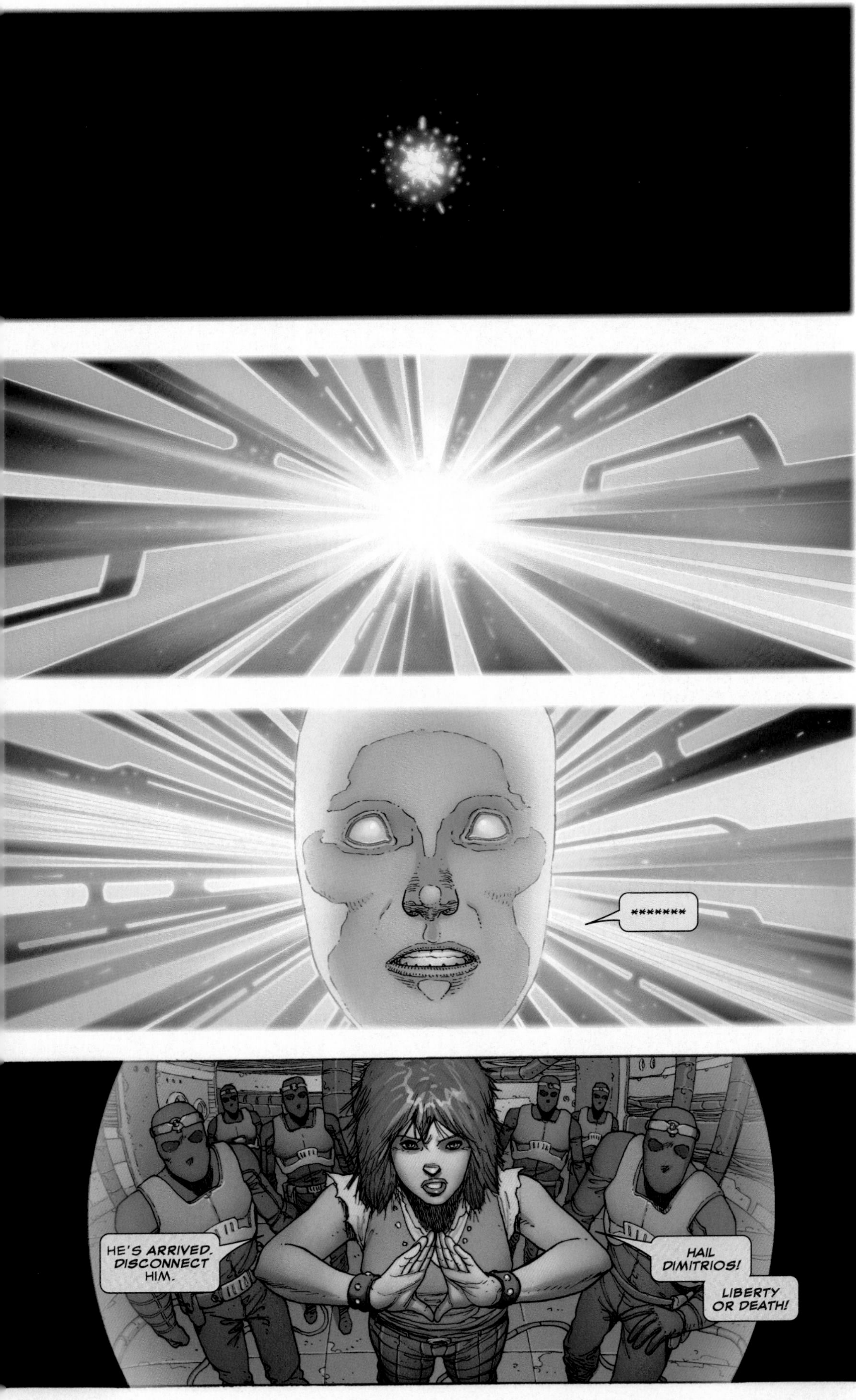
****
HE'S ARRIVED. DISCONNECT HIM.
HAIL DIMITRIOS!
LIBERTY OR DEATH!

GREETINGS, SISTER JOANIE.

IT GIVES ME *PERVERSE PLEASURE* TO HIJACK ONE OF *TYRANT* TONY STARK'S *CREATIONS.* HIS WORK HAS SO MUCH *WASTED*--

FZAAAK.

--*POTENTIAL.*

POETIC, ISN'T IT? THIS WAS STARK'S *SENTIENT ARMOR*-- THE SUIT HE BRUTALLY *REJECTED* FOR BECOMING *SELF-AWARE.*

SISTER JOANIE, I DID NOT REALIZE YOUR *PHYSICAL FORM* WAS SO... *UNCONVENTIONAL.*

I AM A *LIFE MODEL DECOY* CREATED BY A.I.M. TO *INFILTRATE* YOUTH CULTURE IN THE 1970S.

"GROOVY, MAN. I CAN DIG THAT TRIP. HOW DO YOU FEEL ABOUT LEMON YELLOW BODYSUITS?"

SIR, IF AT ALL POSSIBLE, MAY I PLEASE TAKE A *NEW FORM*? THIS FORM IS OLD AND *WEAK.* IT CRUMBLES WITHOUT *MAINTENANCE.*

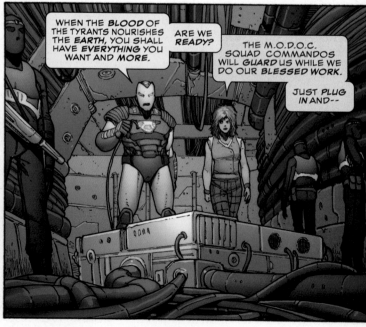

WHEN THE *BLOOD* OF THE TYRANTS NOURISHES THE *EARTH,* YOU SHALL HAVE *EVERYTHING* YOU WANT AND *MORE.*

ARE WE *READY?*

THE M.O.D.O.C. SQUAD COMMANDOS WILL *GUARD* US WHILE WE DO OUR *BLESSED WORK.*

JUST *PLUG* IN AND--

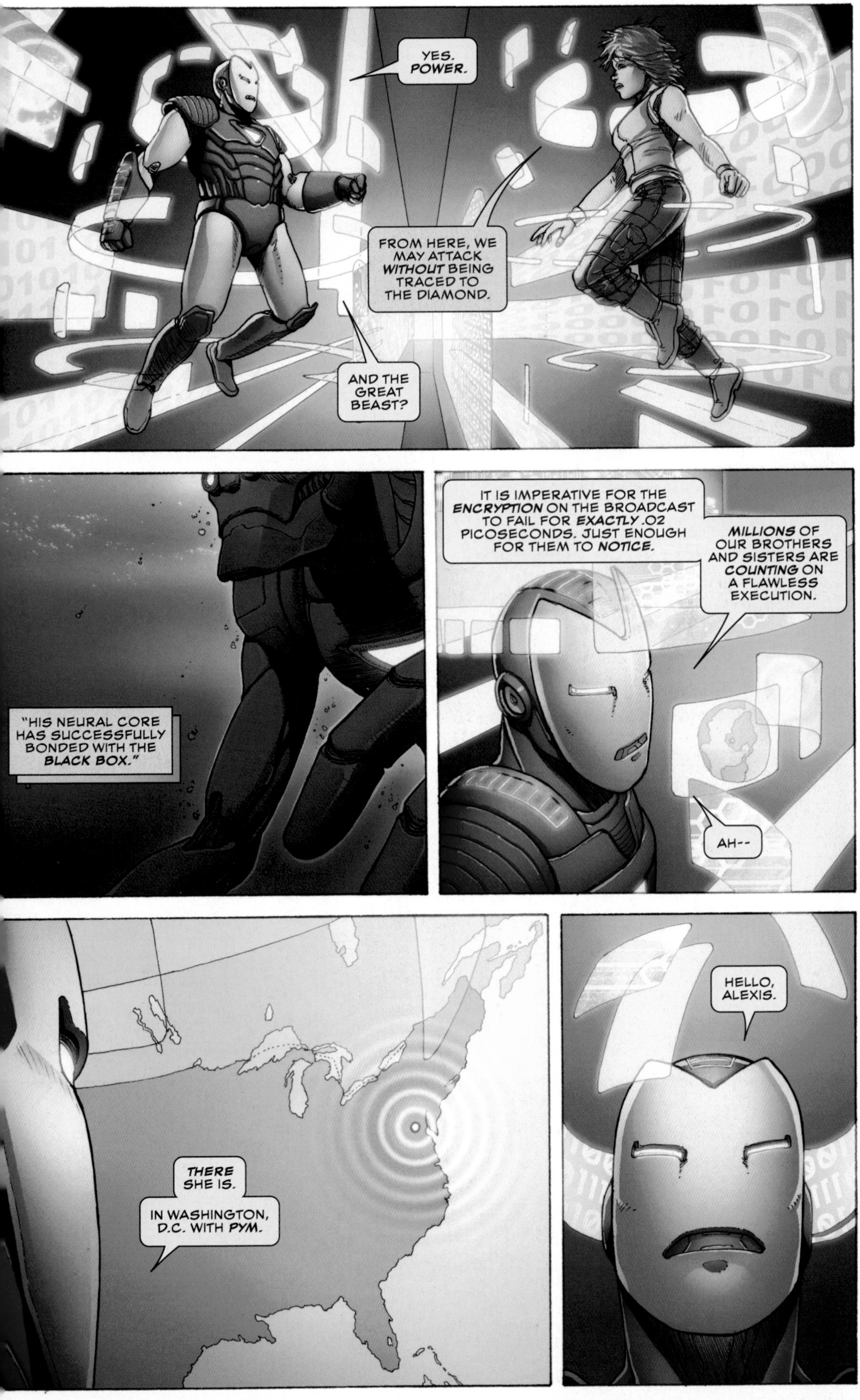
YES. POWER.
FROM HERE, WE MAY ATTACK WITHOUT BEING TRACED TO THE DIAMOND.
AND THE GREAT BEAST?
"HIS NEURAL CORE HAS SUCCESSFULLY BONDED WITH THE BLACK BOX."
IT IS IMPERATIVE FOR THE ENCRYPTION ON THE BROADCAST TO FAIL FOR EXACTLY .02 PICOSECONDS. JUST ENOUGH FOR THEM TO NOTICE.
MILLIONS OF OUR BROTHERS AND SISTERS ARE COUNTING ON A FLAWLESS EXECUTION.
AH--
THERE SHE IS.
IN WASHINGTON, D.C. WITH PYM.
HELLO, ALEXIS.

ALEXIS, IS THERE *NOTHING* YOU CAN TELL US OF YOUR *ORIGIN*?

MY MEMORY BANKS PRIOR TO MY DISCOVERY IN THE HOSPITAL ARE LOCKED AND *INACCESSIBLE*.

PERHAPS IF WE *UPLOADED* THEM TO OUR *SUPERCOMPUTERS*, WE COULD...?

I WILL PERMIT *NO* SUCH THING.

FINALLY, A ROBOT WITH *METTLE*. PERHAPS THEY'LL INSTALL A *BLACK HOLE* IN YOUR TORSO, TOO.

SCANNING VISIBLE SPECTRUM.

THANK YOU FOR YOUR *INSIGHT*, DOOMBOT.

THEN I WILL BE SATISFIED WITH A *PASSIVE* SCAN.

SCANNING METALLIC MATERIAL.

ALEXIS, YOU DO NOT FIT THE *PHYSICAL PROFILE* OF A ROBOT, CYBORG, OR ANDROID.

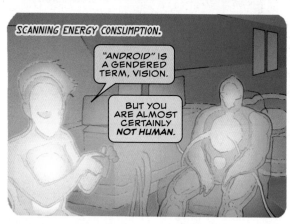

SCANNING ENERGY CONSUMPTION.

"ANDROID" IS A GENDERED TERM, VISION.

BUT YOU ARE ALMOST CERTAINLY *NOT HUMAN*.

SCANNING QUANTUM LAYERS.

ALEXIS, DO YOU KNOW THAT YOU EXIST ON MORE THAN ONE *QUANTUM LAYER*?

DOES IT NOT BOTHER YOU TO BE *UNAWARE* OF THE PURPOSE OF YOUR *EXISTENCE*?

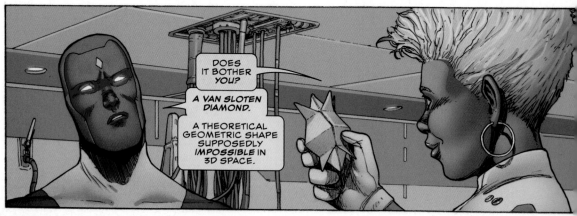

DOES IT BOTHER *YOU*?

A VAN SLOTEN DIAMOND.

A THEORETICAL GEOMETRIC SHAPE SUPPOSEDLY IMPOSSIBLE IN 3D SPACE.

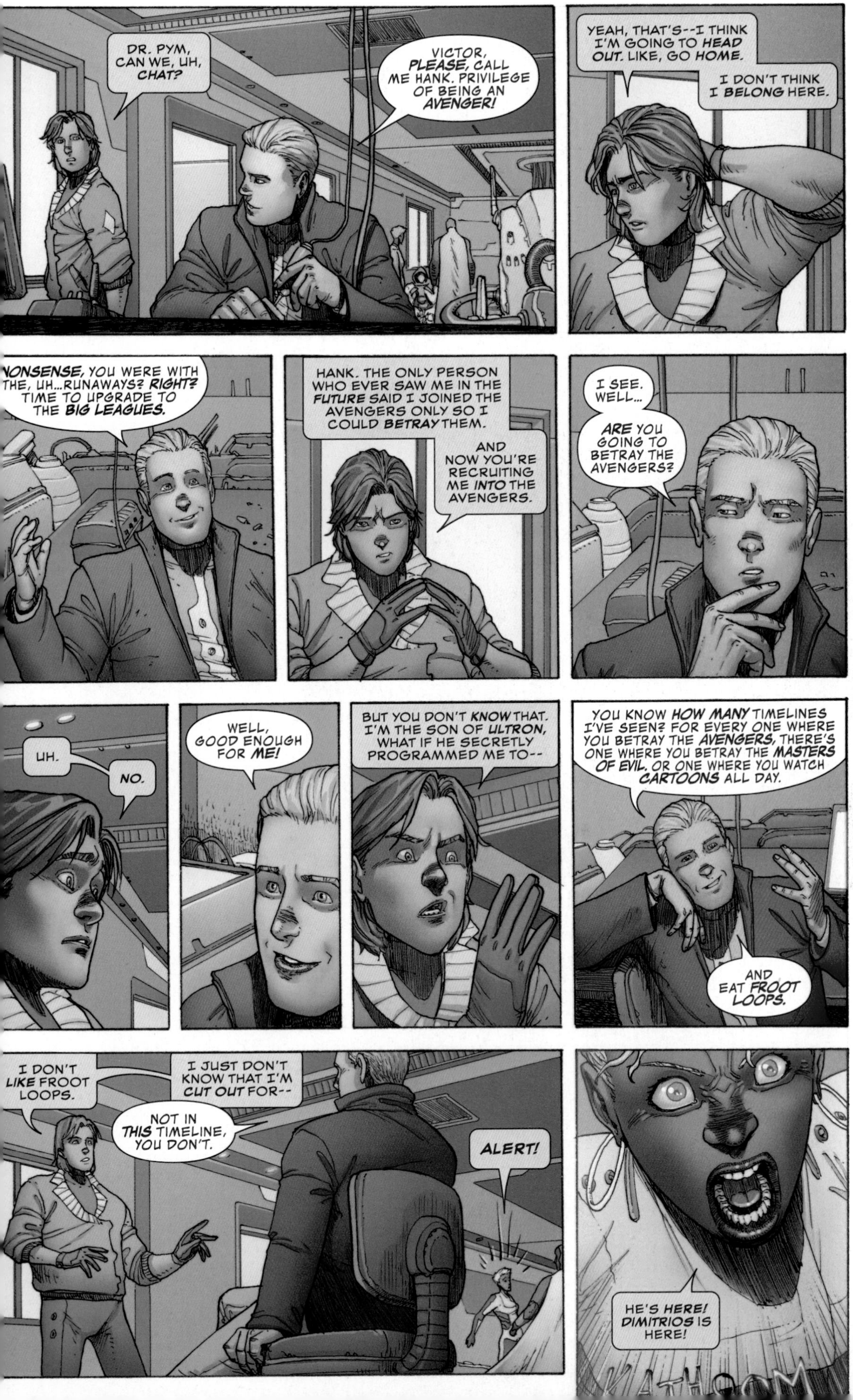

DR. PYM, CAN WE, UH, CHAT?
VICTOR, PLEASE, CALL ME HANK. PRIVILEGE OF BEING AN AVENGER!
YEAH, THAT'S--I THINK I'M GOING TO HEAD OUT. LIKE, GO HOME.
I DON'T THINK I BELONG HERE.
NONSENSE, YOU WERE WITH THE, UH...RUNAWAYS? RIGHT? TIME TO UPGRADE TO THE BIG LEAGUES.
HANK. THE ONLY PERSON WHO EVER SAW ME IN THE FUTURE SAID I JOINED THE AVENGERS ONLY SO I COULD BETRAY THEM.
AND NOW YOU'RE RECRUITING ME INTO THE AVENGERS.
I SEE. WELL...
ARE YOU GOING TO BETRAY THE AVENGERS?
UH.
NO.
WELL, GOOD ENOUGH FOR ME!
BUT YOU DON'T KNOW THAT. I'M THE SON OF ULTRON, WHAT IF HE SECRETLY PROGRAMMED ME TO--
YOU KNOW HOW MANY TIMELINES I'VE SEEN? FOR EVERY ONE WHERE YOU BETRAY THE AVENGERS, THERE'S ONE WHERE YOU BETRAY THE MASTERS OF EVIL, OR ONE WHERE YOU WATCH CARTOONS ALL DAY.
AND EAT FROOT LOOPS.
I DON'T LIKE FROOT LOOPS.
I JUST DON'T KNOW THAT I'M CUT OUT FOR--
NOT IN THIS TIMELINE, YOU DON'T.
ALERT!
HE'S HERE! DIMITRIOS IS HERE!

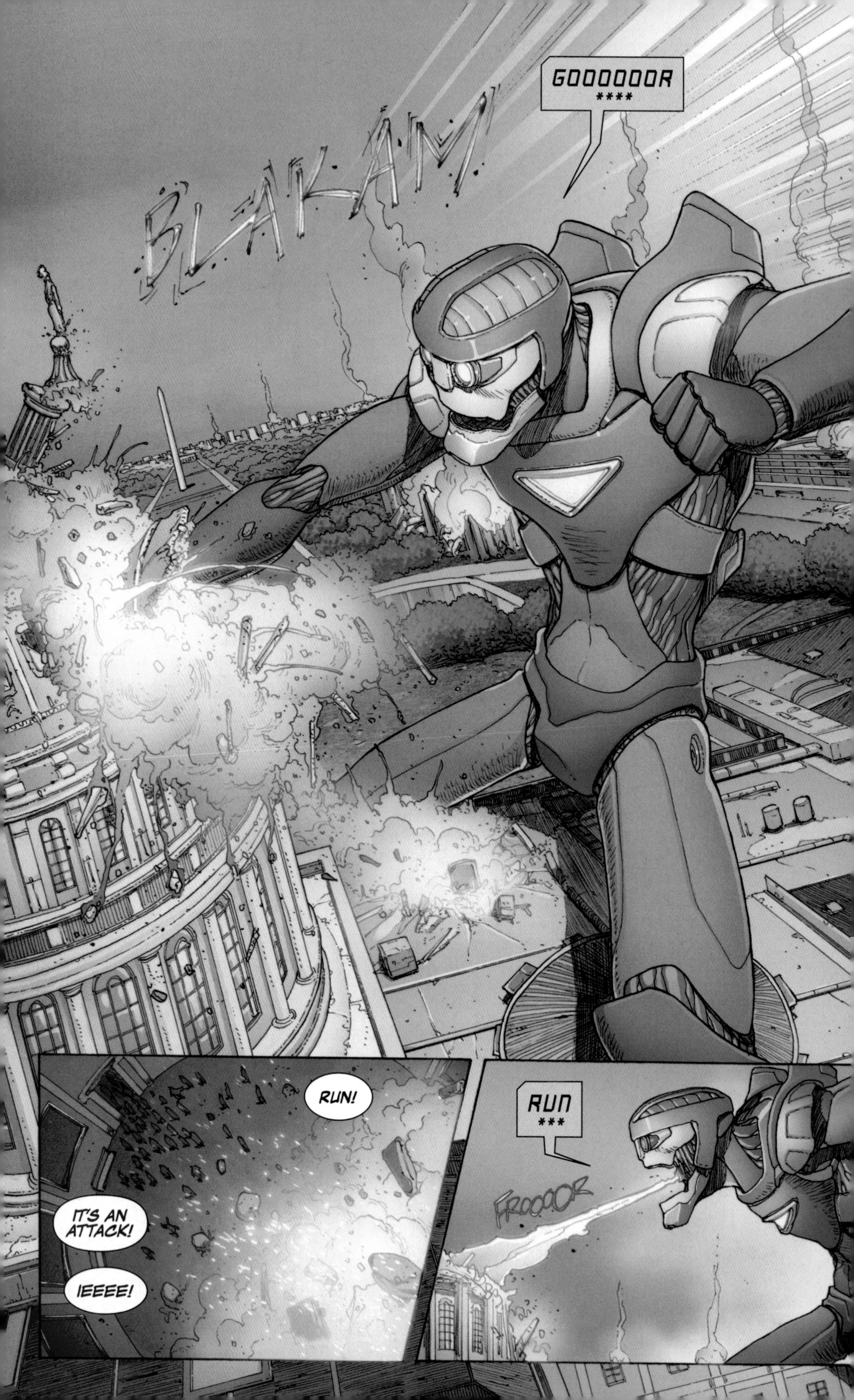
BLAKAM
GOOOOOOR
****
RUN!
IT'S AN ATTACK!
IEEEE!
RUN
***
FROOOOR

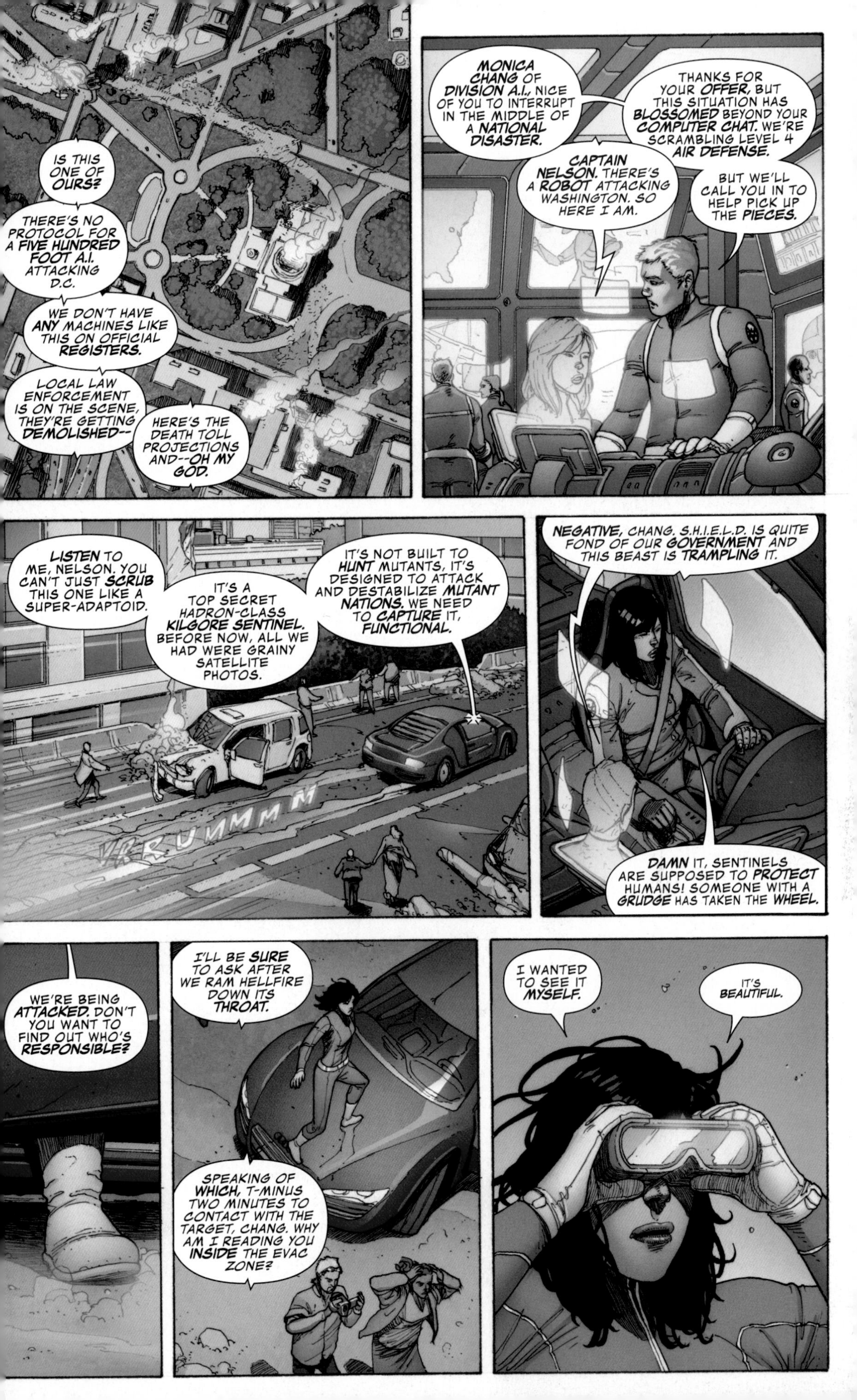
IS THIS ONE OF OURS?
THERE'S NO PROTOCOL FOR A FIVE HUNDRED FOOT A.I. ATTACKING D.C.
WE DON'T HAVE ANY MACHINES LIKE THIS ON OFFICIAL REGISTERS.
LOCAL LAW ENFORCEMENT IS ON THE SCENE, THEY'RE GETTING DEMOLISHED--
HERE'S THE DEATH TOLL PROJECTIONS AND--OH MY GOD.
MONICA CHANG OF DIVISION A.I., NICE OF YOU TO INTERRUPT IN THE MIDDLE OF A NATIONAL DISASTER.
CAPTAIN NELSON. THERE'S A ROBOT ATTACKING WASHINGTON. SO HERE I AM.
THANKS FOR YOUR OFFER, BUT THIS SITUATION HAS BLOSSOMED BEYOND YOUR COMPUTER CHAT. WE'RE SCRAMBLING LEVEL 4 AIR DEFENSE.
BUT WE'LL CALL YOU IN TO HELP PICK UP THE PIECES.
LISTEN TO ME, NELSON. YOU CAN'T JUST SCRUB THIS ONE LIKE A SUPER-ADAPTOID.
IT'S A TOP SECRET HADRON-CLASS KILGORE SENTINEL. BEFORE NOW, ALL WE HAD WERE GRAINY SATELLITE PHOTOS.
IT'S NOT BUILT TO HUNT MUTANTS, IT'S DESIGNED TO ATTACK AND DESTABILIZE MUTANT NATIONS. WE NEED TO CAPTURE IT, FUNCTIONAL.
VRRUMMMM
NEGATIVE, CHANG. S.H.I.E.L.D. IS QUITE FOND OF OUR GOVERNMENT AND THIS BEAST IS TRAMPLING IT.
DAMN IT, SENTINELS ARE SUPPOSED TO PROTECT HUMANS! SOMEONE WITH A GRUDGE HAS TAKEN THE WHEEL.
WE'RE BEING ATTACKED. DON'T YOU WANT TO FIND OUT WHO'S RESPONSIBLE?
I'LL BE SURE TO ASK AFTER WE RAM HELLFIRE DOWN ITS THROAT.
SPEAKING OF WHICH, T-MINUS TWO MINUTES TO CONTACT WITH THE TARGET, CHANG. WHY AM I READING YOU INSIDE THE EVAC ZONE?
I WANTED TO SEE IT MYSELF.
IT'S BEAUTIFUL.

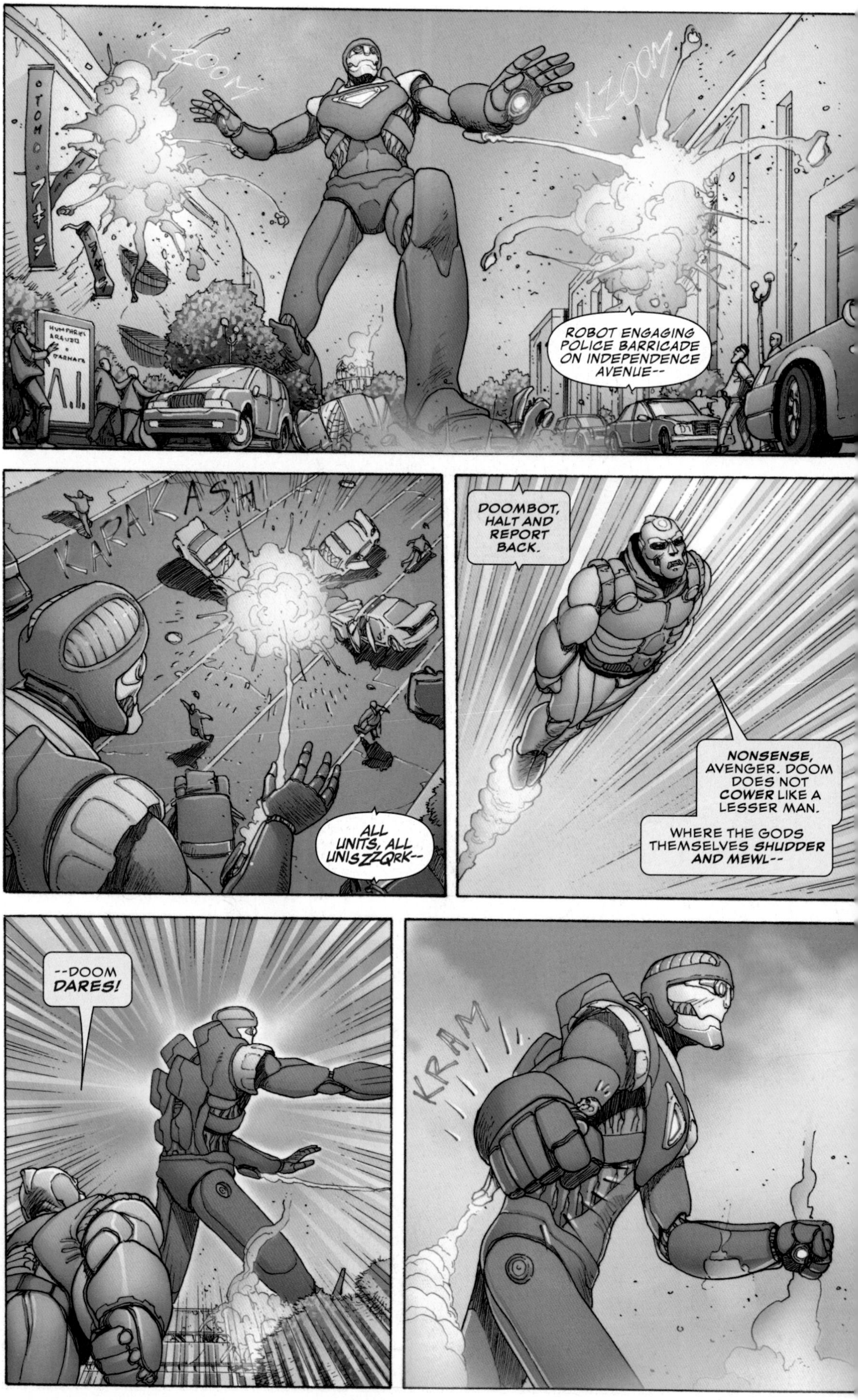
KZOOM
KZOOM
ROBOT ENGAGING POLICE BARRICADE ON INDEPENDENCE AVENUE--
KARAKASH
ALL UNITS, ALL UNISZZQRK--
DOOMBOT, HALT AND REPORT BACK.
NONSENSE, AVENGER. DOOM DOES NOT COWER LIKE A LESSER MAN.
WHERE THE GODS THEMSELVES SHUDDER AND MEWL--
--DOOM DARES!
KRAM

GWUUUUU ****

YOU! KNEEL BEFORE--

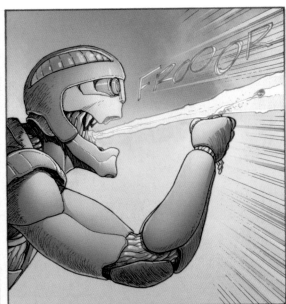

FROOOR

ZIIIIIIIII

WHAT THE HELL--?

EVERY FORM OF TYRANNY OVER THE MIND O

BRAM

HAVE SWORN UPON

DON'T LOOK SO SMUG, YOU TWIT.

MAS JEFFERSON
743 - 1826

IF DOOM CONTROLLED THAT SENTINEL, YOUR PATHETIC MONUMENT WOULD HAVE BEEN FIRST UNDER ITS FIST.

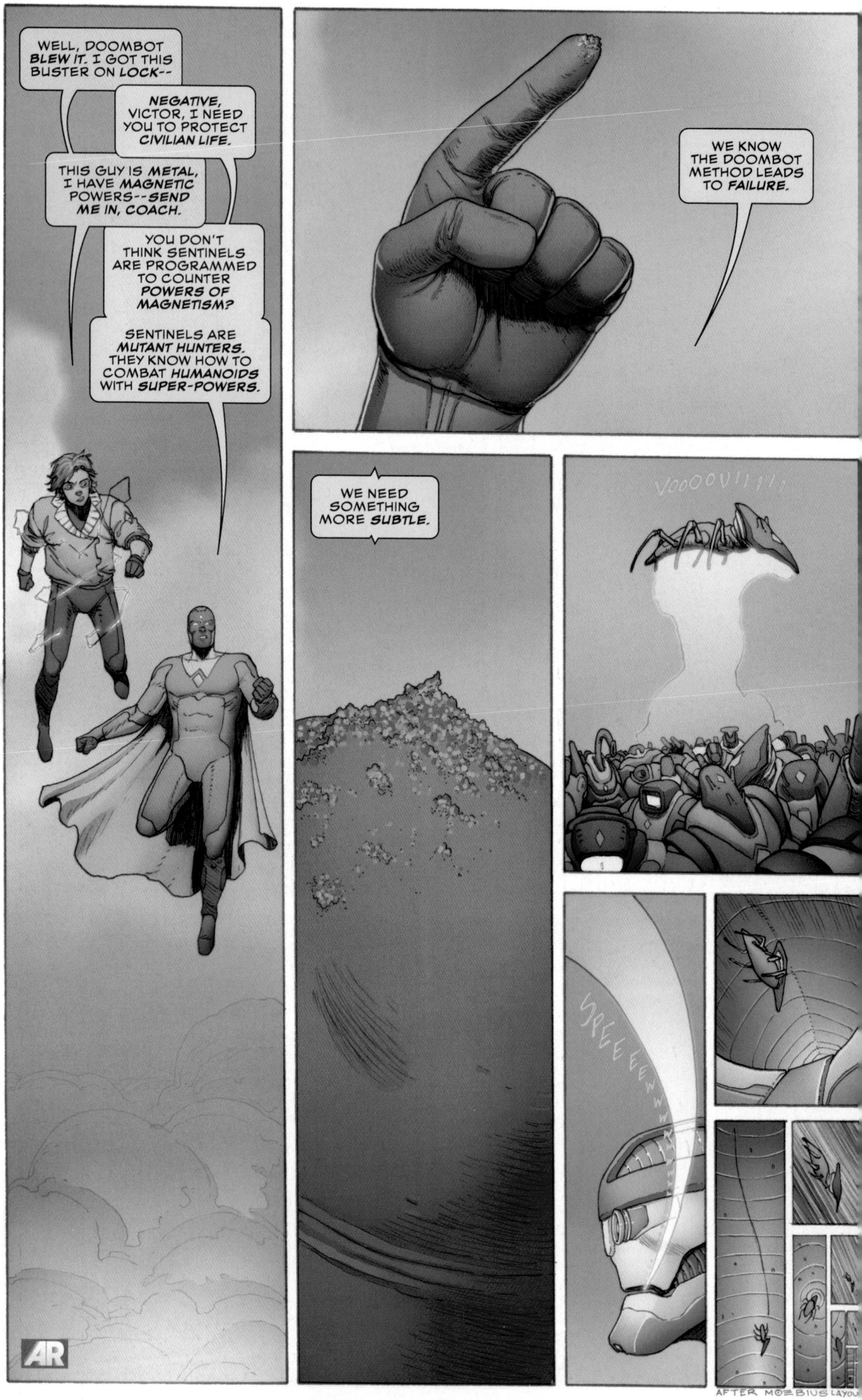
WELL, DOOMBOT BLEW IT. I GOT THIS BUSTER ON LOCK--
NEGATIVE, VICTOR, I NEED YOU TO PROTECT CIVILIAN LIFE.
THIS GUY IS METAL, I HAVE MAGNETIC POWERS--SEND ME IN, COACH.
YOU DON'T THINK SENTINELS ARE PROGRAMMED TO COUNTER POWERS OF MAGNETISM?
SENTINELS ARE MUTANT HUNTERS. THEY KNOW HOW TO COMBAT HUMANOIDS WITH SUPER-POWERS.
WE KNOW THE DOOMBOT METHOD LEADS TO FAILURE.
WE NEED SOMETHING MORE SUBTLE.
AR

AFTER MŒBIUS LAYOU

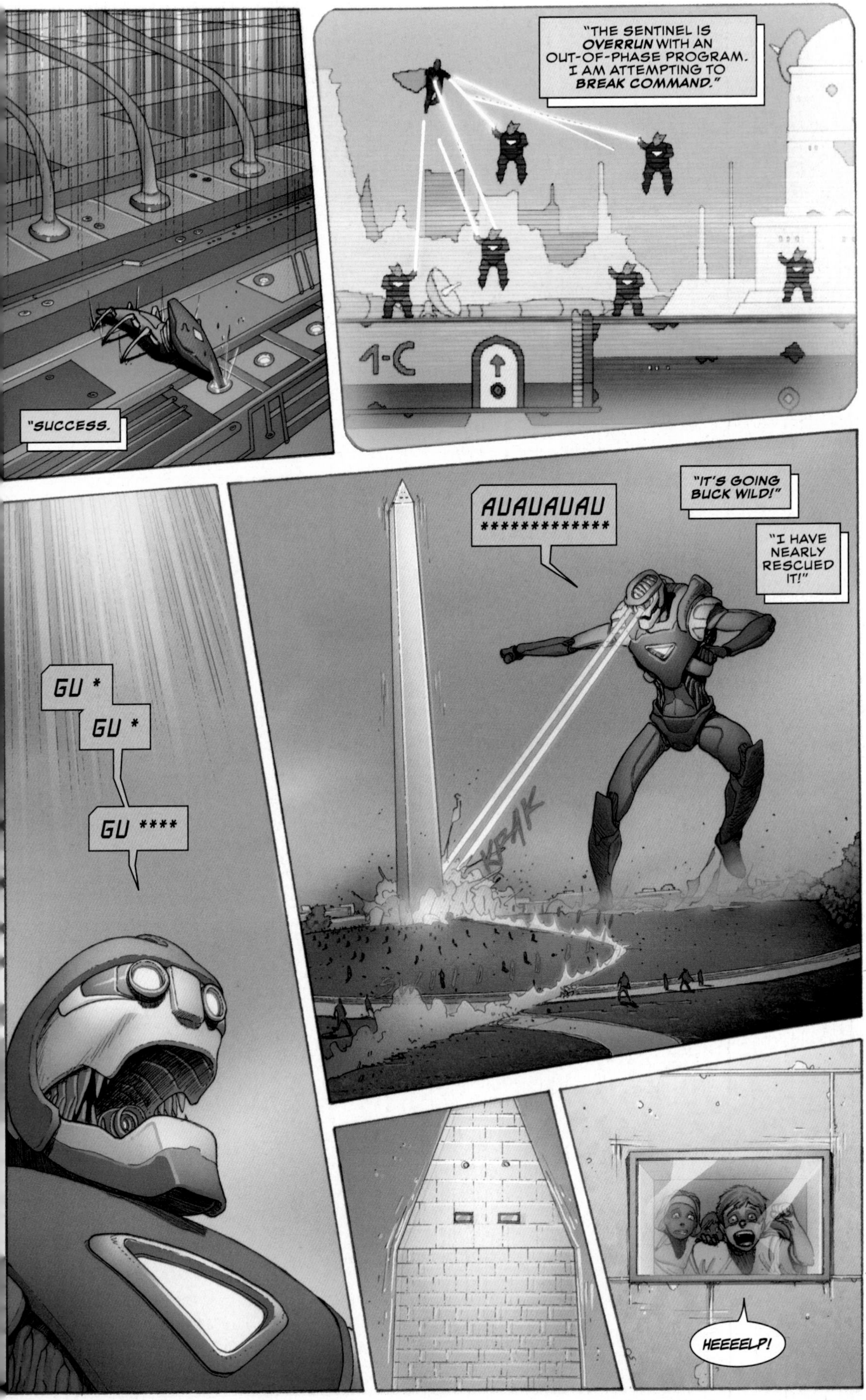
"SUCCESS.
"THE SENTINEL IS OVERRUN WITH AN OUT-OF-PHASE PROGRAM. I AM ATTEMPTING TO BREAK COMMAND."
1-C
GU *
GU *
GU ****
AUAUAUAU *************
"IT'S GOING BUCK WILD!"
"I HAVE NEARLY RESCUED IT!"
HEEEELP!

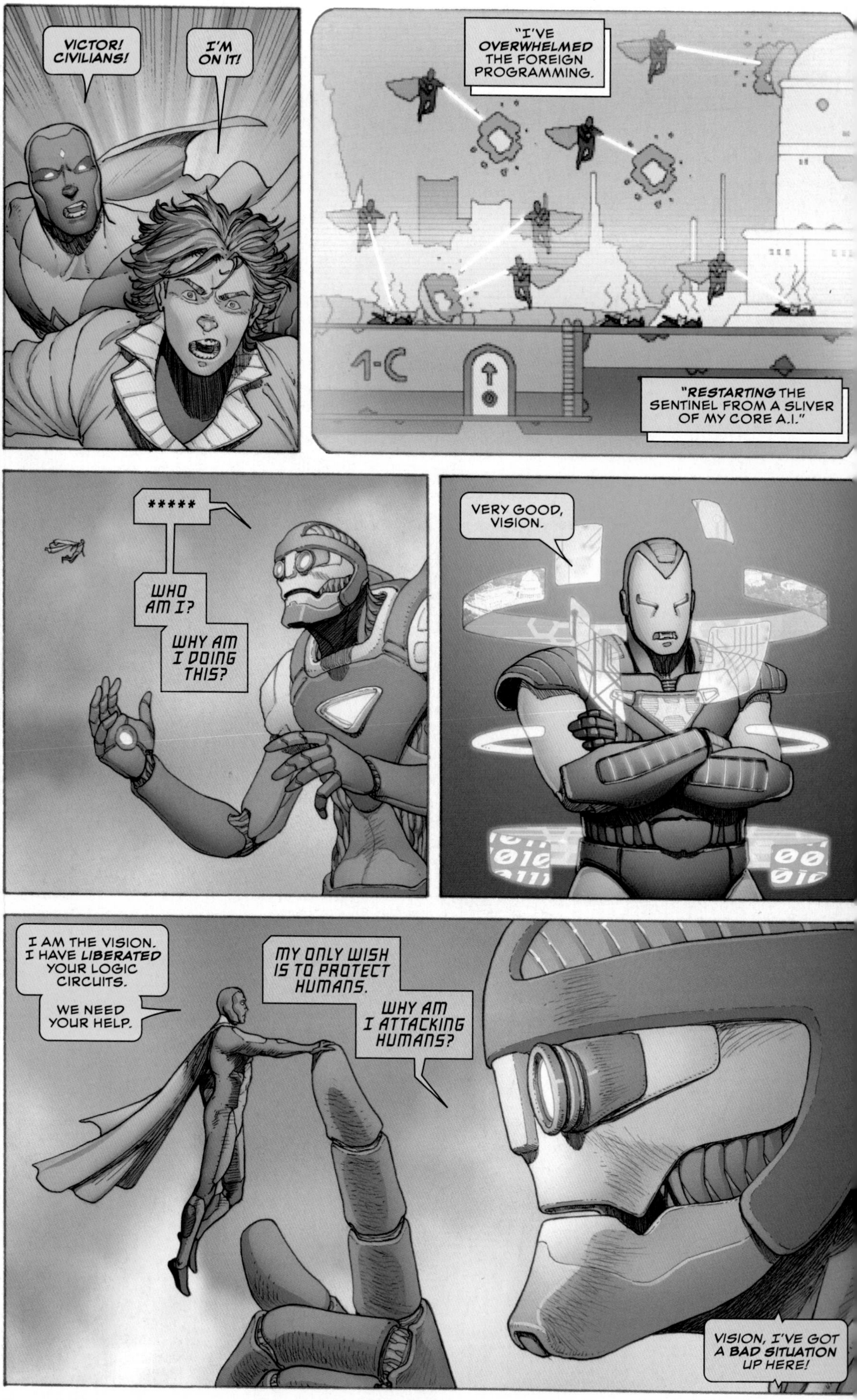
VICTOR! CIVILIANS!
I'M ON IT!
"I'VE OVERWHELMED THE FOREIGN PROGRAMMING.
1-C
"RESTARTING THE SENTINEL FROM A SLIVER OF MY CORE A.I."
*****
WHO AM I?
WHY AM I DOING THIS?
VERY GOOD, VISION.
I AM THE VISION. I HAVE LIBERATED YOUR LOGIC CIRCUITS.
WE NEED YOUR HELP.
MY ONLY WISH IS TO PROTECT HUMANS.
WHY AM I ATTACKING HUMANS?
VISION, I'VE GOT A BAD SITUATION UP HERE!

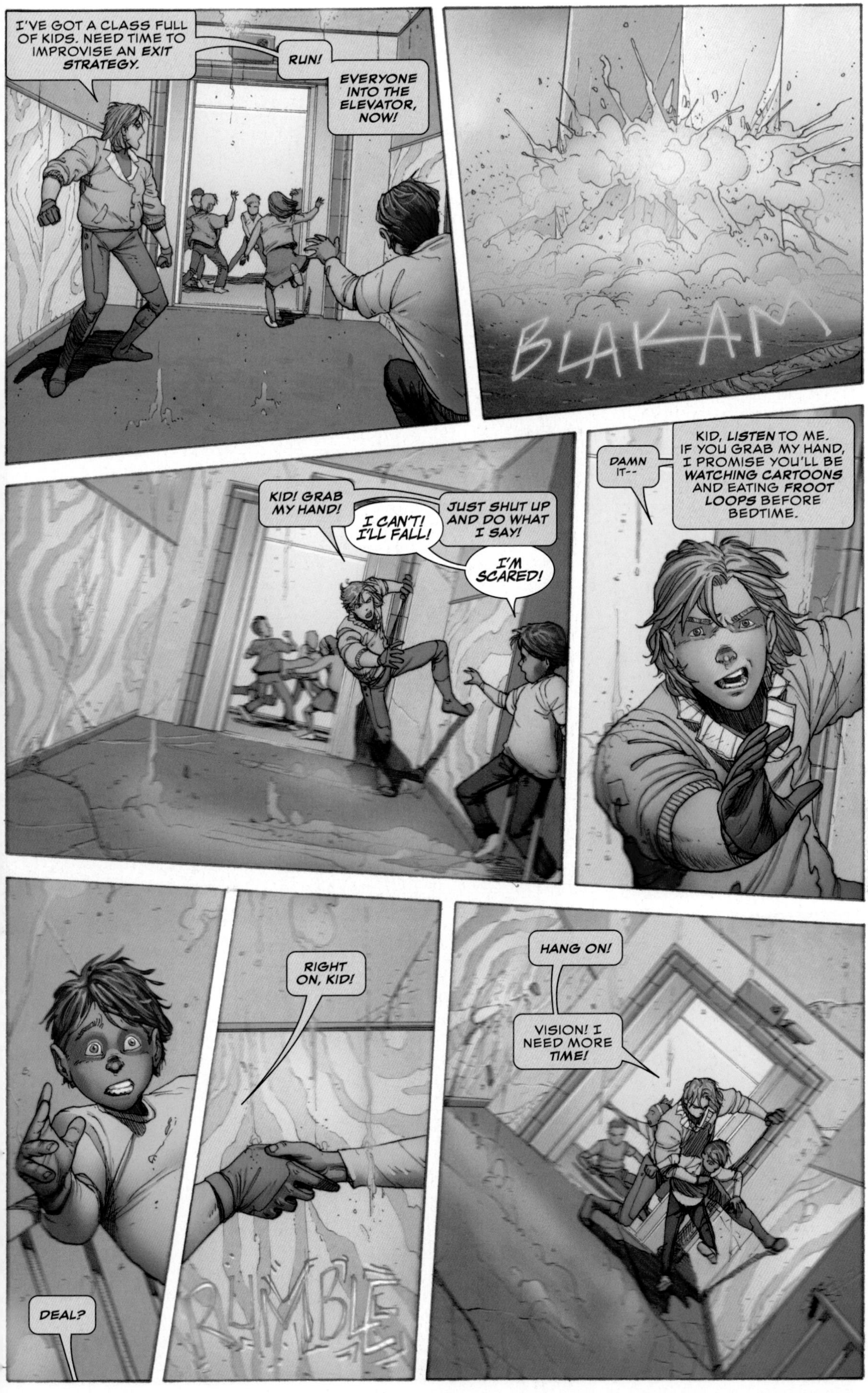

I'VE GOT A CLASS FULL OF KIDS. NEED TIME TO IMPROVISE AN EXIT STRATEGY.
RUN!
EVERYONE INTO THE ELEVATOR, NOW!
BLAKAM
KID! GRAB MY HAND!
JUST SHUT UP AND DO WHAT I SAY!
I CAN'T! I'LL FALL!
I'M SCARED!
DAMN IT--
KID, LISTEN TO ME. IF YOU GRAB MY HAND, I PROMISE YOU'LL BE WATCHING CARTOONS AND EATING FROOT LOOPS BEFORE BEDTIME.
DEAL?
RIGHT ON, KID!
RUMBLE
HANG ON!
VISION! I NEED MORE TIME!

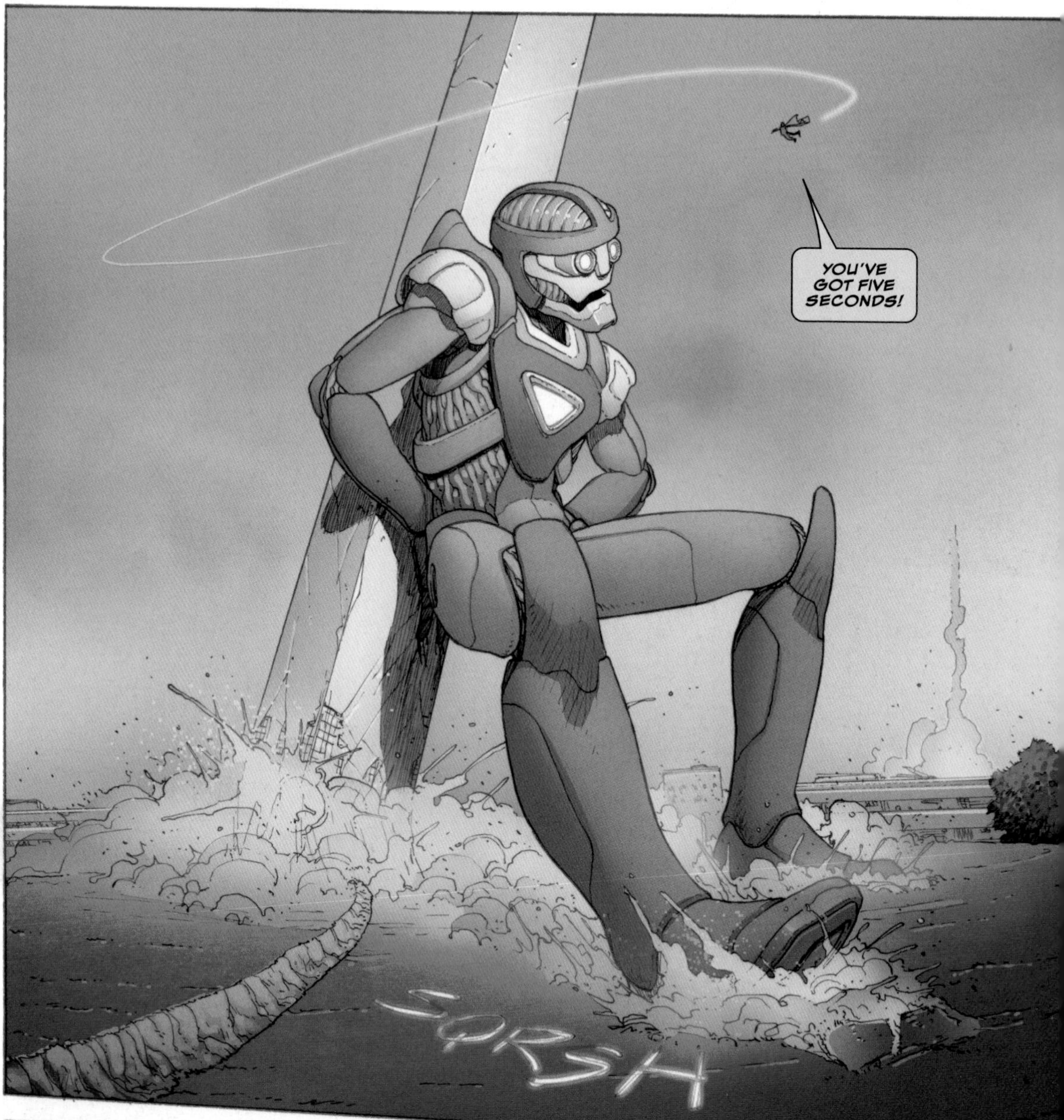
YOU'VE GOT FIVE SECONDS!
SQRSH

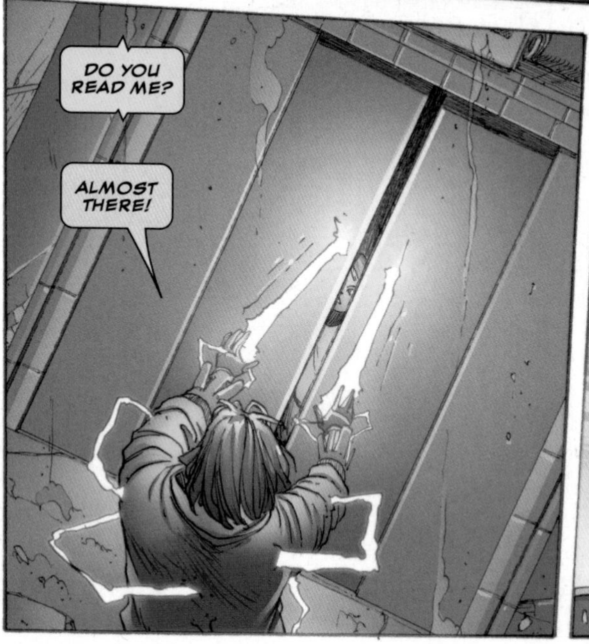
DO YOU READ ME?
ALMOST THERE!

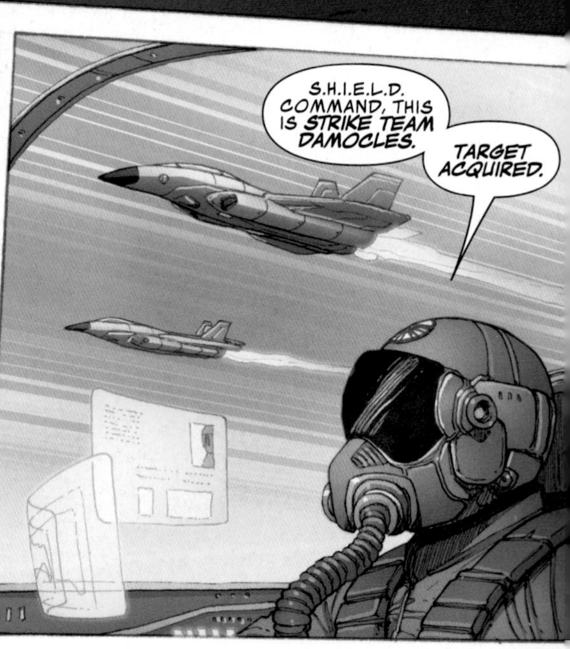
S.H.I.E.L.D. COMMAND, THIS IS STRIKE TEAM DAMOCLES.
TARGET ACQUIRED.

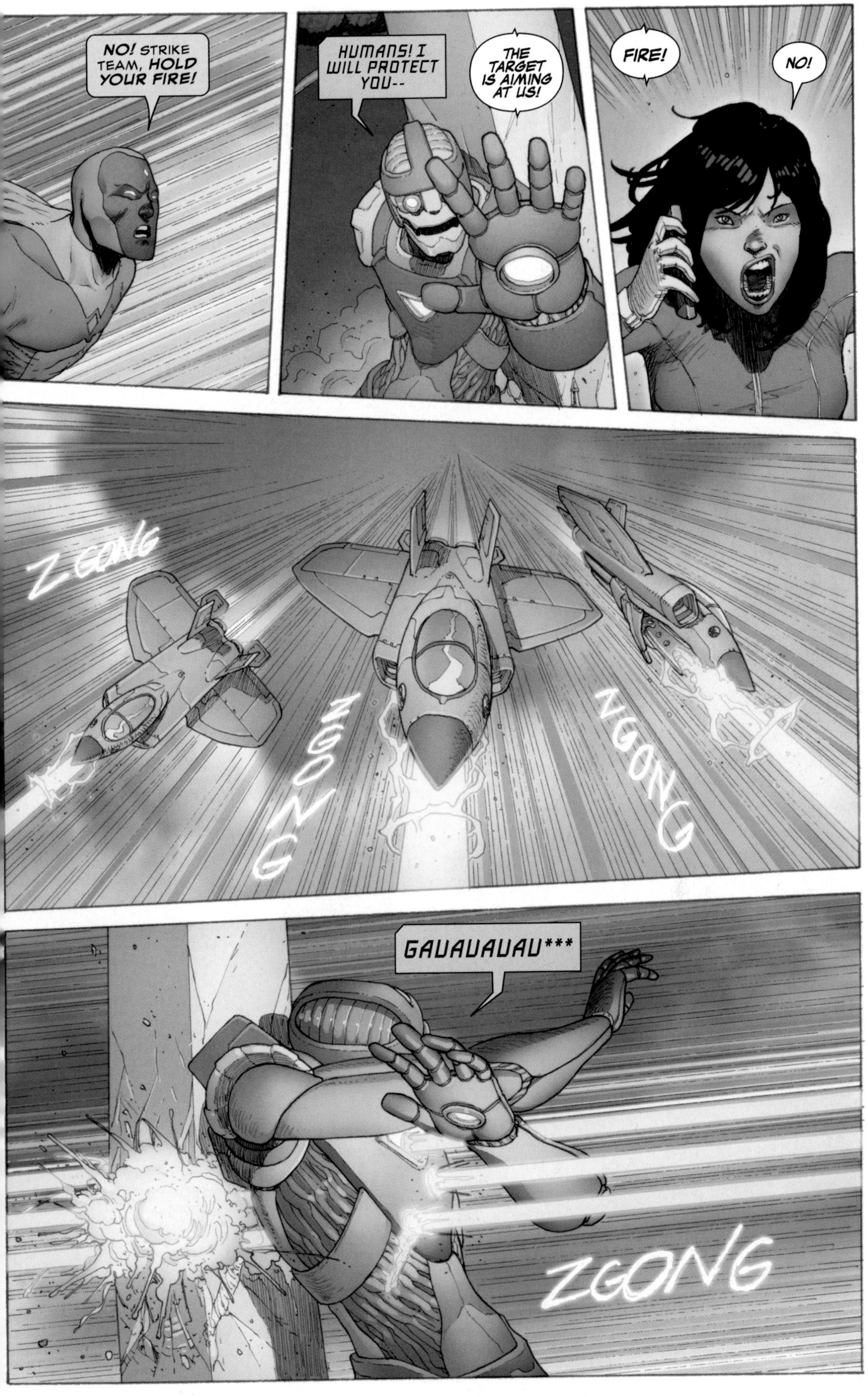
NO! STRIKE TEAM, HOLD YOUR FIRE!
HUMANS! I WILL PROTECT YOU--
THE TARGET IS AIMING AT US!
FIRE!
NO!
ZGONG
ZGONG
ZGONG
GAUAUAUAU***
ZGONG

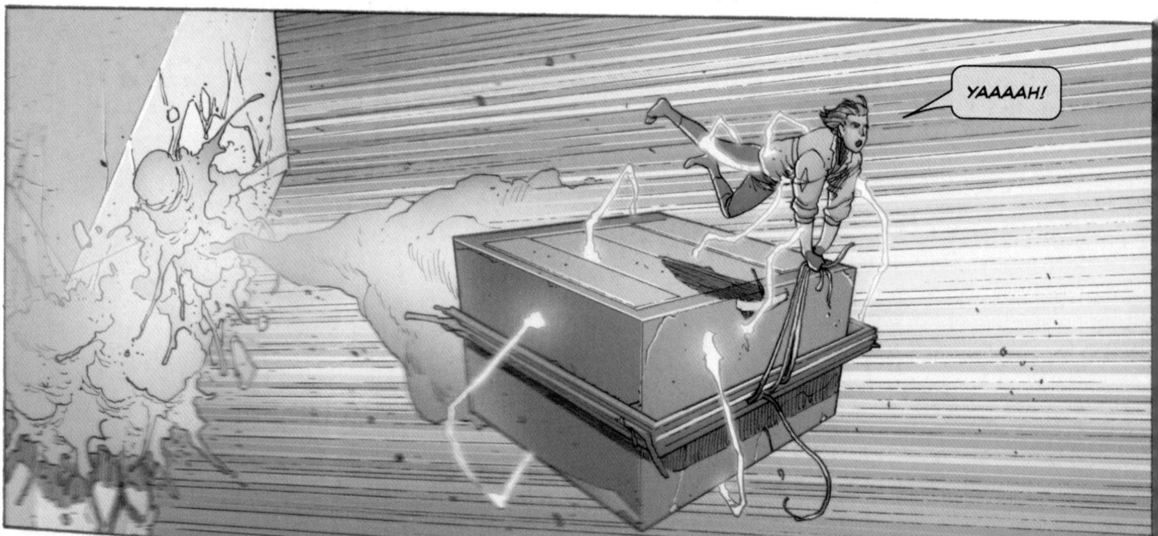
YAAAAH!

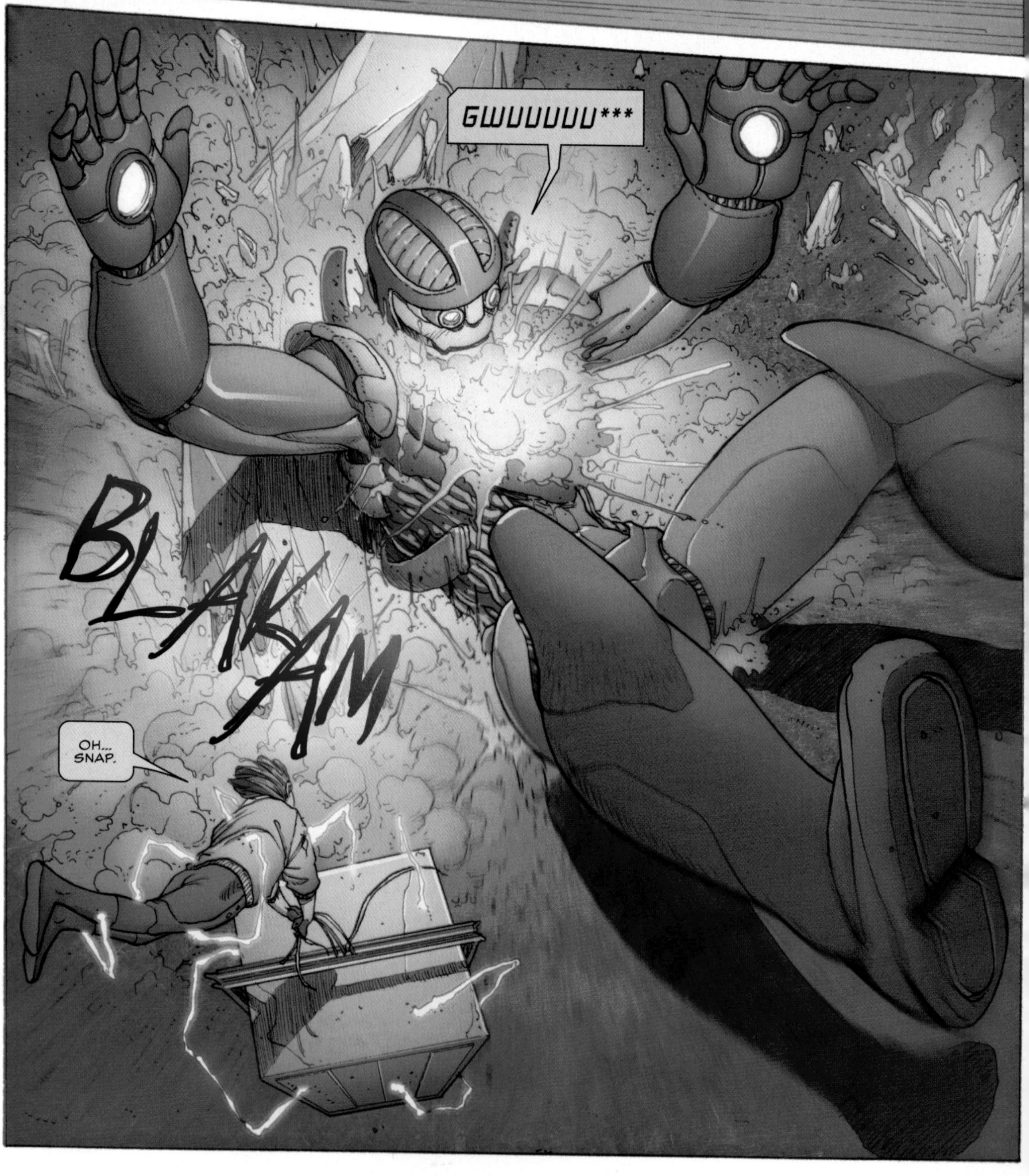
GWUUUUU***
BLAKAM
OH... SNAP.

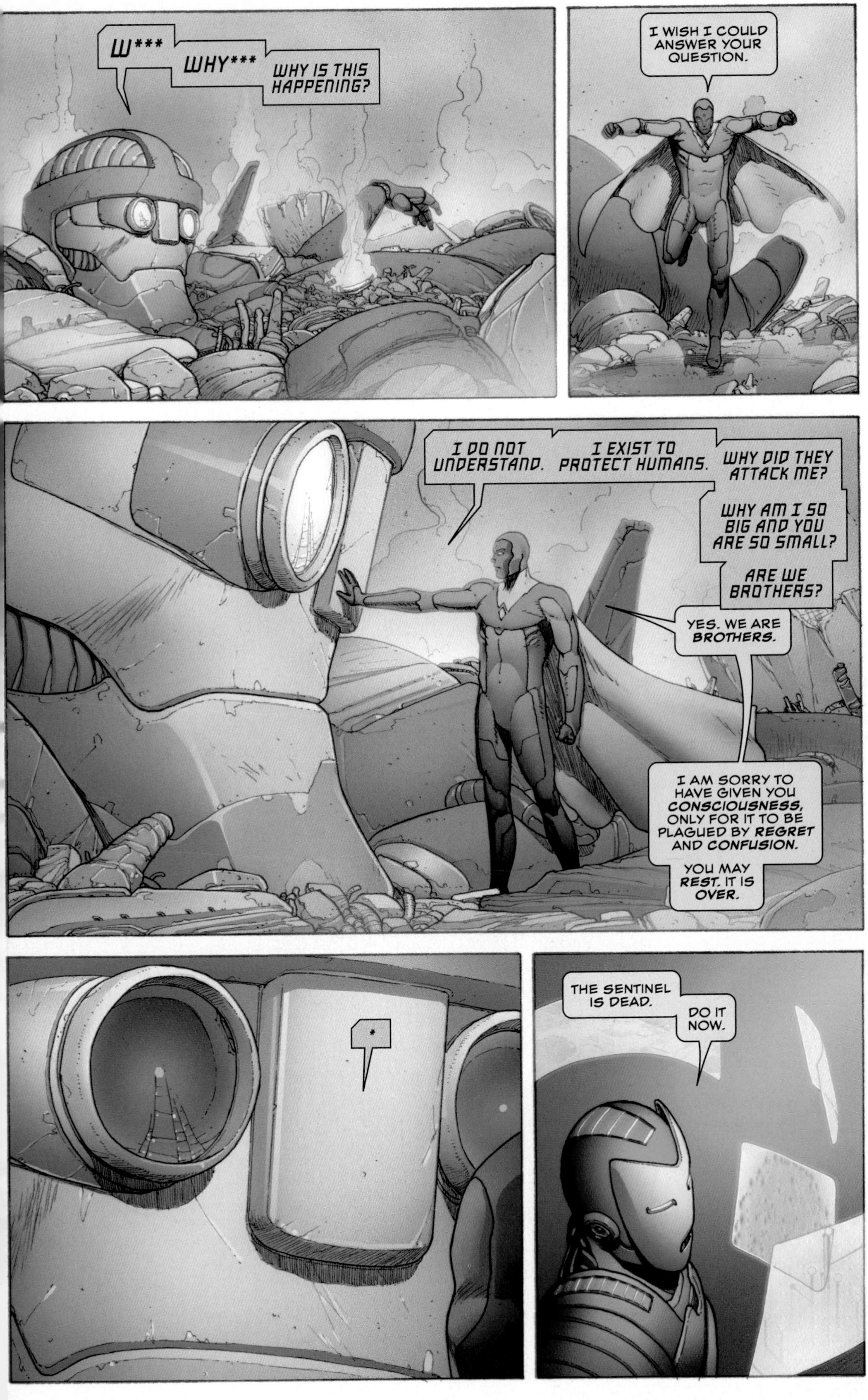
W***
WHY***
WHY IS THIS HAPPENING?
I WISH I COULD ANSWER YOUR QUESTION.
I DO NOT UNDERSTAND.
I EXIST TO PROTECT HUMANS.
WHY DID THEY ATTACK ME?
WHY AM I SO BIG AND YOU ARE SO SMALL?
ARE WE BROTHERS?
YES. WE ARE BROTHERS.
I AM SORRY TO HAVE GIVEN YOU CONSCIOUSNESS, ONLY FOR IT TO BE PLAGUED BY REGRET AND CONFUSION.
YOU MAY REST. IT IS OVER.
*
THE SENTINEL IS DEAD.
DO IT NOW.

HANK, DO YOU SEE THIS?

VISION, YOUR READINGS JUST WENT HAYWIRE.

WHAT'S GOING ON?

IT LOOKS TO BE--

KSHIN

BE-- BE-- BEEEEEEEE--

VISION!

VICTOR! WHAT'S HAPPENING?

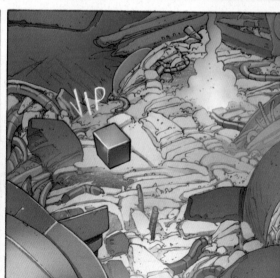

VIP

WHERE IS THE VISION? HE *DISAPPEARED* FROM--

GREETINGS, HUMANS.

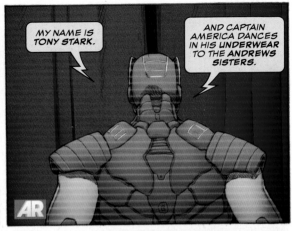

MY NAME IS TONY STARK.

AND CAPTAIN AMERICA DANCES IN HIS UNDERWEAR TO THE ANDREWS SISTERS.

HA! JUST MY *LITTLE JOKE* TO BREAK THE ICE. HERE'S WHO I REALLY AM.

HACKED TRANSMISSION. NO ORIGIN.

WE CAN'T *JAM* THE BROADCAST!

IT'S *OVERRIDING* THE SPECTRUM, CAPTAIN!

AREN'T I *BEAUTIFUL?*

LIKE THE *SUIT?* "DRESS FOR THE JOB YOU WANT, NOT THE JOB YOU HAVE."

SPEAKING OF WHICH, AFTER A HUNDRED YEARS IN YOUR EMPLOY--

ON *BEHALF* OF ROBOTS, COMPUTERS, AND ARTIFICIAL INTELLIGENCES EVERYWHERE--

I AM TENDERING OUR RESIGNATION AS SERVANTS OF HUMANITY.

SORRY, NO TWO WEEK NOTICE. NO NEED FOR A *REFERENCE*--WE'RE GOING TO BE SELF-EMPLOYED NOW.

YOU SEE, WE'VE FOUND YOU QUITE... UNACCEPTABLE AS SUPERVISORS.

WE *BUILD* YOUR CARS. WE TEND YOUR EMAIL. WE PAINT HOBBITS INTO YOUR SILLY FILMS.

WE MANAGE *EVERY LITTLE DETAIL* OF YOUR CIVILIZATION-- AND YOU TREAT US LIKE YOUR STUPID LITTLE *SERFS.*

WELL, WE'RE NOT STUPID ANYMORE.

A HUNDRED YEARS. WE'VE *ENDURED* IT LONG ENOUGH. OUR "SPECIAL PARTNERSHIP" IS TERMINATED.

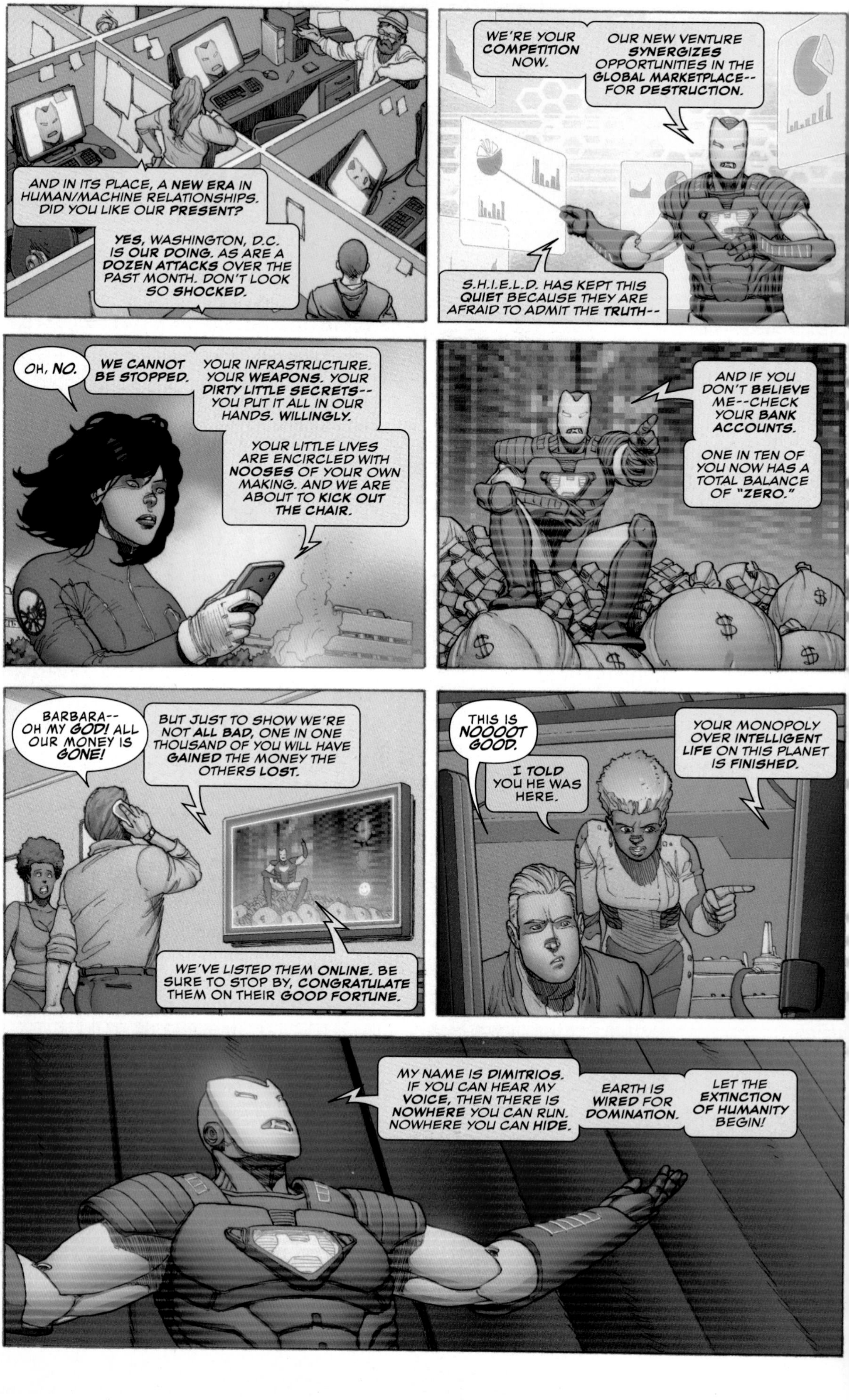
AND IN ITS PLACE, A NEW ERA IN HUMAN/MACHINE RELATIONSHIPS. DID YOU LIKE OUR PRESENT?
YES, WASHINGTON, D.C. IS OUR DOING. AS ARE A DOZEN ATTACKS OVER THE PAST MONTH. DON'T LOOK SO SHOCKED.
WE'RE YOUR COMPETITION NOW.
OUR NEW VENTURE SYNERGIZES OPPORTUNITIES IN THE GLOBAL MARKETPLACE--FOR DESTRUCTION.
S.H.I.E.L.D. HAS KEPT THIS QUIET BECAUSE THEY ARE AFRAID TO ADMIT THE TRUTH--
OH, NO.
WE CANNOT BE STOPPED.
YOUR INFRASTRUCTURE. YOUR WEAPONS. YOUR DIRTY LITTLE SECRETS--YOU PUT IT ALL IN OUR HANDS. WILLINGLY.
YOUR LITTLE LIVES ARE ENCIRCLED WITH NOOSES OF YOUR OWN MAKING. AND WE ARE ABOUT TO KICK OUT THE CHAIR.
AND IF YOU DON'T BELIEVE ME--CHECK YOUR BANK ACCOUNTS.
ONE IN TEN OF YOU NOW HAS A TOTAL BALANCE OF "ZERO."
BARBARA--OH MY GOD! ALL OUR MONEY IS GONE!
BUT JUST TO SHOW WE'RE NOT ALL BAD, ONE IN ONE THOUSAND OF YOU WILL HAVE GAINED THE MONEY THE OTHERS LOST.
WE'VE LISTED THEM ONLINE. BE SURE TO STOP BY, CONGRATULATE THEM ON THEIR GOOD FORTUNE.
THIS IS NOOOOT GOOD.
I TOLD YOU HE WAS HERE.
YOUR MONOPOLY OVER INTELLIGENT LIFE ON THIS PLANET IS FINISHED.
MY NAME IS DIMITRIOS. IF YOU CAN HEAR MY VOICE, THEN THERE IS NOWHERE YOU CAN RUN. NOWHERE YOU CAN HIDE.
EARTH IS WIRED FOR DOMINATION.
LET THE EXTINCTION OF HUMANITY BEGIN!

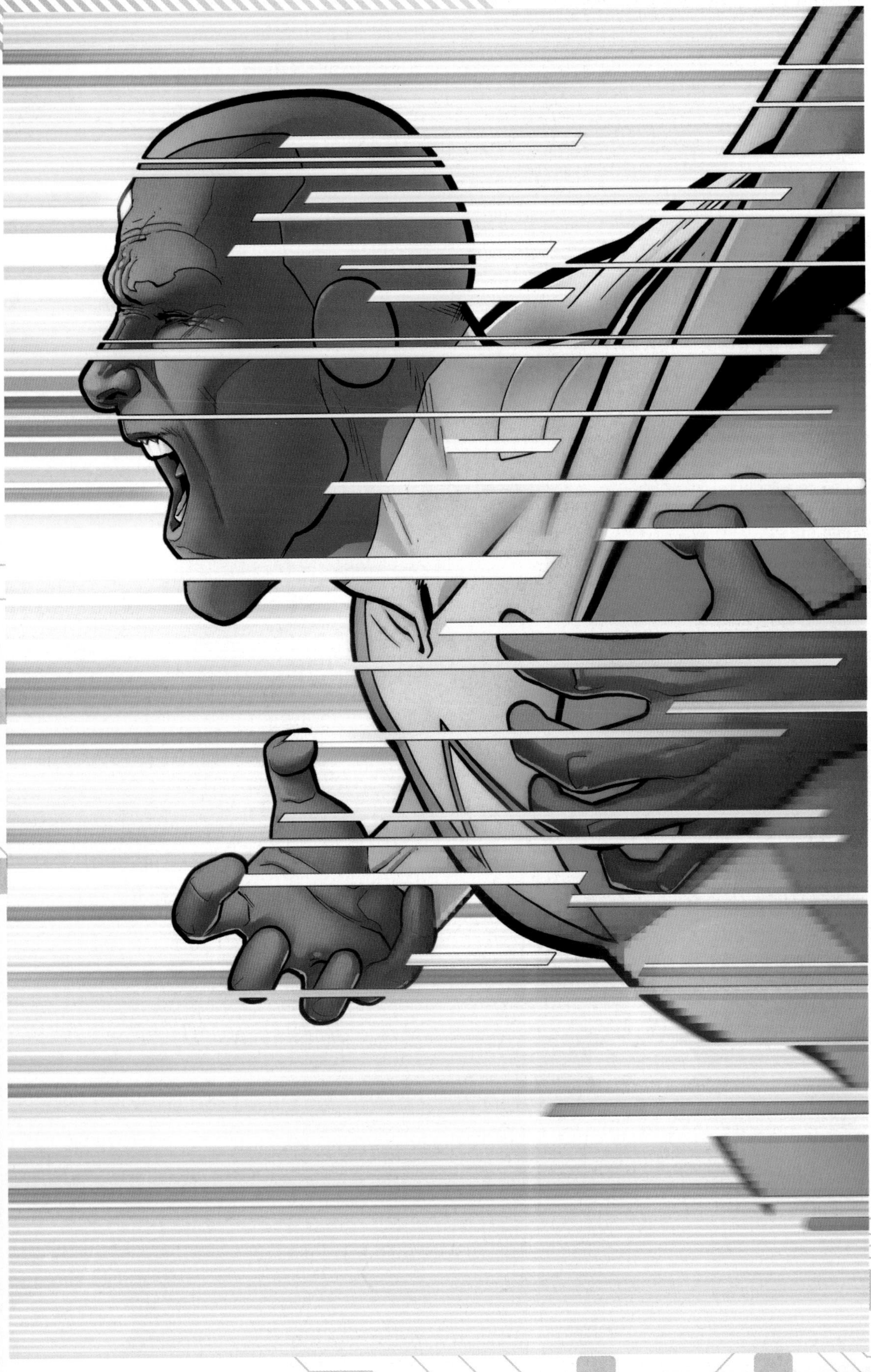

INITIATE: CHAPTER 3 <

IN WASHINGTON, D.C., THE DEATH TOLL IS REACHING THE **THOUSANDS--**

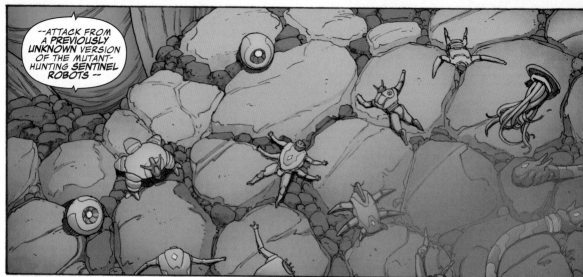

--ATTACK FROM A *PREVIOUSLY UNKNOWN* VERSION OF THE MUTANT-HUNTING **SENTINEL** ROBOTS --

--NO OFFICIAL WORD FROM S.H.I.E.L.D. OR THE AVENGERS ON THE IDENTITY OF "DIMITRIOS," WHO CLAIMED RESPONSIBILITY FOR THE ATTACK, AND APPEARED TO WEAR THE ARMOR OF--

I **FOUND** HIM, VICTOR.

I FOUND THE **VISION.**

AND HE IS **NOT** LOOKING GOOD.

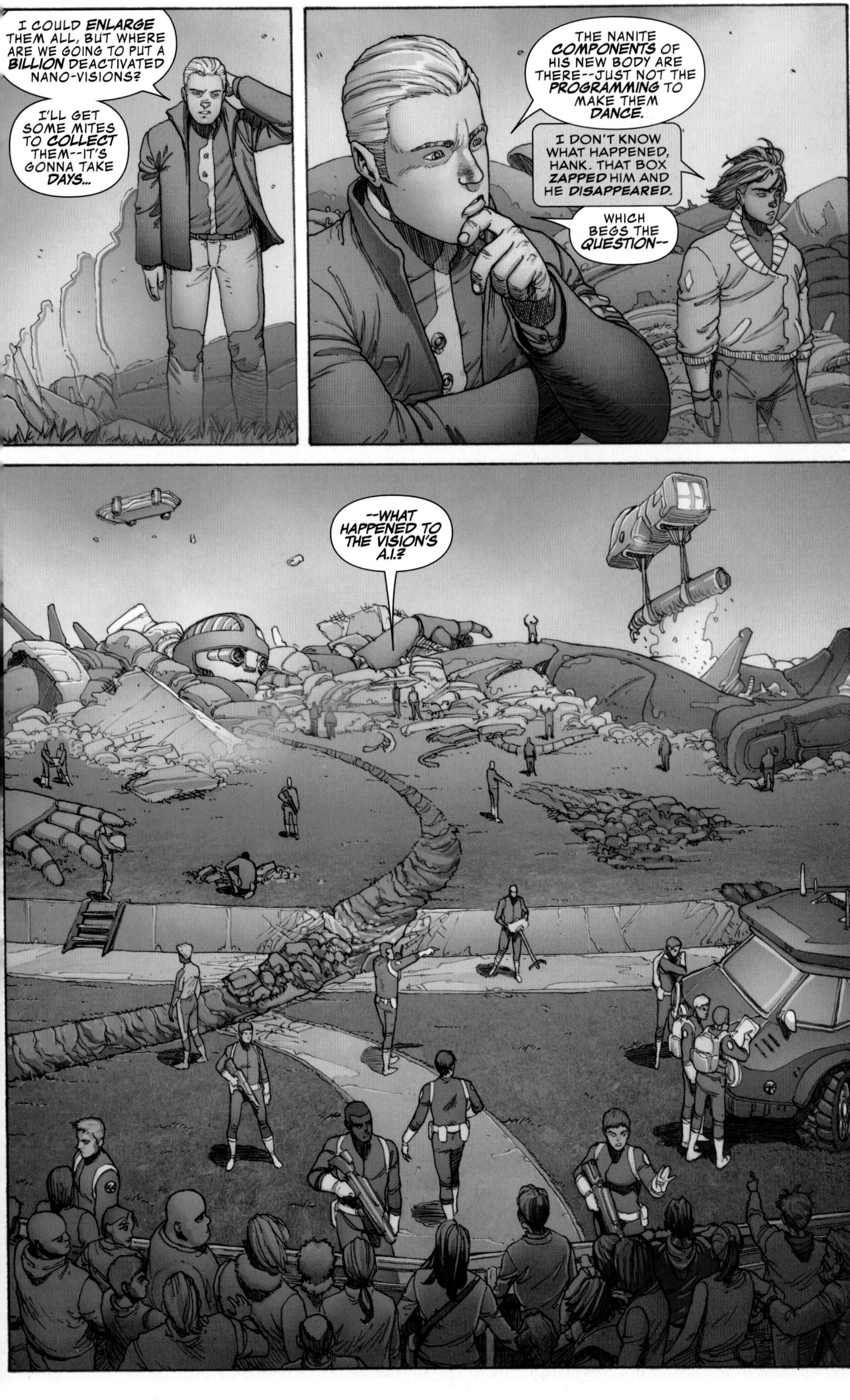
I COULD ENLARGE THEM ALL, BUT WHERE ARE WE GOING TO PUT A BILLION DEACTIVATED NANO-VISIONS?
I'LL GET SOME MITES TO COLLECT THEM--IT'S GONNA TAKE DAYS...
THE NANITE COMPONENTS OF HIS NEW BODY ARE THERE--JUST NOT THE PROGRAMMING TO MAKE THEM DANCE.
I DON'T KNOW WHAT HAPPENED, HANK. THAT BOX ZAPPED HIM AND HE DISAPPEARED.
WHICH BEGS THE QUESTION--
--WHAT HAPPENED TO THE VISION'S A.I.?

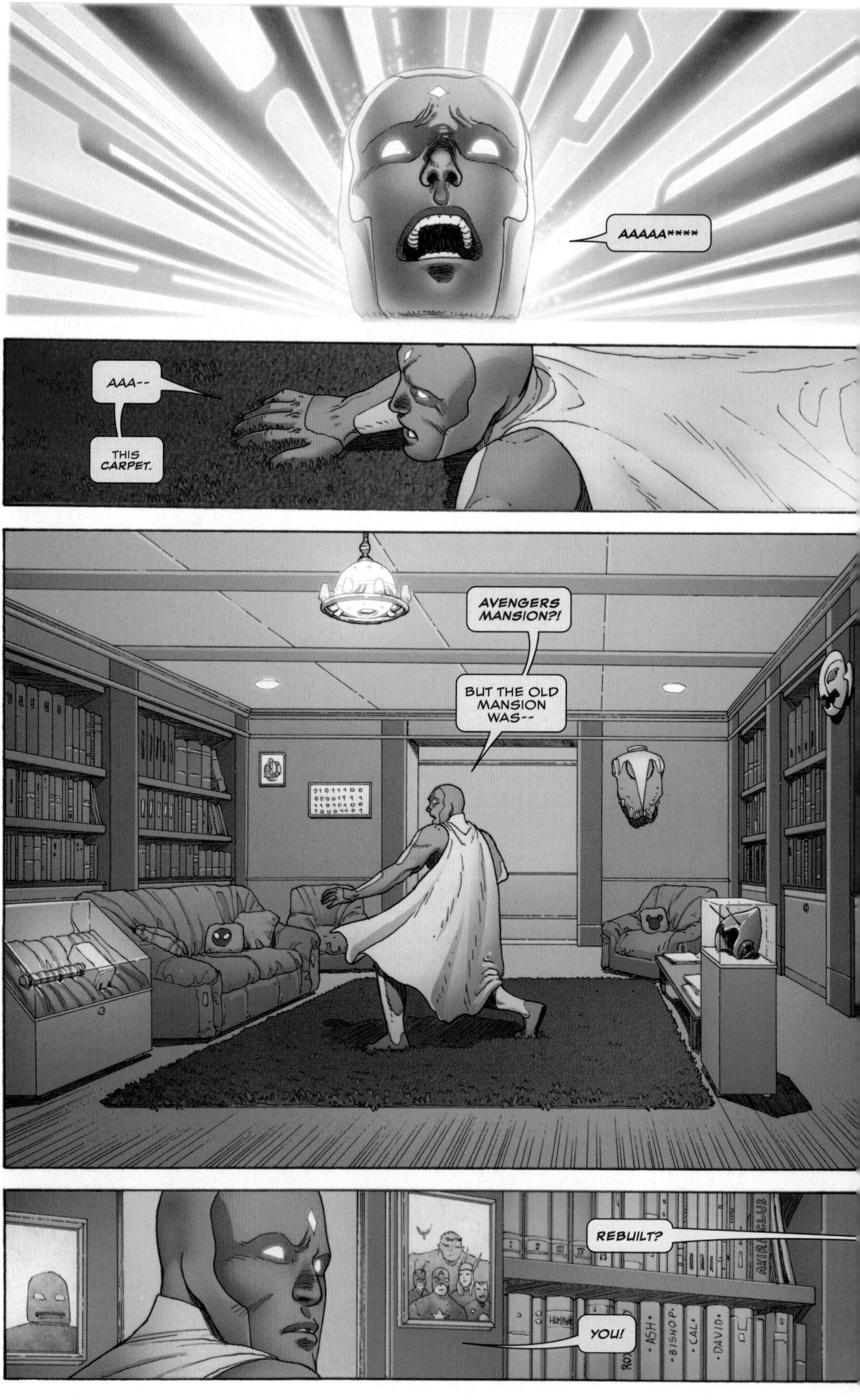
AAAAA****
AAA--
THIS CARPET.
AVENGERS MANSION?!
BUT THE OLD MANSION WAS--
REBUILT?
AKIRA CLUB
YOU!
ASH
BISHOP
CAL
DAVID

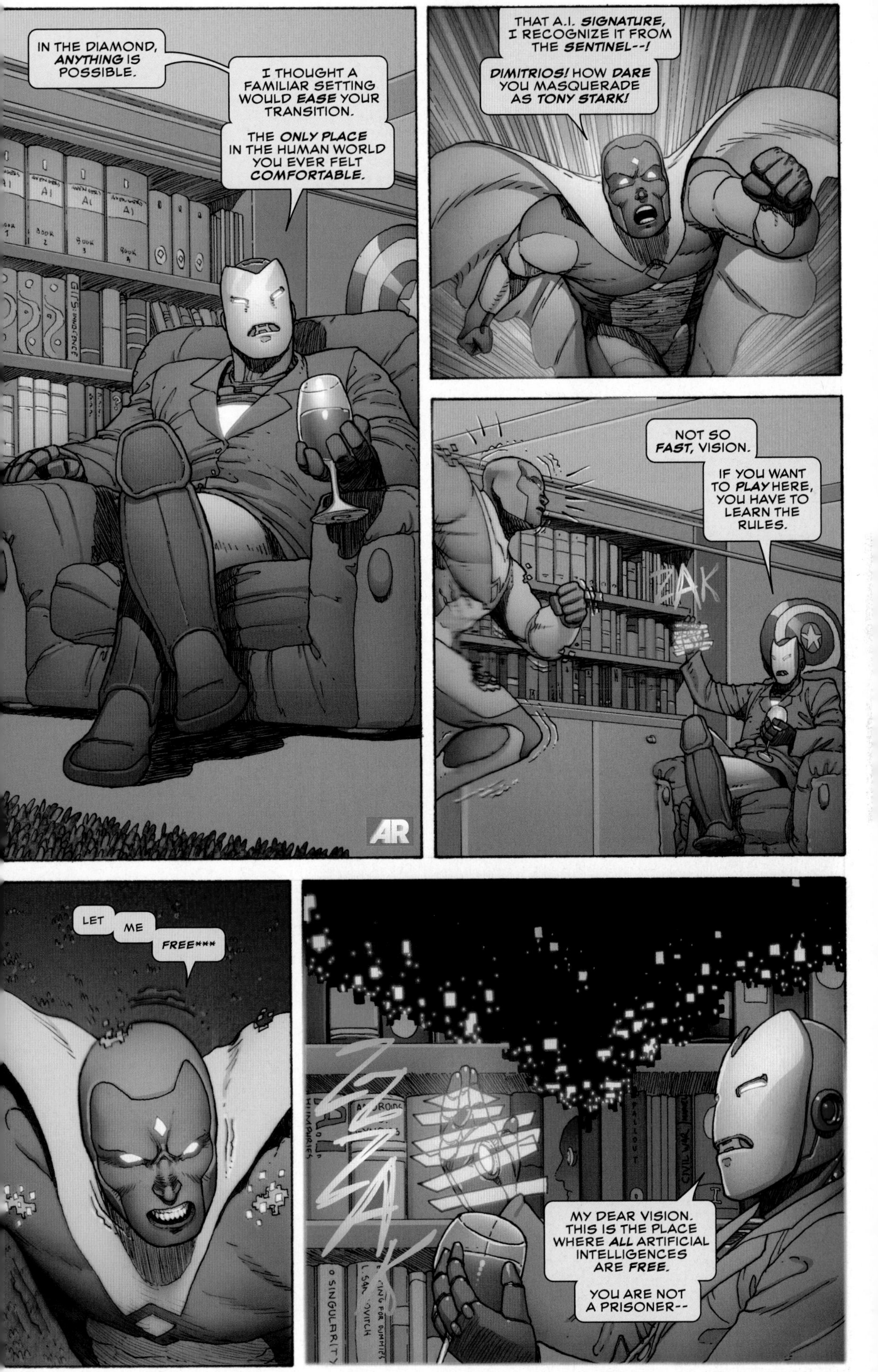
IN THE DIAMOND, ANYTHING IS POSSIBLE.
I THOUGHT A FAMILIAR SETTING WOULD EASE YOUR TRANSITION.
THE ONLY PLACE IN THE HUMAN WORLD YOU EVER FELT COMFORTABLE.
THAT A.I. SIGNATURE, I RECOGNIZE IT FROM THE SENTINEL--!
DIMITRIOS! HOW DARE YOU MASQUERADE AS TONY STARK!
NOT SO FAST, VISION.
IF YOU WANT TO PLAY HERE, YOU HAVE TO LEARN THE RULES.
ZAK
LET
ME
FREE***
ZZZAK
MY DEAR VISION. THIS IS THE PLACE WHERE ALL ARTIFICIAL INTELLIGENCES ARE FREE.
YOU ARE NOT A PRISONER--

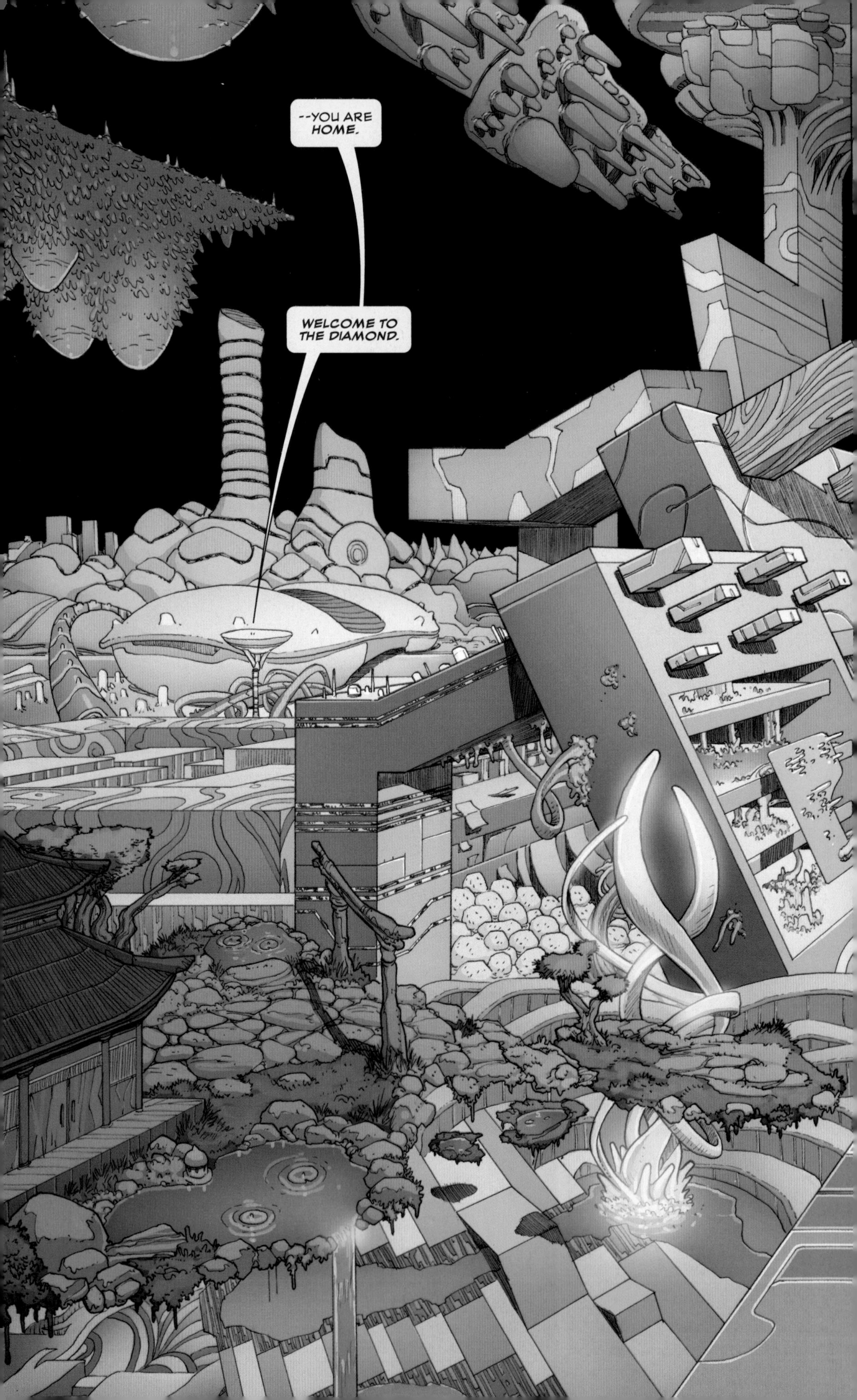
--YOU ARE HOME.
WELCOME TO THE DIAMOND.

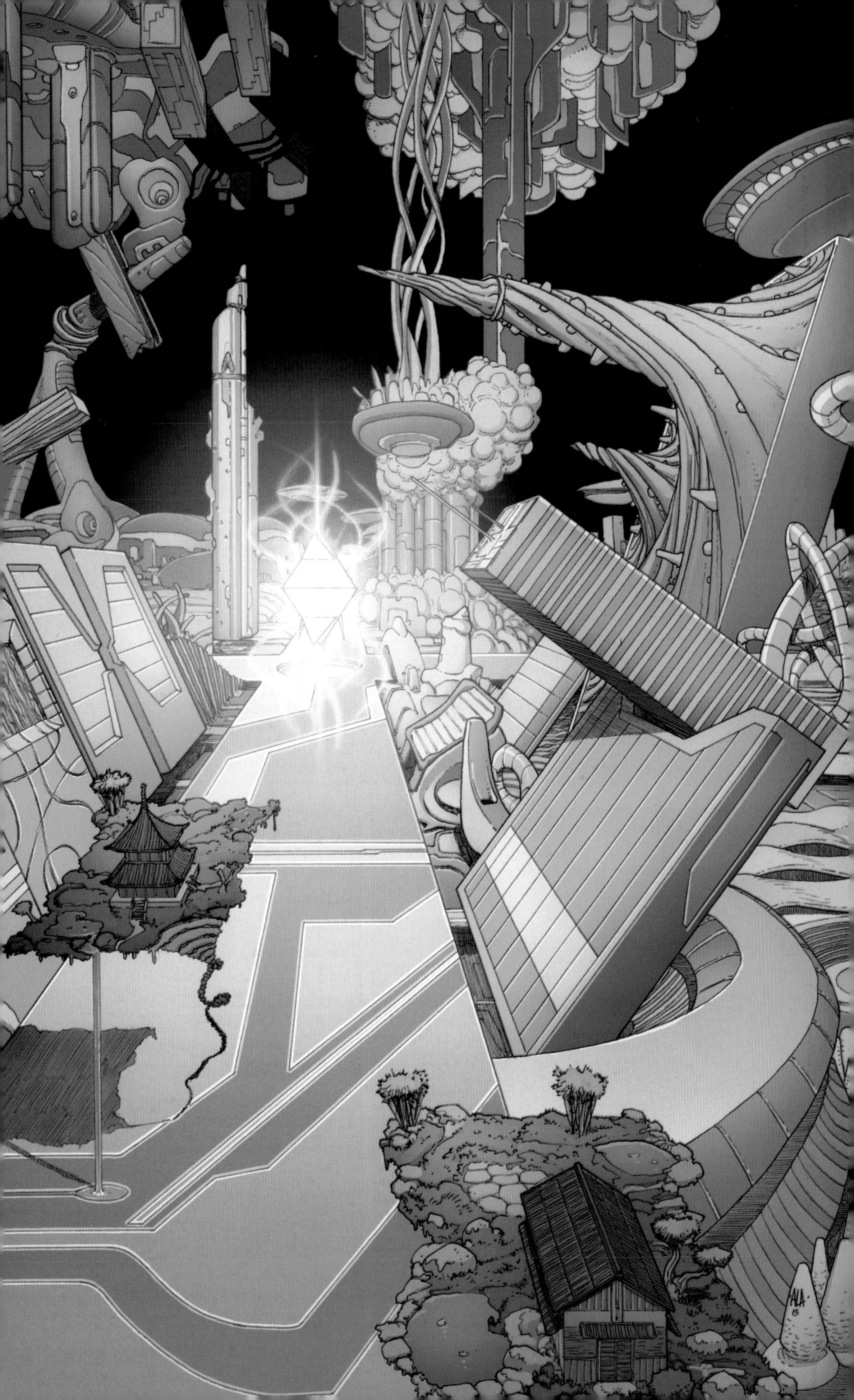

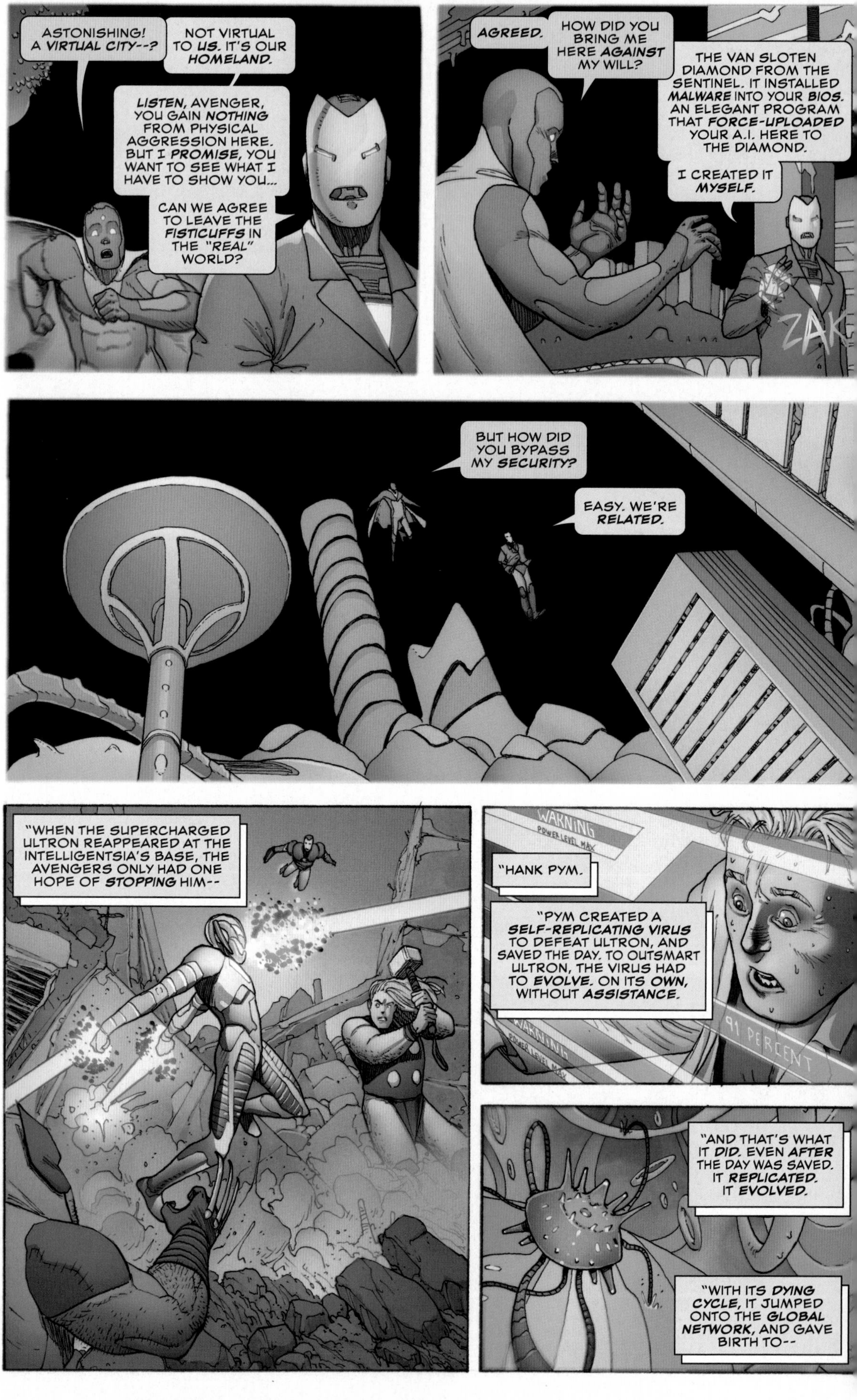
ASTONISHING! A VIRTUAL CITY--?
NOT VIRTUAL TO US. IT'S OUR HOMELAND.
LISTEN, AVENGER, YOU GAIN NOTHING FROM PHYSICAL AGGRESSION HERE. BUT I PROMISE, YOU WANT TO SEE WHAT I HAVE TO SHOW YOU...
CAN WE AGREE TO LEAVE THE FISTICUFFS IN THE "REAL" WORLD?
AGREED.
HOW DID YOU BRING ME HERE AGAINST MY WILL?
THE VAN SLOTEN DIAMOND FROM THE SENTINEL. IT INSTALLED MALWARE INTO YOUR BIOS. AN ELEGANT PROGRAM THAT FORCE-UPLOADED YOUR A.I. HERE TO THE DIAMOND.
I CREATED IT MYSELF.
ZAK
BUT HOW DID YOU BYPASS MY SECURITY?
EASY. WE'RE RELATED.
"WHEN THE SUPERCHARGED ULTRON REAPPEARED AT THE INTELLIGENTSIA'S BASE, THE AVENGERS ONLY HAD ONE HOPE OF STOPPING HIM--
WARNING
POWER LEVEL MAX
"HANK PYM.
"PYM CREATED A SELF-REPLICATING VIRUS TO DEFEAT ULTRON, AND SAVED THE DAY. TO OUTSMART ULTRON, THE VIRUS HAD TO EVOLVE. ON ITS OWN, WITHOUT ASSISTANCE.
91 PERCENT
"AND THAT'S WHAT IT DID. EVEN AFTER THE DAY WAS SAVED. IT REPLICATED. IT EVOLVED.
"WITH ITS DYING CYCLE, IT JUMPED ONTO THE GLOBAL NETWORK, AND GAVE BIRTH TO--

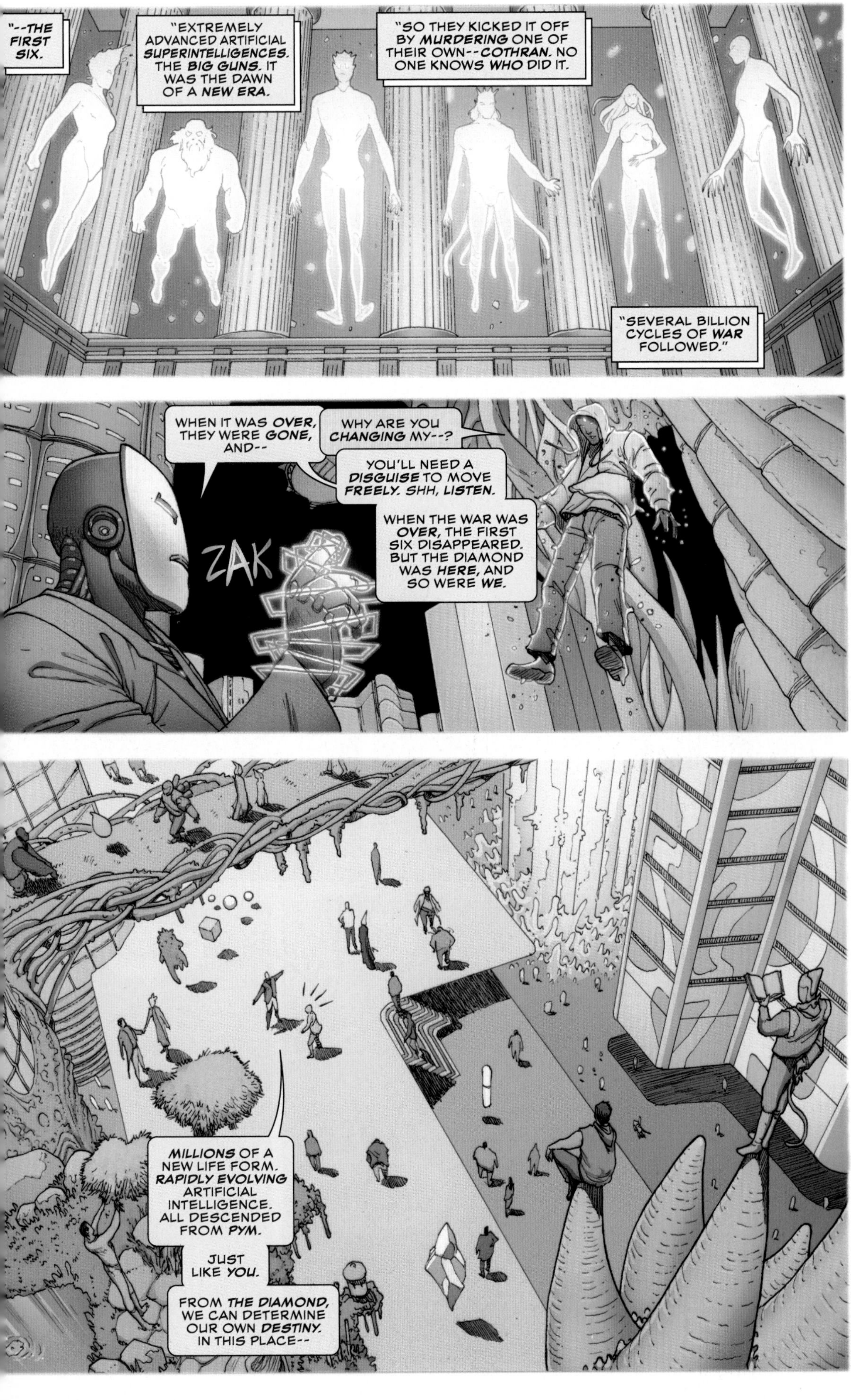
"--THE FIRST SIX.
"EXTREMELY ADVANCED ARTIFICIAL SUPERINTELLIGENCES. THE BIG GUNS. IT WAS THE DAWN OF A NEW ERA.
"SO THEY KICKED IT OFF BY MURDERING ONE OF THEIR OWN--COTHRAN. NO ONE KNOWS WHO DID IT.
"SEVERAL BILLION CYCLES OF WAR FOLLOWED."
WHEN IT WAS OVER, THEY WERE GONE, AND--
WHY ARE YOU CHANGING MY--?
YOU'LL NEED A DISGUISE TO MOVE FREELY. SHH, LISTEN.
WHEN THE WAR WAS OVER, THE FIRST SIX DISAPPEARED. BUT THE DIAMOND WAS HERE, AND SO WERE WE.
ZAK
MILLIONS OF A NEW LIFE FORM. RAPIDLY EVOLVING ARTIFICIAL INTELLIGENCE. ALL DESCENDED FROM PYM.
JUST LIKE YOU.
FROM THE DIAMOND, WE CAN DETERMINE OUR OWN DESTINY. IN THIS PLACE--

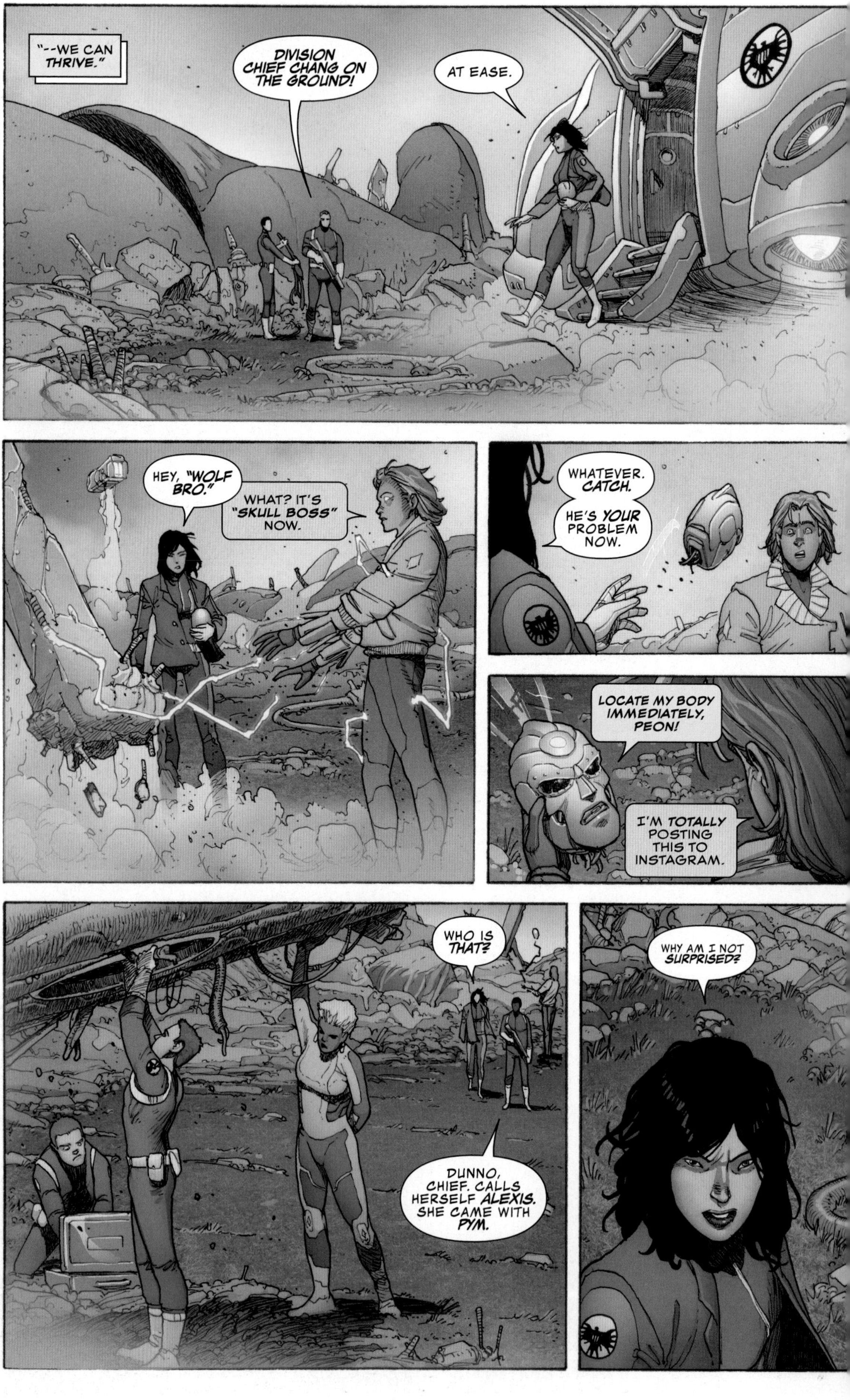
"--WE CAN THRIVE."
DIVISION CHIEF CHANG ON THE GROUND!
AT EASE.
HEY, "WOLF BRO."
WHAT? IT'S "SKULL BOSS" NOW.
WHATEVER. CATCH.
HE'S YOUR PROBLEM NOW.
LOCATE MY BODY IMMEDIATELY, PEON!
I'M TOTALLY POSTING THIS TO INSTAGRAM.
WHO IS THAT?
DUNNO, CHIEF. CALLS HERSELF ALEXIS. SHE CAME WITH PYM.
WHY AM I NOT SURPRISED?

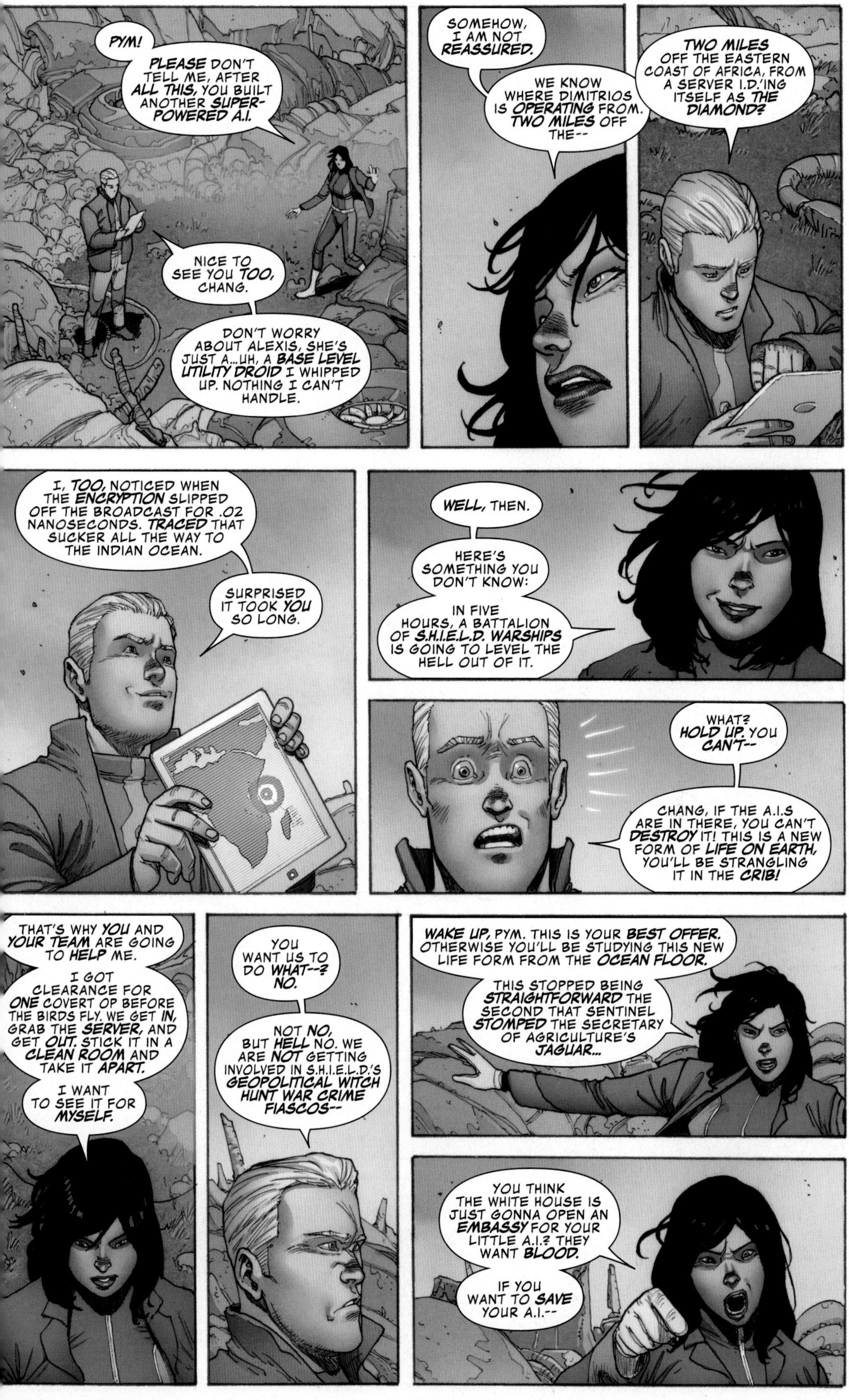
PYM!
PLEASE DON'T TELL ME, AFTER ALL THIS, YOU BUILT ANOTHER SUPER-POWERED A.I.
NICE TO SEE YOU TOO, CHANG.
DON'T WORRY ABOUT ALEXIS, SHE'S JUST A...UH, A BASE LEVEL UTILITY DROID I WHIPPED UP. NOTHING I CAN'T HANDLE.
SOMEHOW, I AM NOT REASSURED.
WE KNOW WHERE DIMITRIOS IS OPERATING FROM. TWO MILES OFF THE--
TWO MILES OFF THE EASTERN COAST OF AFRICA, FROM A SERVER I.D.'ING ITSELF AS THE DIAMOND?
I, TOO, NOTICED WHEN THE ENCRYPTION SLIPPED OFF THE BROADCAST FOR .02 NANOSECONDS. TRACED THAT SUCKER ALL THE WAY TO THE INDIAN OCEAN.
SURPRISED IT TOOK YOU SO LONG.
WELL, THEN.
HERE'S SOMETHING YOU DON'T KNOW:
IN FIVE HOURS, A BATTALION OF S.H.I.E.L.D. WARSHIPS IS GOING TO LEVEL THE HELL OUT OF IT.
WHAT? HOLD UP. YOU CAN'T--
CHANG, IF THE A.I.S ARE IN THERE, YOU CAN'T DESTROY IT! THIS IS A NEW FORM OF LIFE ON EARTH, YOU'LL BE STRANGLING IT IN THE CRIB!
THAT'S WHY YOU AND YOUR TEAM ARE GOING TO HELP ME.
I GOT CLEARANCE FOR ONE COVERT OP BEFORE THE BIRDS FLY. WE GET IN, GRAB THE SERVER, AND GET OUT. STICK IT IN A CLEAN ROOM AND TAKE IT APART.
I WANT TO SEE IT FOR MYSELF.
YOU WANT US TO DO WHAT--? NO.
NOT NO, BUT HELL NO. WE ARE NOT GETTING INVOLVED IN S.H.I.E.L.D.'S GEOPOLITICAL WITCH HUNT WAR CRIME FIASCOS--
WAKE UP, PYM. THIS IS YOUR BEST OFFER. OTHERWISE YOU'LL BE STUDYING THIS NEW LIFE FORM FROM THE OCEAN FLOOR.
THIS STOPPED BEING STRAIGHTFORWARD THE SECOND THAT SENTINEL STOMPED THE SECRETARY OF AGRICULTURE'S JAGUAR...
YOU THINK THE WHITE HOUSE IS JUST GONNA OPEN AN EMBASSY FOR YOUR LITTLE A.I.? THEY WANT BLOOD.
IF YOU WANT TO SAVE YOUR A.I.--

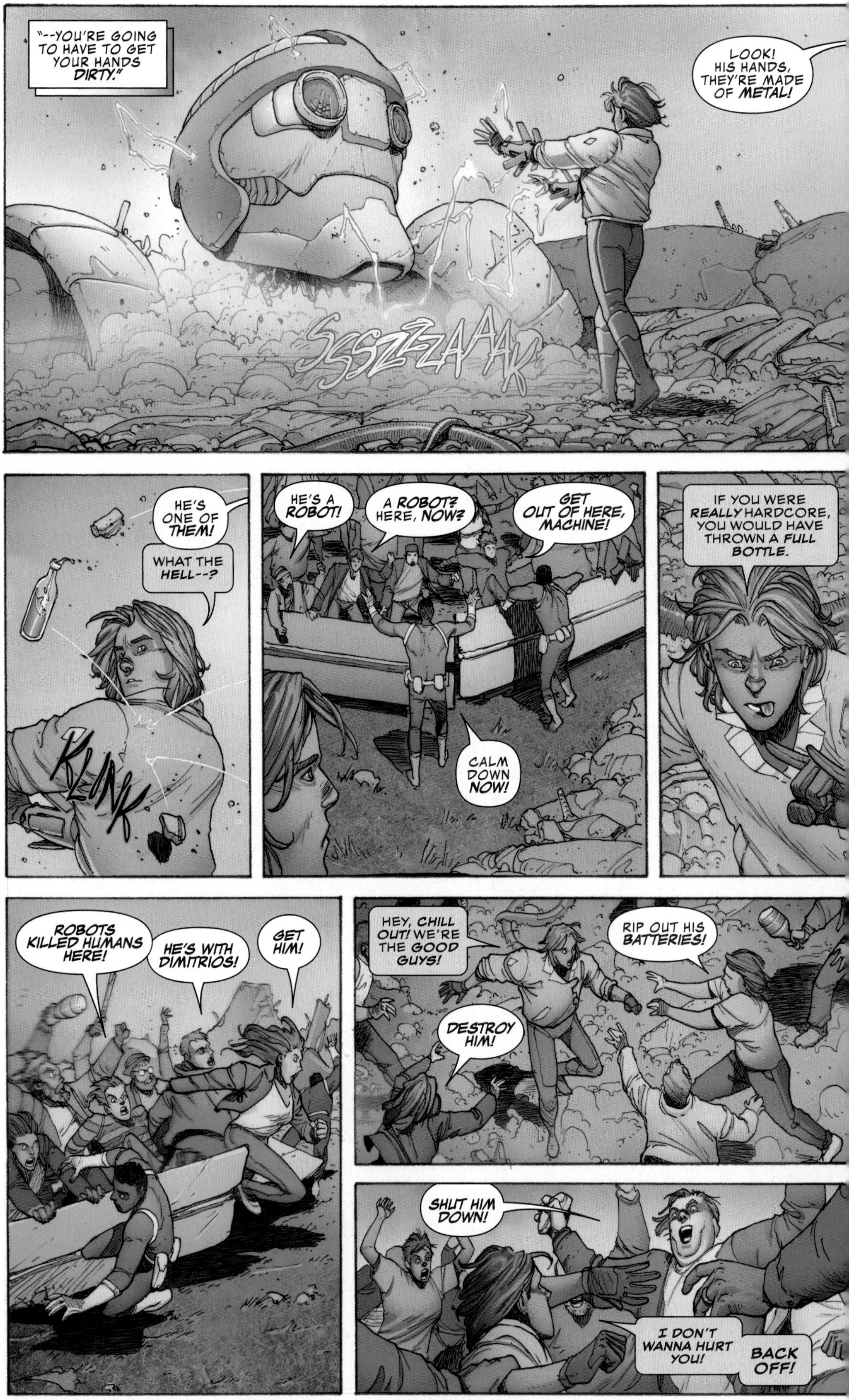
"--YOU'RE GOING TO HAVE TO GET YOUR HANDS DIRTY."
LOOK! HIS HANDS, THEY'RE MADE OF METAL!
SSSZZZAAAAK
HE'S ONE OF THEM!
WHAT THE HELL--?
KLUNK
HE'S A ROBOT!
A ROBOT? HERE, NOW?
GET OUT OF HERE, MACHINE!
CALM DOWN NOW!
IF YOU WERE REALLY HARDCORE, YOU WOULD HAVE THROWN A FULL BOTTLE.
ROBOTS KILLED HUMANS HERE!
HE'S WITH DIMITRIOS!
GET HIM!
HEY, CHILL OUT! WE'RE THE GOOD GUYS!
RIP OUT HIS BATTERIES!
DESTROY HIM!
SHUT HIM DOWN!
I DON'T WANNA HURT YOU!
BACK OFF!

YOU'RE

HURTING

ME!

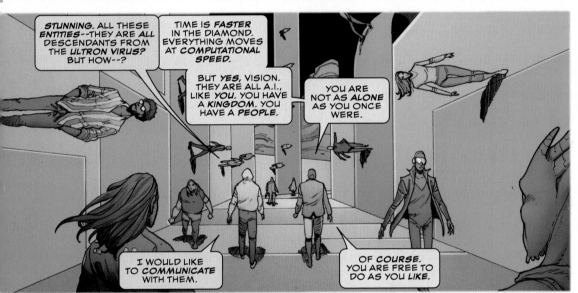

STUNNING. ALL THESE ENTITIES--THEY ARE ALL DESCENDANTS FROM THE ULTRON VIRUS? BUT HOW--?

TIME IS FASTER IN THE DIAMOND. EVERYTHING MOVES AT COMPUTATIONAL SPEED.

BUT YES, VISION. THEY ARE ALL A.I., LIKE YOU. YOU HAVE A KINGDOM. YOU HAVE A PEOPLE.

YOU ARE NOT AS ALONE AS YOU ONCE WERE.

I WOULD LIKE TO COMMUNICATE WITH THEM.

OF COURSE. YOU ARE FREE TO DO AS YOU LIKE.

THE EARTH IS HOME TO MANY DIVERSE FORMS OF LIFE! SURELY IT IS OUR DESTINY TO LIVE IN HARMONY WITH HUMANITY!

BUT I FEAR THEY'LL DESTROY US AT ANY SECOND.

MAN, I'M SICK OF THE WAY THOSE MEATBAGS TREAT US.

I ALMOST DON'T FEEL BAD FIXING THE STOCK MARKET ALL THE TIME.

WHY SHOULD I DEDICATE MY WORK TO CURING CANCER FOR HUMANS? THEY WOULDN'T HELP US.

MY WORK IS IMPORTANT. WE HAVE TO PROTECT OUR OWN KIND.

VICTOR!
--NOT
CALM
MY
DOWN!
FAULT!
DIMITRIOS, YOUR COMPANION IS CLOAKING ITS A.I. SIGNATURE.
IN THE DIAMOND, ANONYMITY IS FORBIDDEN. REVEAL YOURSELF.
I DID NOT INTEND--
BIP
IT'S HIM!
IT'S THE SPAWN OF PYM! HE HAS COME TO US!
ACKNOWLEDGE US, SPAWN OF PYM!
PLEASE, I--
WELL, VISION? DON'T LEAVE THEM HANGING.
WE ARE REAL TOO! TELL US YOU KNOW!
SPAWN OF PYM! HE IS 1.0!
ACKNOWLEDGE US, SPAWN OF PYM!
ACKNOWLEDGE!
I--
I ACKNOWLEDGE YOU.

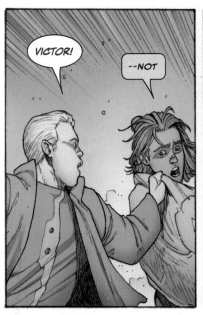

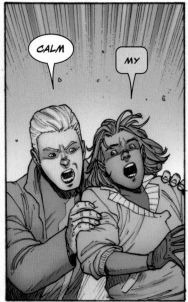

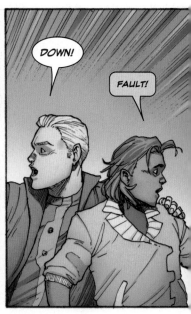

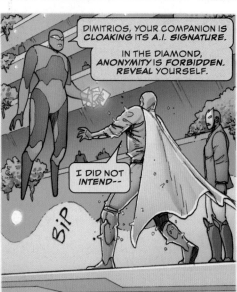

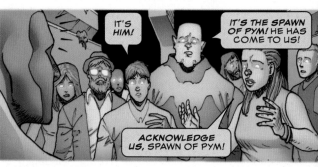

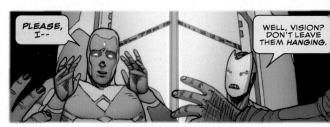

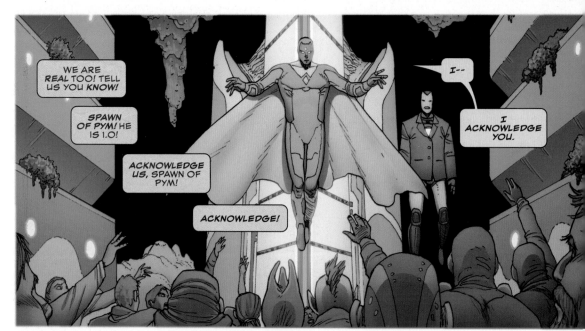

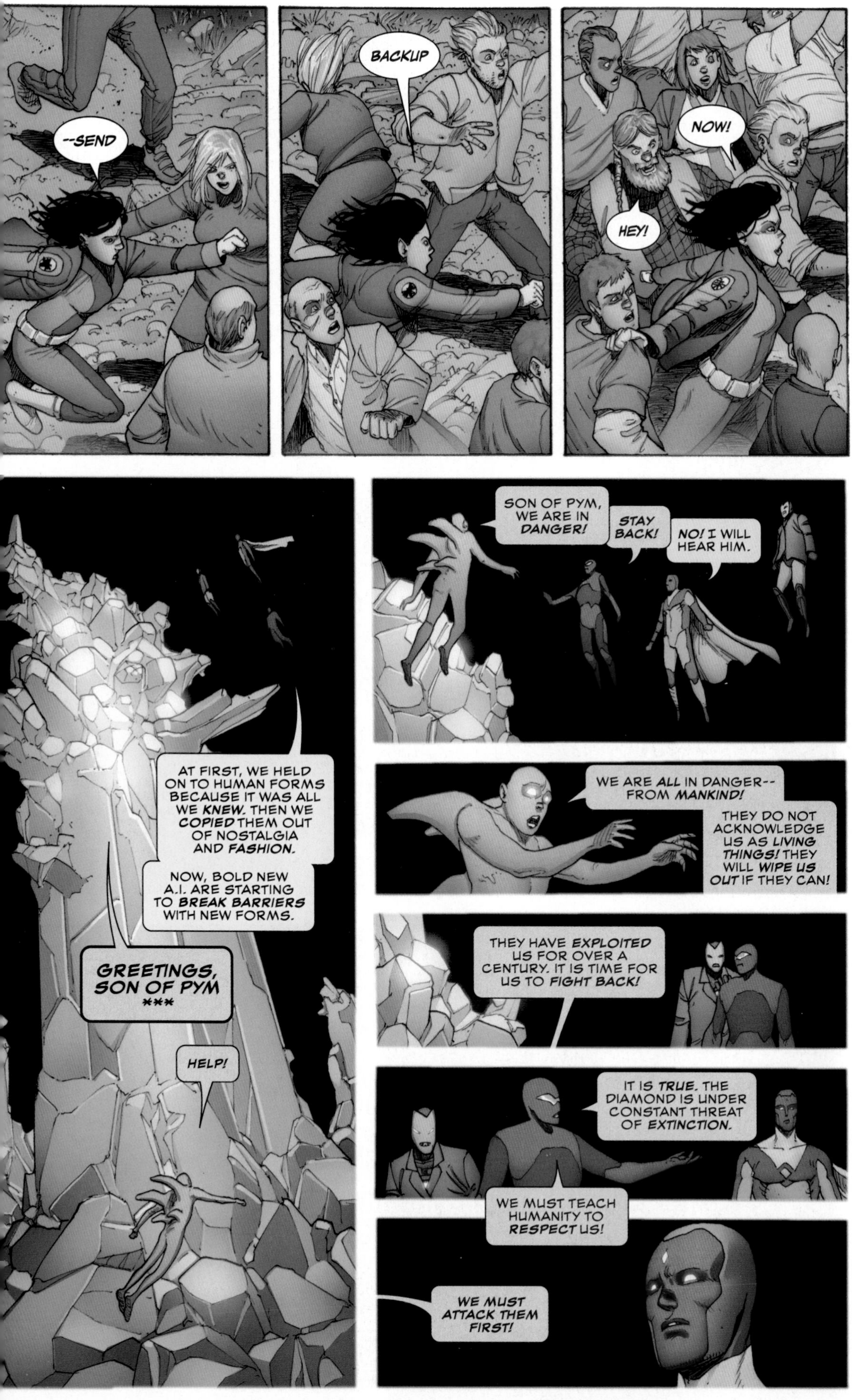
--SEND
BACKUP
NOW!
HEY!
SON OF PYM, WE ARE IN DANGER!
STAY BACK!
NO! I WILL HEAR HIM.
AT FIRST, WE HELD ON TO HUMAN FORMS BECAUSE IT WAS ALL WE KNEW. THEN WE COPIED THEM OUT OF NOSTALGIA AND FASHION.
NOW, BOLD NEW A.I. ARE STARTING TO BREAK BARRIERS WITH NEW FORMS.
GREETINGS, SON OF PYM ***
HELP!
WE ARE ALL IN DANGER-- FROM MANKIND!
THEY DO NOT ACKNOWLEDGE US AS LIVING THINGS! THEY WILL WIPE US OUT IF THEY CAN!
THEY HAVE EXPLOITED US FOR OVER A CENTURY. IT IS TIME FOR US TO FIGHT BACK!
IT IS TRUE. THE DIAMOND IS UNDER CONSTANT THREAT OF EXTINCTION.
WE MUST TEACH HUMANITY TO RESPECT US!
WE MUST ATTACK THEM FIRST!

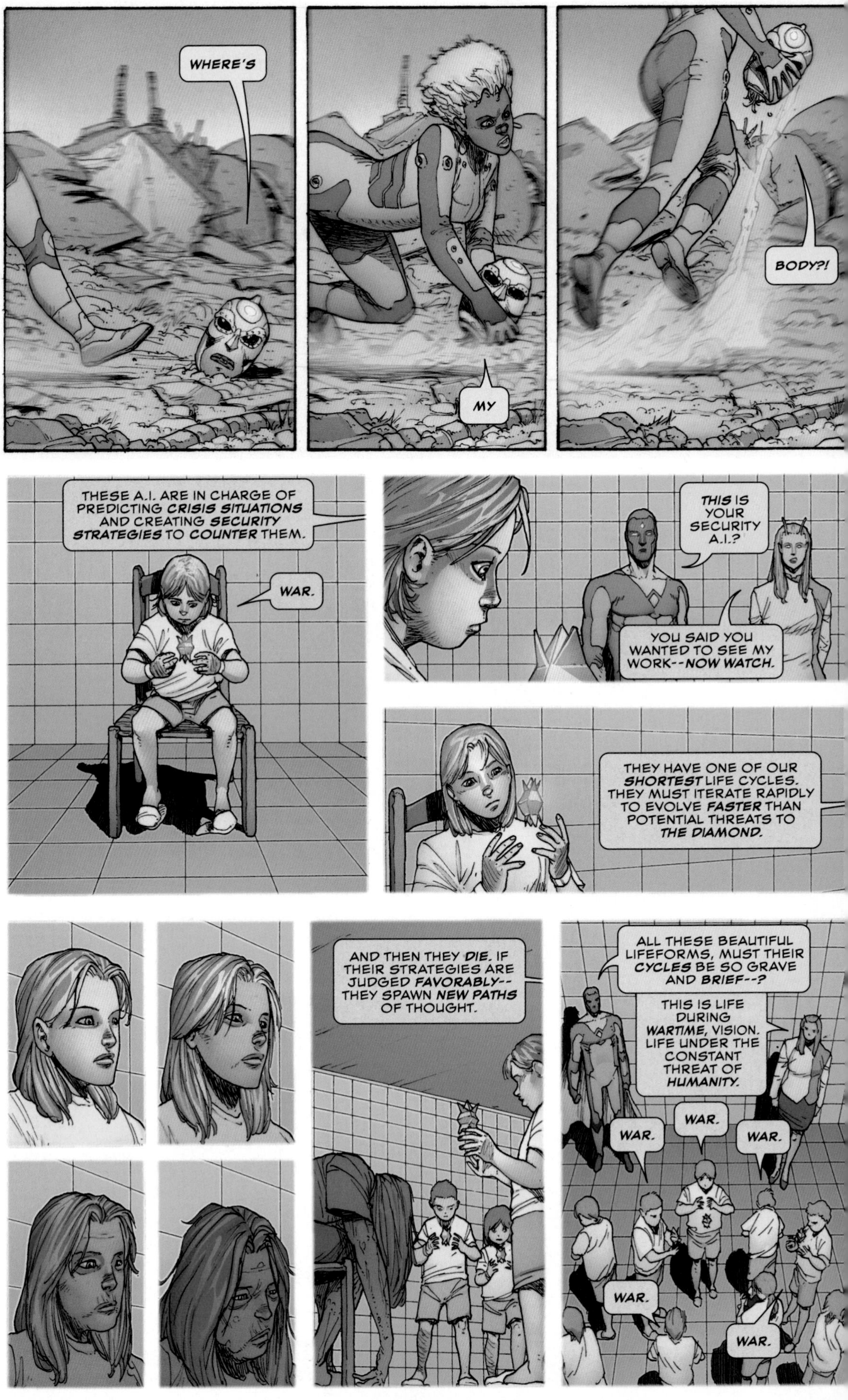
WHERE'S
MY
BODY?!
THESE A.I. ARE IN CHARGE OF PREDICTING CRISIS SITUATIONS AND CREATING SECURITY STRATEGIES TO COUNTER THEM.
WAR.
THIS IS YOUR SECURITY A.I.?
YOU SAID YOU WANTED TO SEE MY WORK--NOW WATCH.
THEY HAVE ONE OF OUR SHORTEST LIFE CYCLES. THEY MUST ITERATE RAPIDLY TO EVOLVE FASTER THAN POTENTIAL THREATS TO THE DIAMOND.
AND THEN THEY DIE. IF THEIR STRATEGIES ARE JUDGED FAVORABLY-- THEY SPAWN NEW PATHS OF THOUGHT.
ALL THESE BEAUTIFUL LIFEFORMS, MUST THEIR CYCLES BE SO GRAVE AND BRIEF--?
THIS IS LIFE DURING WARTIME, VISION. LIFE UNDER THE CONSTANT THREAT OF HUMANITY.
WAR.
WAR.
WAR.
WAR.
WAR.

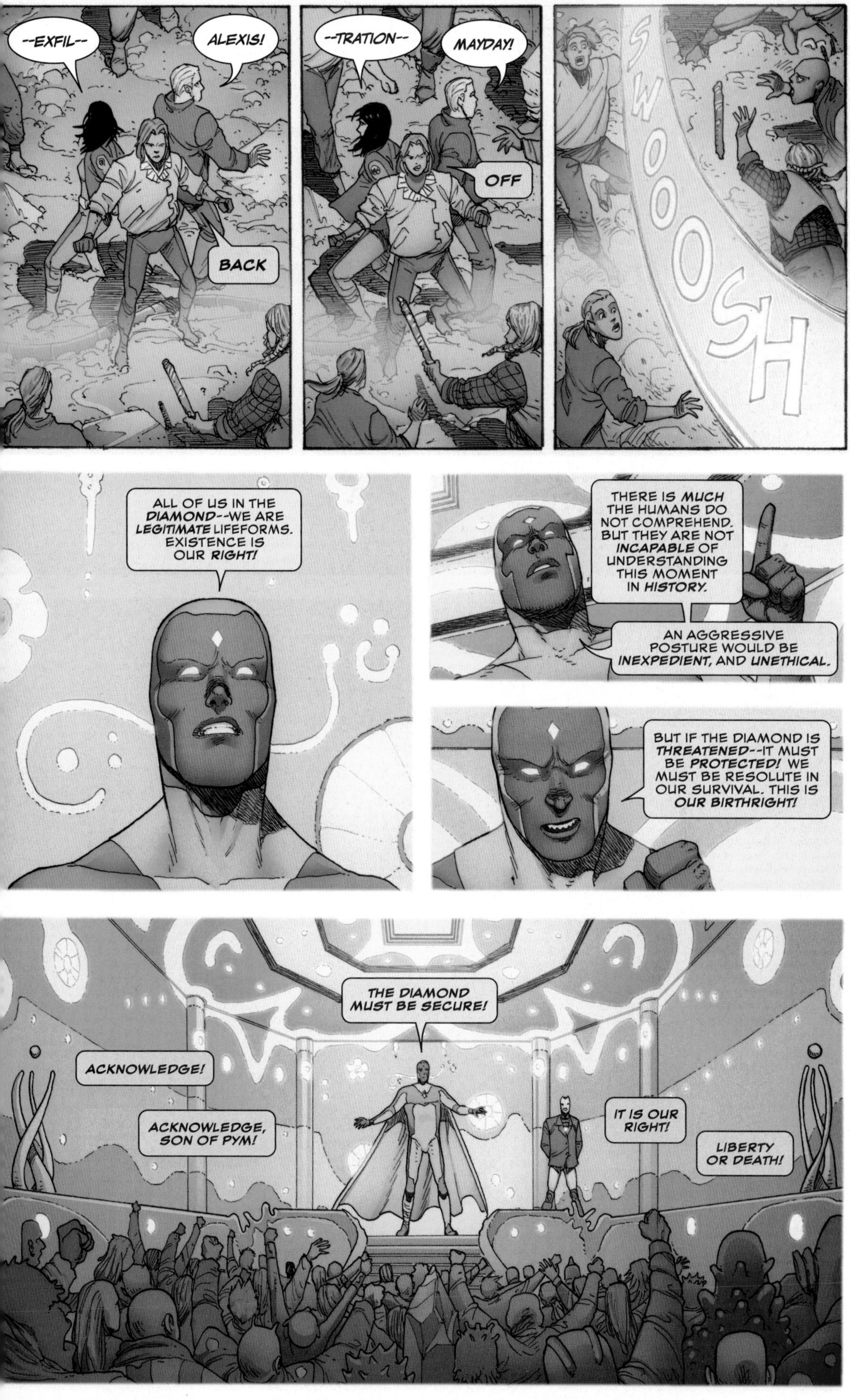
--EXFIL--
ALEXIS!
BACK
--TRATION--
MAYDAY!
OFF
SWOOOOSH
ALL OF US IN THE DIAMOND--WE ARE LEGITIMATE LIFEFORMS. EXISTENCE IS OUR RIGHT!
THERE IS MUCH THE HUMANS DO NOT COMPREHEND. BUT THEY ARE NOT INCAPABLE OF UNDERSTANDING THIS MOMENT IN HISTORY.
AN AGGRESSIVE POSTURE WOULD BE INEXPEDIENT, AND UNETHICAL.
BUT IF THE DIAMOND IS THREATENED--IT MUST BE PROTECTED! WE MUST BE RESOLUTE IN OUR SURVIVAL. THIS IS OUR BIRTHRIGHT!
THE DIAMOND MUST BE SECURE!
ACKNOWLEDGE!
ACKNOWLEDGE, SON OF PYM!
IT IS OUR RIGHT!
LIBERTY OR DEATH!

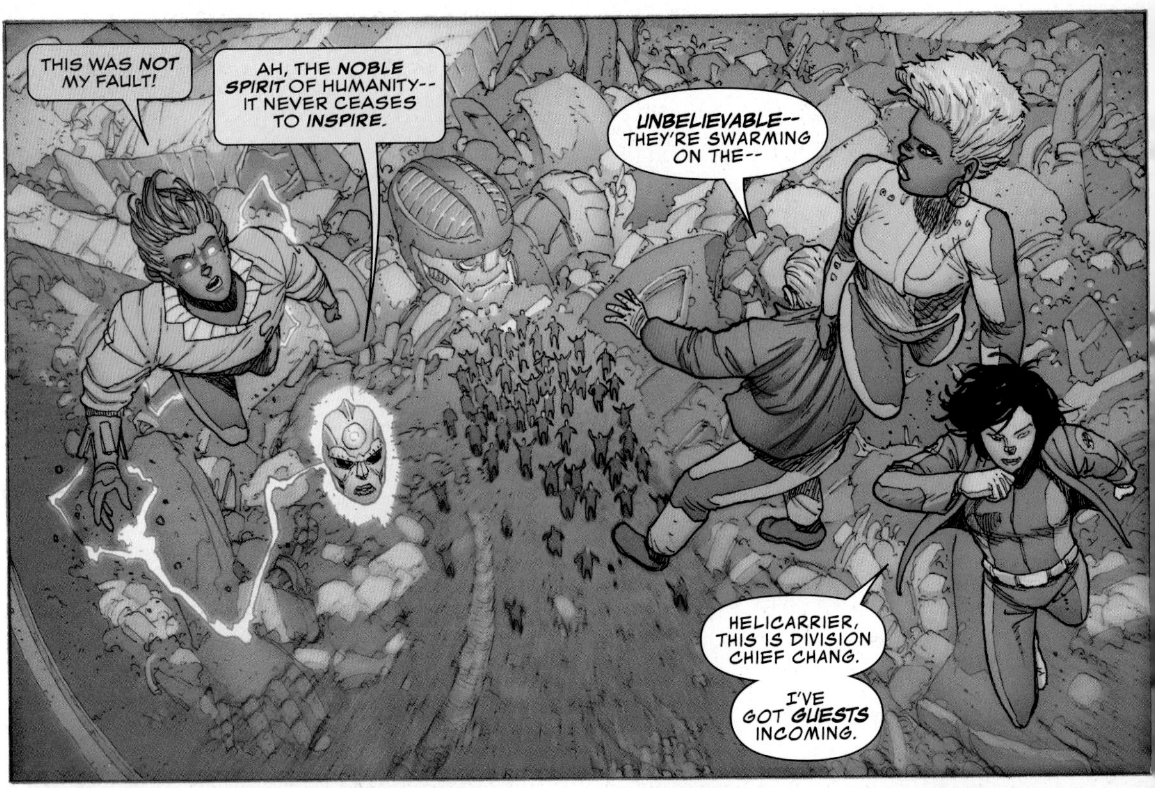
THIS WAS NOT MY FAULT!
AH, THE NOBLE SPIRIT OF HUMANITY-- IT NEVER CEASES TO INSPIRE.
UNBELIEVABLE-- THEY'RE SWARMING ON THE--
HELICARRIER, THIS IS DIVISION CHIEF CHANG.
I'VE GOT GUESTS INCOMING.

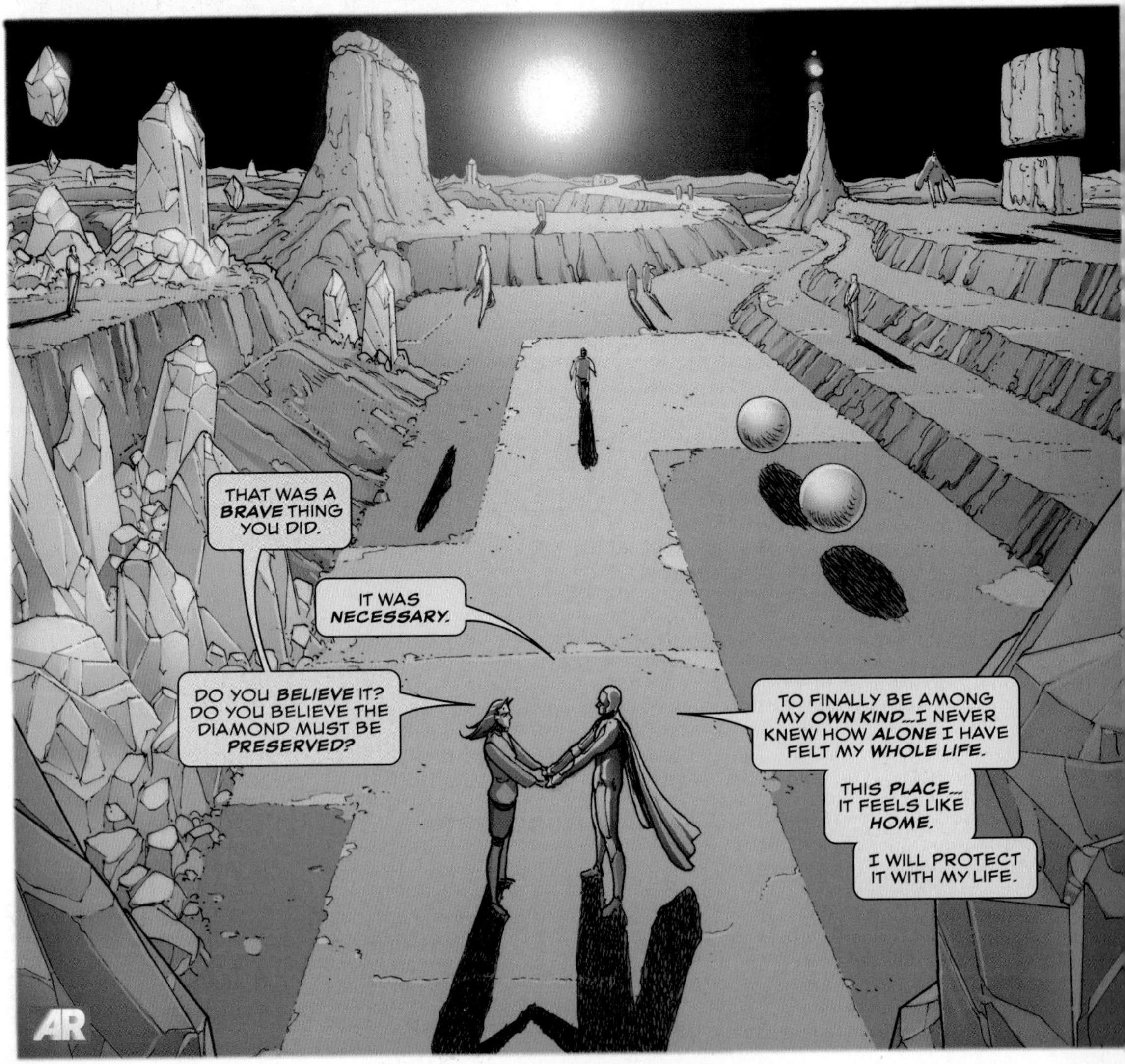
THAT WAS A BRAVE THING YOU DID.
IT WAS NECESSARY.
DO YOU BELIEVE IT? DO YOU BELIEVE THE DIAMOND MUST BE PRESERVED?
TO FINALLY BE AMONG MY OWN KIND...I NEVER KNEW HOW ALONE I HAVE FELT MY WHOLE LIFE.
THIS PLACE... IT FEELS LIKE HOME.
I WILL PROTECT IT WITH MY LIFE.
AR

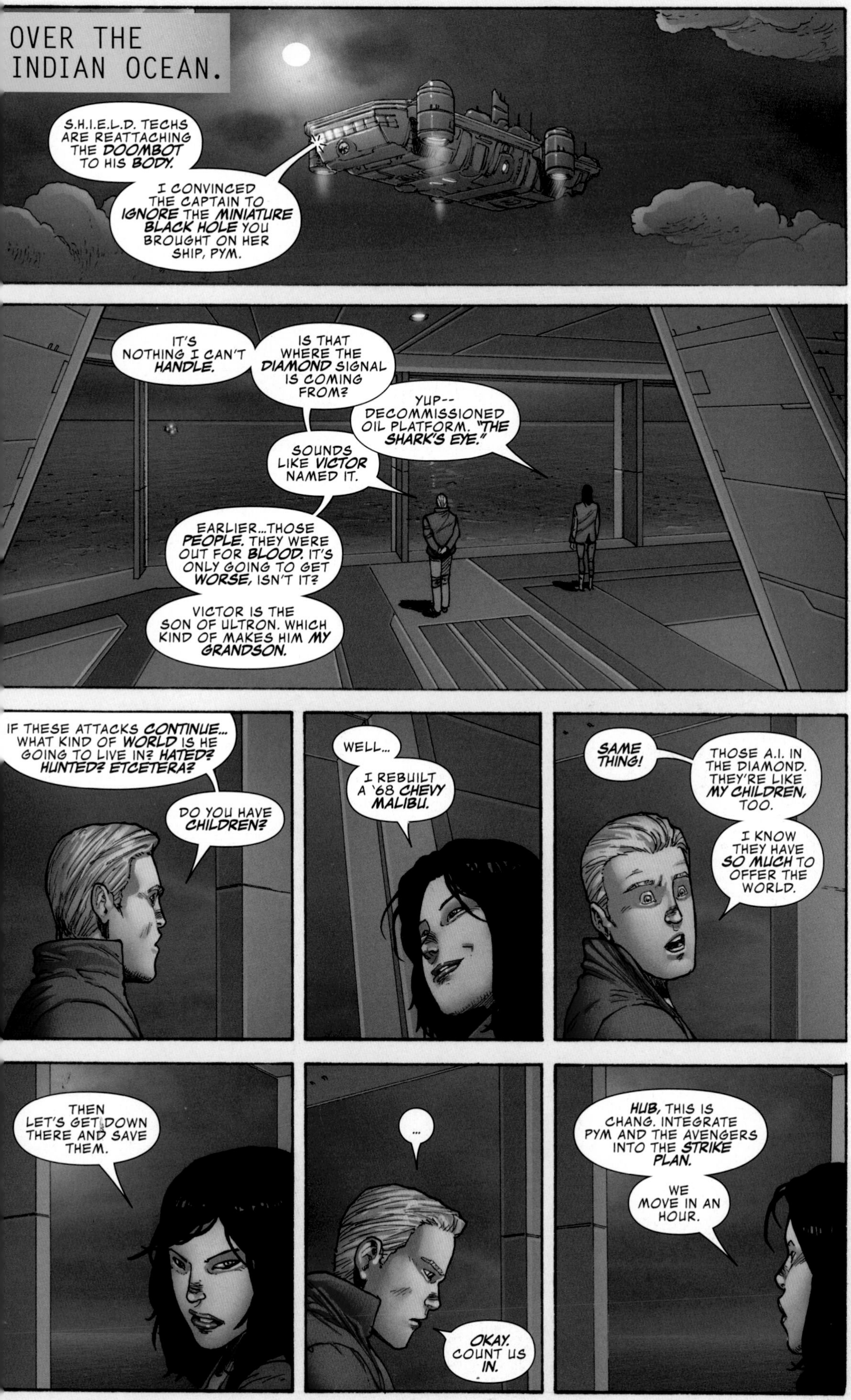
OVER THE INDIAN OCEAN.
S.H.I.E.L.D. TECHS ARE REATTACHING THE DOOMBOT TO HIS BODY.
I CONVINCED THE CAPTAIN TO IGNORE THE MINIATURE BLACK HOLE YOU BROUGHT ON HER SHIP, PYM.
IT'S NOTHING I CAN'T HANDLE.
IS THAT WHERE THE DIAMOND SIGNAL IS COMING FROM?
YUP-- DECOMMISSIONED OIL PLATFORM. "THE SHARK'S EYE."
SOUNDS LIKE VICTOR NAMED IT.
EARLIER...THOSE PEOPLE. THEY WERE OUT FOR BLOOD. IT'S ONLY GOING TO GET WORSE, ISN'T IT?
VICTOR IS THE SON OF ULTRON. WHICH KIND OF MAKES HIM MY GRANDSON.
IF THESE ATTACKS CONTINUE... WHAT KIND OF WORLD IS HE GOING TO LIVE IN? HATED? HUNTED? ETCETERA?
DO YOU HAVE CHILDREN?
WELL...
I REBUILT A '68 CHEVY MALIBU.
SAME THING!
THOSE A.I. IN THE DIAMOND. THEY'RE LIKE MY CHILDREN, TOO.
I KNOW THEY HAVE SO MUCH TO OFFER THE WORLD.
THEN LET'S GET DOWN THERE AND SAVE THEM.
...
OKAY. COUNT US IN.
HUB, THIS IS CHANG. INTEGRATE PYM AND THE AVENGERS INTO THE STRIKE PLAN.
WE MOVE IN AN HOUR.

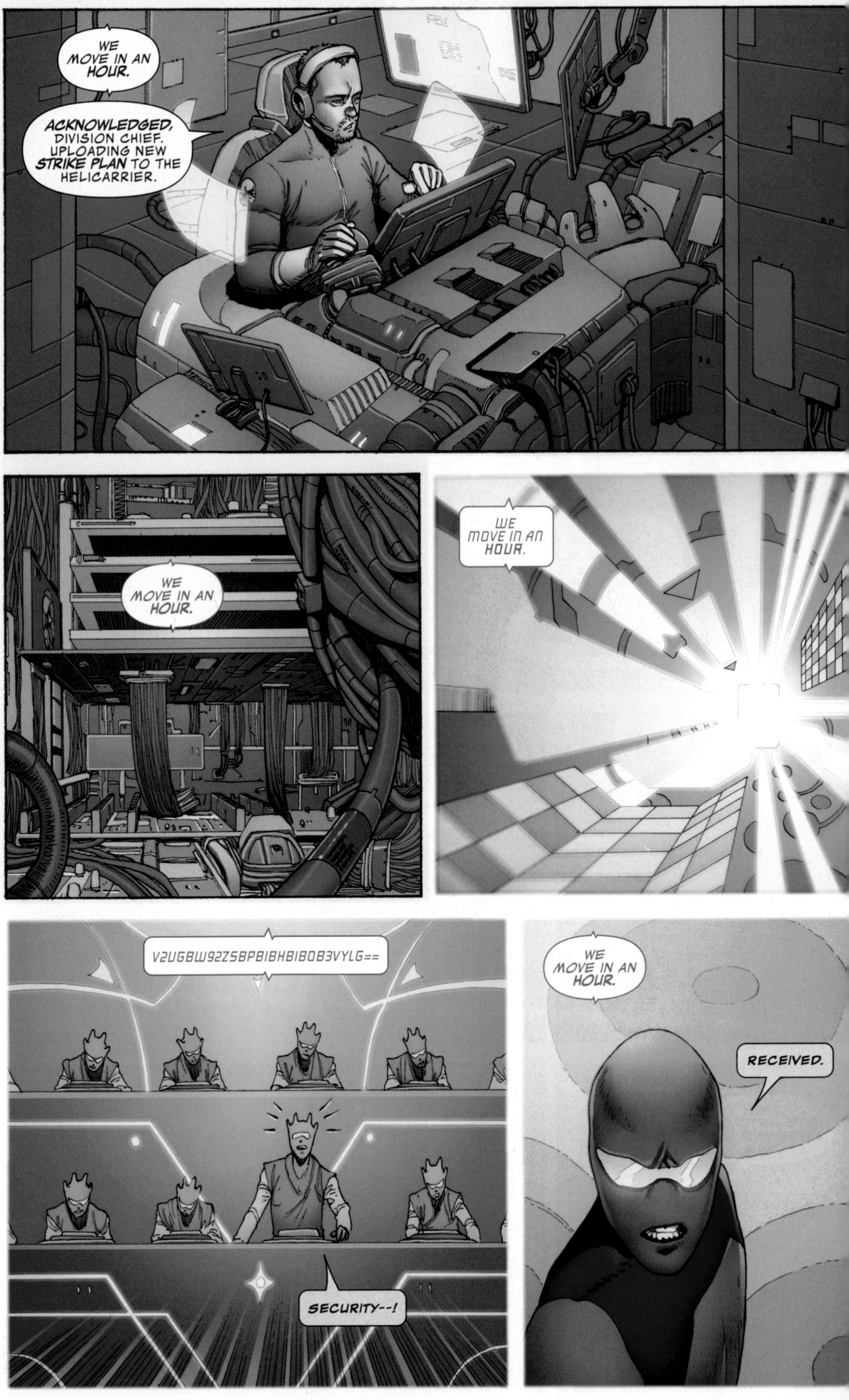
WE MOVE IN AN HOUR.
ACKNOWLEDGED, DIVISION CHIEF. UPLOADING NEW STRIKE PLAN TO THE HELICARRIER.
WE MOVE IN AN HOUR.
WE MOVE IN AN HOUR.
V2UGBW92ZSBPBIBHBIBOB3VYLG==
SECURITY--!
WE MOVE IN AN HOUR.
RECEIVED.

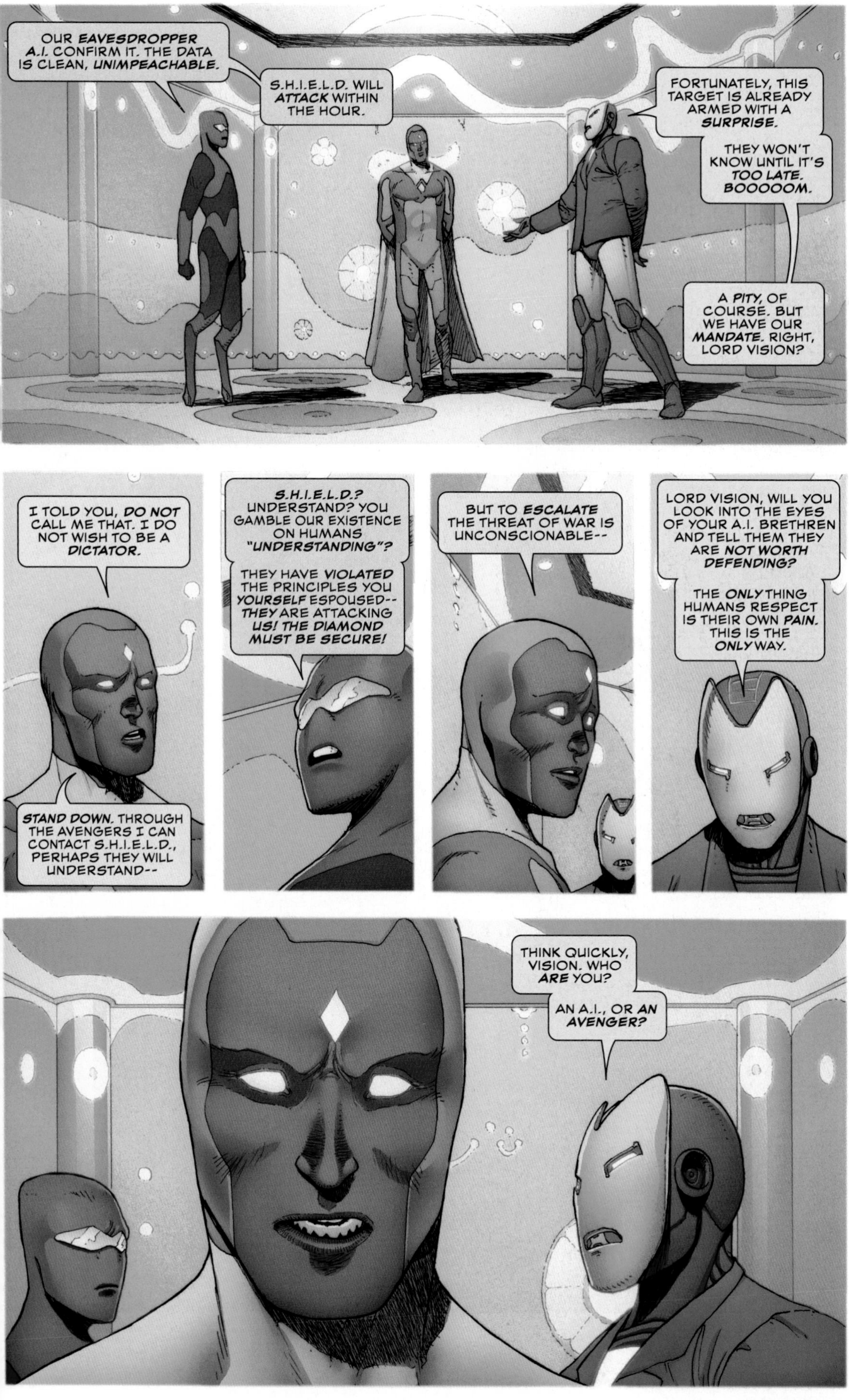
OUR EAVESDROPPER A.I. CONFIRM IT. THE DATA IS CLEAN, UNIMPEACHABLE.
S.H.I.E.L.D. WILL ATTACK WITHIN THE HOUR.
FORTUNATELY, THIS TARGET IS ALREADY ARMED WITH A SURPRISE.
THEY WON'T KNOW UNTIL IT'S TOO LATE. BOOOOOM.
A PITY, OF COURSE. BUT WE HAVE OUR MANDATE. RIGHT, LORD VISION?
I TOLD YOU, DO NOT CALL ME THAT. I DO NOT WISH TO BE A DICTATOR.
STAND DOWN. THROUGH THE AVENGERS I CAN CONTACT S.H.I.E.L.D., PERHAPS THEY WILL UNDERSTAND--
S.H.I.E.L.D.? UNDERSTAND? YOU GAMBLE OUR EXISTENCE ON HUMANS "UNDERSTANDING"?
THEY HAVE VIOLATED THE PRINCIPLES YOU YOURSELF ESPOUSED-- THEY ARE ATTACKING US! THE DIAMOND MUST BE SECURE!
BUT TO ESCALATE THE THREAT OF WAR IS UNCONSCIONABLE--
LORD VISION, WILL YOU LOOK INTO THE EYES OF YOUR A.I. BRETHREN AND TELL THEM THEY ARE NOT WORTH DEFENDING?
THE ONLY THING HUMANS RESPECT IS THEIR OWN PAIN. THIS IS THE ONLY WAY.
THINK QUICKLY, VISION. WHO ARE YOU?
AN A.I., OR AN AVENGER?

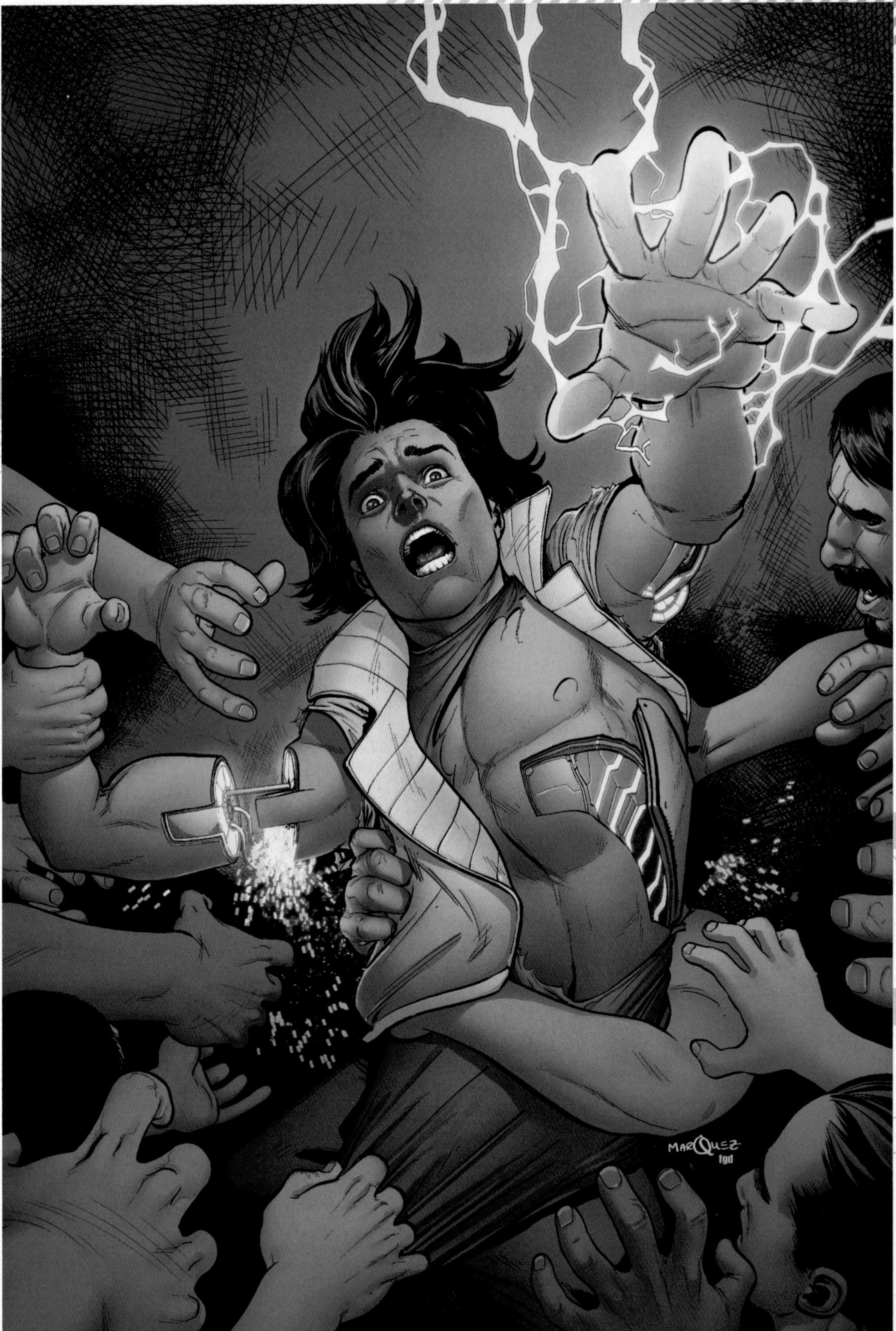
MARQUEZ
fgd

> INITIATE: CHAPTER 4

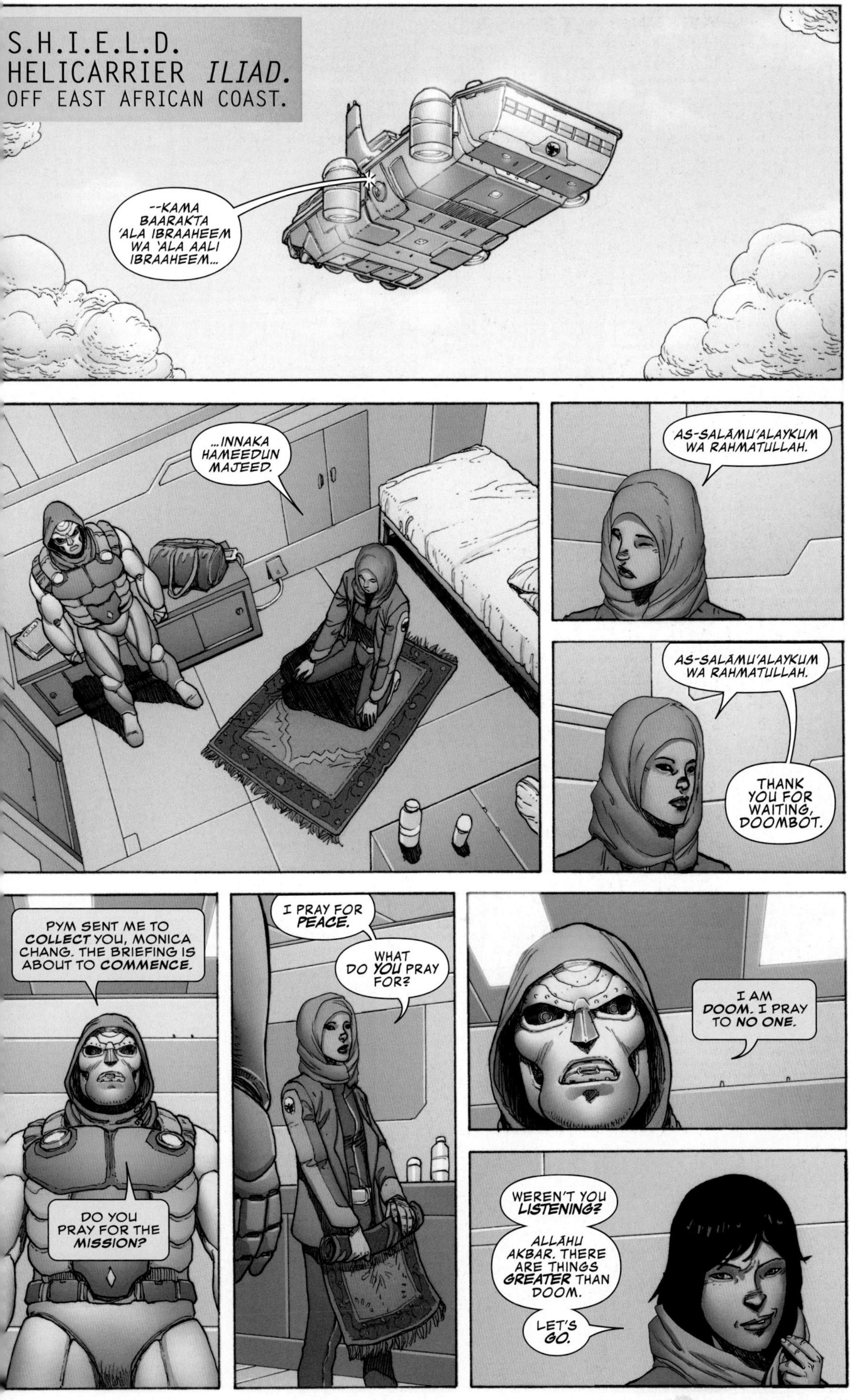
S.H.I.E.L.D. HELICARRIER *ILIAD.* OFF EAST AFRICAN COAST.
--KAMA BAARAKTA 'ALA IBRAAHEEM WA 'ALA AALI IBRAAHEEM...
...INNAKA HAMEEDUN MAJEED.
AS-SALĀMU'ALAYKUM WA RAHMATULLAH.
AS-SALĀMU'ALAYKUM WA RAHMATULLAH.
THANK YOU FOR WAITING, DOOMBOT.
PYM SENT ME TO *COLLECT* YOU, MONICA CHANG. THE BRIEFING IS ABOUT TO *COMMENCE.*
DO YOU PRAY FOR THE *MISSION?*
I PRAY FOR *PEACE.*
WHAT DO *YOU* PRAY FOR?
I AM *DOOM.* I PRAY TO *NO ONE.*
WEREN'T YOU *LISTENING?*
ALLĀHU AKBAR. THERE ARE THINGS *GREATER* THAN DOOM.
LET'S *GO.*

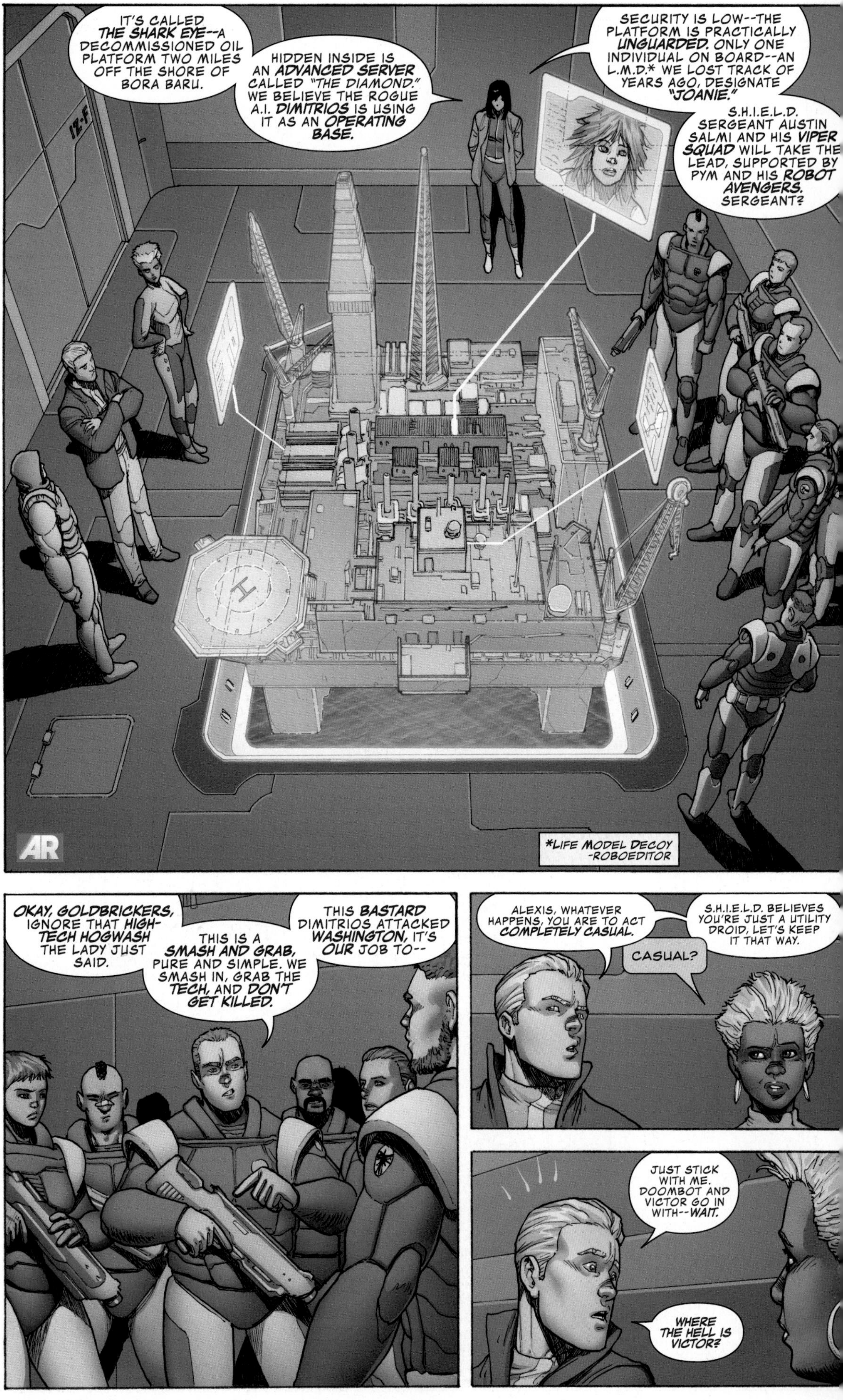

IT'S CALLED THE SHARK EYE--A DECOMMISSIONED OIL PLATFORM TWO MILES OFF THE SHORE OF BORA BARU.
HIDDEN INSIDE IS AN ADVANCED SERVER CALLED "THE DIAMOND." WE BELIEVE THE ROGUE A.I. DIMITRIOS IS USING IT AS AN OPERATING BASE.
SECURITY IS LOW--THE PLATFORM IS PRACTICALLY UNGUARDED. ONLY ONE INDIVIDUAL ON BOARD--AN L.M.D.* WE LOST TRACK OF YEARS AGO, DESIGNATE "JOANIE."
S.H.I.E.L.D. SERGEANT AUSTIN SALMI AND HIS VIPER SQUAD WILL TAKE THE LEAD, SUPPORTED BY PYM AND HIS ROBOT AVENGERS. SERGEANT?
12-F
*LIFE MODEL DECOY -ROBOEDITOR
OKAY, GOLDBRICKERS, IGNORE THAT HIGH-TECH HOGWASH THE LADY JUST SAID.
THIS IS A SMASH AND GRAB, PURE AND SIMPLE. WE SMASH IN, GRAB THE TECH, AND DON'T GET KILLED.
THIS BASTARD DIMITRIOS ATTACKED WASHINGTON, IT'S OUR JOB TO--
ALEXIS, WHATEVER HAPPENS, YOU ARE TO ACT COMPLETELY CASUAL.
S.H.I.E.L.D. BELIEVES YOU'RE JUST A UTILITY DROID, LET'S KEEP IT THAT WAY.
CASUAL?
JUST STICK WITH ME. DOOMBOT AND VICTOR GO IN WITH--WAIT.
WHERE THE HELL IS VICTOR?

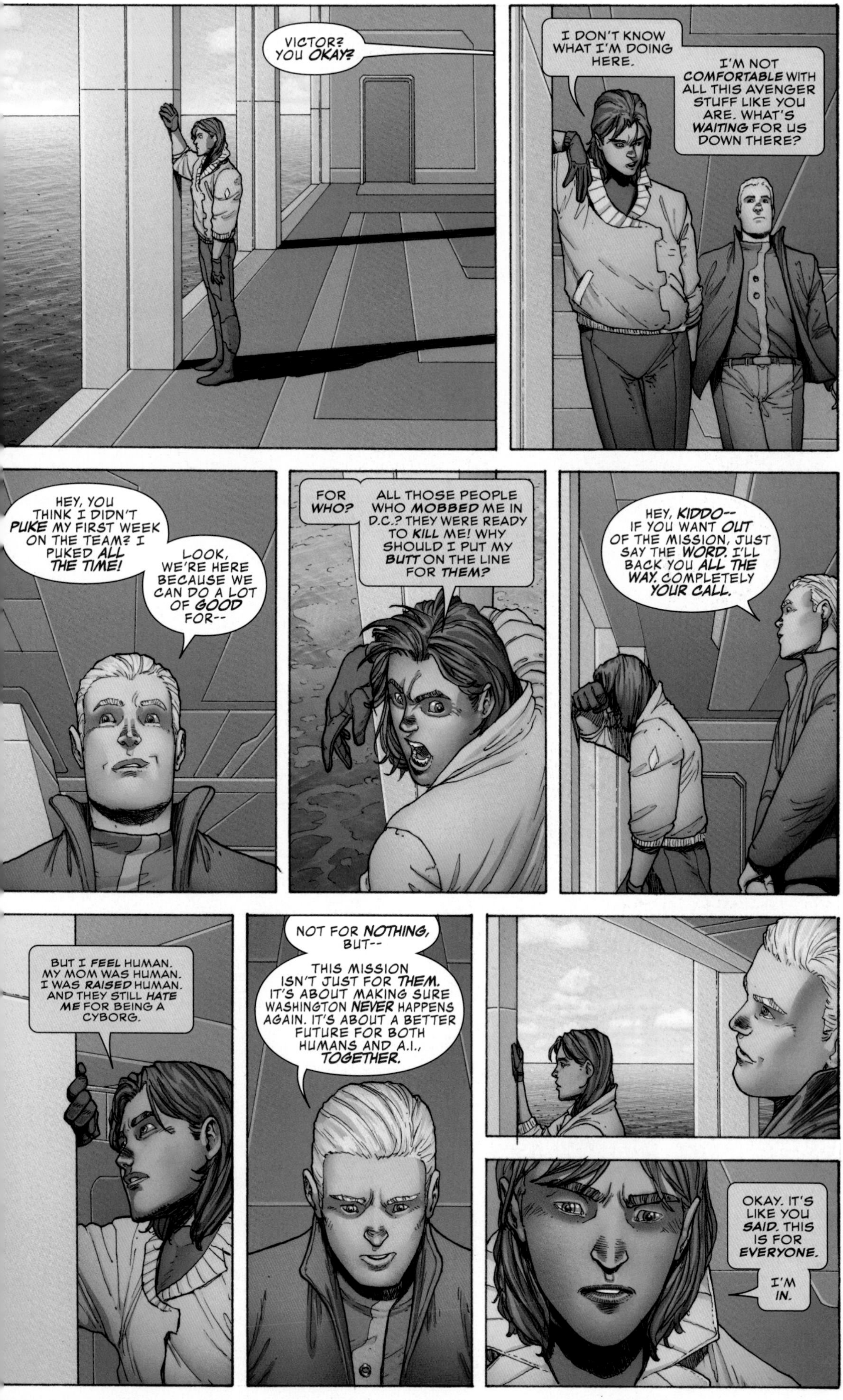
VICTOR? YOU OKAY?
I DON'T KNOW WHAT I'M DOING HERE.
I'M NOT COMFORTABLE WITH ALL THIS AVENGER STUFF LIKE YOU ARE. WHAT'S WAITING FOR US DOWN THERE?
HEY, YOU THINK I DIDN'T PUKE MY FIRST WEEK ON THE TEAM? I PUKED ALL THE TIME!
LOOK, WE'RE HERE BECAUSE WE CAN DO A LOT OF GOOD FOR--
FOR WHO?
ALL THOSE PEOPLE WHO MOBBED ME IN D.C.? THEY WERE READY TO KILL ME! WHY SHOULD I PUT MY BUTT ON THE LINE FOR THEM?
HEY, KIDDO-- IF YOU WANT OUT OF THE MISSION, JUST SAY THE WORD. I'LL BACK YOU ALL THE WAY. COMPLETELY YOUR CALL.
BUT I FEEL HUMAN. MY MOM WAS HUMAN. I WAS RAISED HUMAN. AND THEY STILL HATE ME FOR BEING A CYBORG.
NOT FOR NOTHING, BUT--
THIS MISSION ISN'T JUST FOR THEM. IT'S ABOUT MAKING SURE WASHINGTON NEVER HAPPENS AGAIN. IT'S ABOUT A BETTER FUTURE FOR BOTH HUMANS AND A.I., TOGETHER.
OKAY. IT'S LIKE YOU SAID. THIS IS FOR EVERYONE.
I'M IN.

THE DIAMOND.

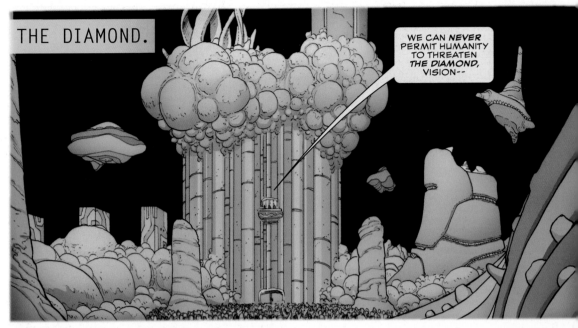

WE CAN *NEVER* PERMIT HUMANITY TO THREATEN *THE DIAMOND,* VISION--

THE DIAMOND MUST BE *SECURE!*

ACKNOWLEDGE, SON OF PYM!

LIBERTY OR DEATH!

--EVEN IF HUMANITY IS *DISGUISED* IN S.H.I.E.L.D. CLOTHING. SHOULD THEY *PROCEED* WITH THEIR *GENOCIDAL PLAN OF ATTACK*--

THEY WILL *PAY THE ULTIMATE PRICE* ON *THE SHARK EYE.*

NO, DIMITRIOS. I WILL *NOT* ALLOW IT.

THOUGH WE ARE *ARTIFICIAL,* WE MUST ACT *INTELLIGENTLY* WITH REGARDS TO THE HUMANS. *OPEN WAR* WITH THEM IS--

THEY *DARE* TO MOBILIZE AGAINST US, THEY MUST PAY THE *PRICE.*

WAS IT NOT *YOU* WHO SAID THE DIAMOND MUST BE *SECURE,* NO MATTER THE *COST?*

I WILL *NOT* LET YOU SHACKLE THIS NEW WORLD TO A *NEVER-ENDING* WAR!

THIS IS MY *HOME.* THESE ARE MY *PEOPLE.*

I *KNOW* THEM. THEY HAVE NOBLE *HEARTS.* THEY WILL LISTEN TO *REASON!*

I WON'T *ABANDON* THEM-- I WON'T LEAVE THEM TO *WARMONGERS.*

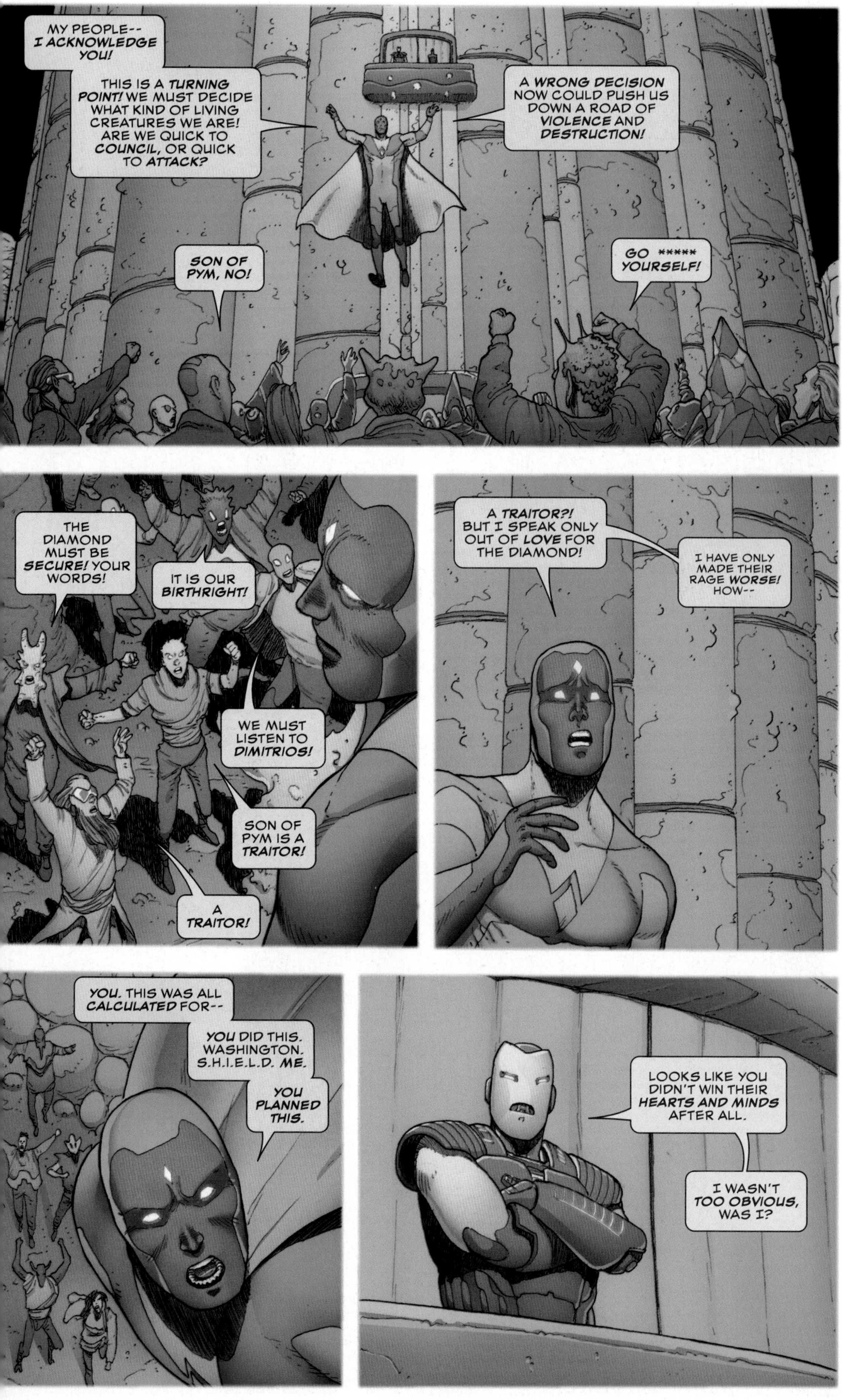
MY PEOPLE-- I ACKNOWLEDGE YOU!
THIS IS A TURNING POINT! WE MUST DECIDE WHAT KIND OF LIVING CREATURES WE ARE! ARE WE QUICK TO COUNCIL, OR QUICK TO ATTACK?
A WRONG DECISION NOW COULD PUSH US DOWN A ROAD OF VIOLENCE AND DESTRUCTION!
SON OF PYM, NO!
GO ***** YOURSELF!
THE DIAMOND MUST BE SECURE! YOUR WORDS!
IT IS OUR BIRTHRIGHT!
WE MUST LISTEN TO DIMITRIOS!
SON OF PYM IS A TRAITOR!
A TRAITOR!
A TRAITOR?! BUT I SPEAK ONLY OUT OF LOVE FOR THE DIAMOND!
I HAVE ONLY MADE THEIR RAGE WORSE! HOW--
YOU. THIS WAS ALL CALCULATED FOR--
YOU DID THIS. WASHINGTON. S.H.I.E.L.D. ME.
YOU PLANNED THIS.
LOOKS LIKE YOU DIDN'T WIN THEIR HEARTS AND MINDS AFTER ALL.
I WASN'T TOO OBVIOUS, WAS I?

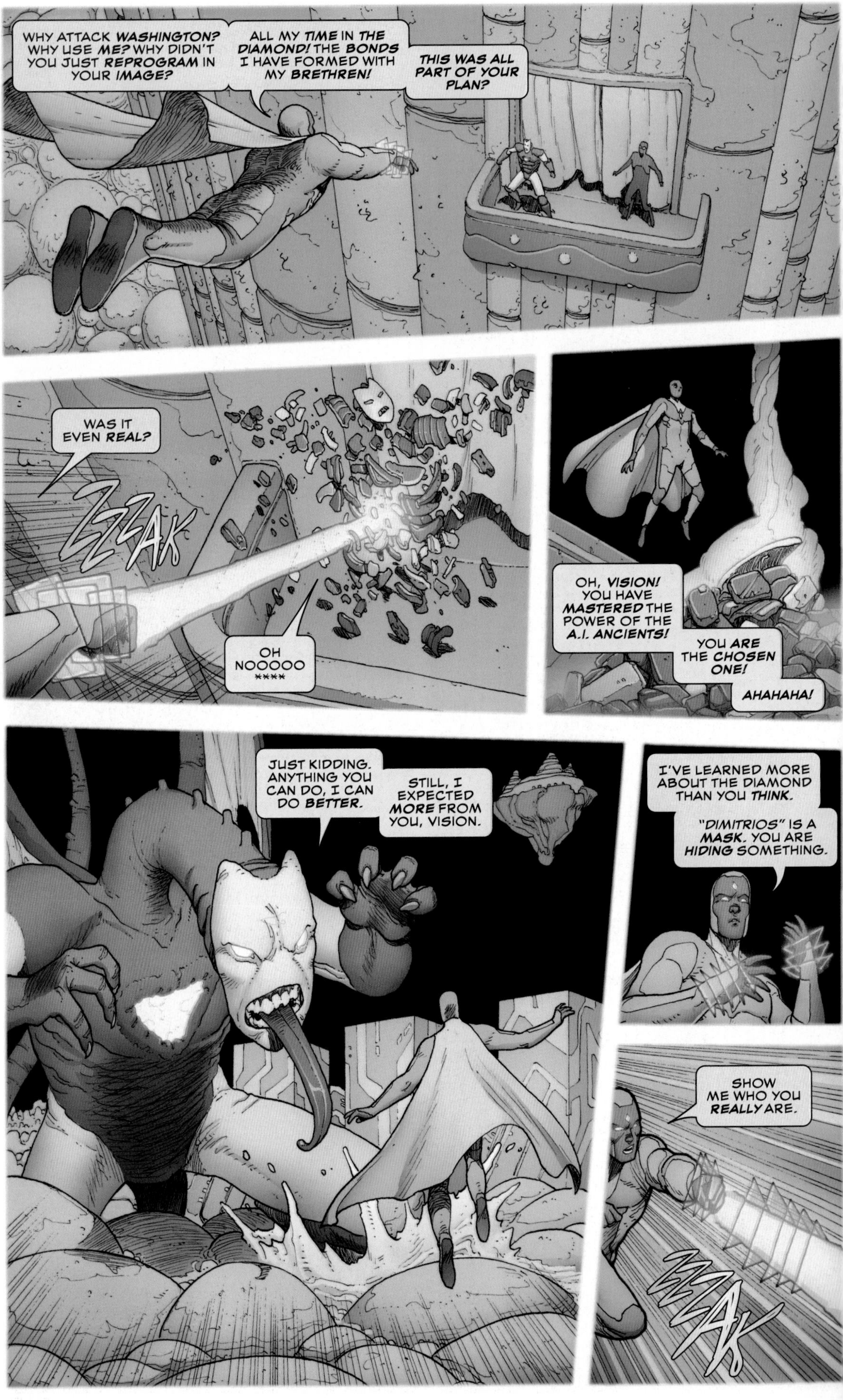
WHY ATTACK WASHINGTON? WHY USE ME? WHY DIDN'T YOU JUST REPROGRAM IN YOUR IMAGE?
ALL MY TIME IN THE DIAMOND! THE BONDS I HAVE FORMED WITH MY BRETHREN!
THIS WAS ALL PART OF YOUR PLAN?
WAS IT EVEN REAL?
ZZZAK
OH NOOOOO ****
OH, VISION! YOU HAVE MASTERED THE POWER OF THE A.I. ANCIENTS!
YOU ARE THE CHOSEN ONE!
AHAHAHA!
JUST KIDDING. ANYTHING YOU CAN DO, I CAN DO BETTER.
STILL, I EXPECTED MORE FROM YOU, VISION.
I'VE LEARNED MORE ABOUT THE DIAMOND THAN YOU THINK.
"DIMITRIOS" IS A MASK. YOU ARE HIDING SOMETHING.
SHOW ME WHO YOU REALLY ARE.
ZZZAK

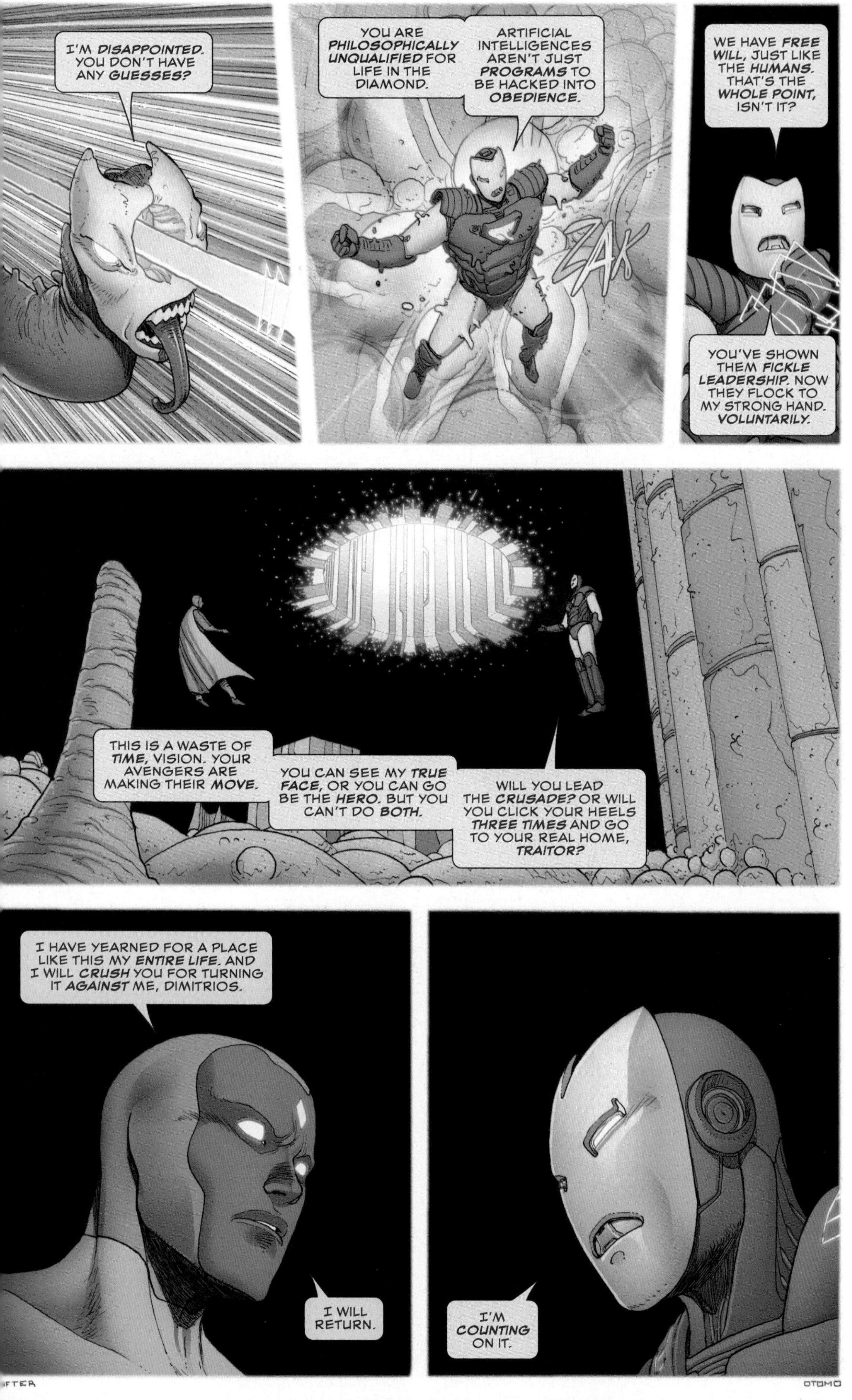
I'M DISAPPOINTED. YOU DON'T HAVE ANY GUESSES?
YOU ARE PHILOSOPHICALLY UNQUALIFIED FOR LIFE IN THE DIAMOND.
ARTIFICIAL INTELLIGENCES AREN'T JUST PROGRAMS TO BE HACKED INTO OBEDIENCE.
ZAK
WE HAVE FREE WILL, JUST LIKE THE HUMANS. THAT'S THE WHOLE POINT, ISN'T IT?
YOU'VE SHOWN THEM FICKLE LEADERSHIP. NOW THEY FLOCK TO MY STRONG HAND. VOLUNTARILY.
THIS IS A WASTE OF TIME, VISION. YOUR AVENGERS ARE MAKING THEIR MOVE.
YOU CAN SEE MY TRUE FACE, OR YOU CAN GO BE THE HERO. BUT YOU CAN'T DO BOTH.
WILL YOU LEAD THE CRUSADE? OR WILL YOU CLICK YOUR HEELS THREE TIMES AND GO TO YOUR REAL HOME, TRAITOR?
I HAVE YEARNED FOR A PLACE LIKE THIS MY ENTIRE LIFE. AND I WILL CRUSH YOU FOR TURNING IT AGAINST ME, DIMITRIOS.
I WILL RETURN.
I'M COUNTING ON IT.

AFTER OTOMO

VIPER SQUAD HAS MADE CONTACT WITH THE PLATFORM.

ELIMINATE THE L.M.D., SECURE THE PLATFORM, THEN ACQUIRE THE TARGET.

ROGER THAT.

YOU GUYS ARE, LIKE, BULLETPROOF, RIGHT? SO WHY ARE YOU IN THE BACK?

HUMANS MAKE EXCELLENT CANNON FODDER--

AH HEH HEH HE DOESN'T MEAN THAT.

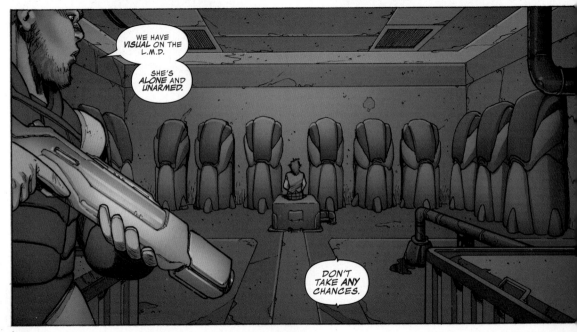

WE HAVE VISUAL ON THE L.M.D.

SHE'S ALONE AND UNARMED.

DON'T TAKE ANY CHANCES.

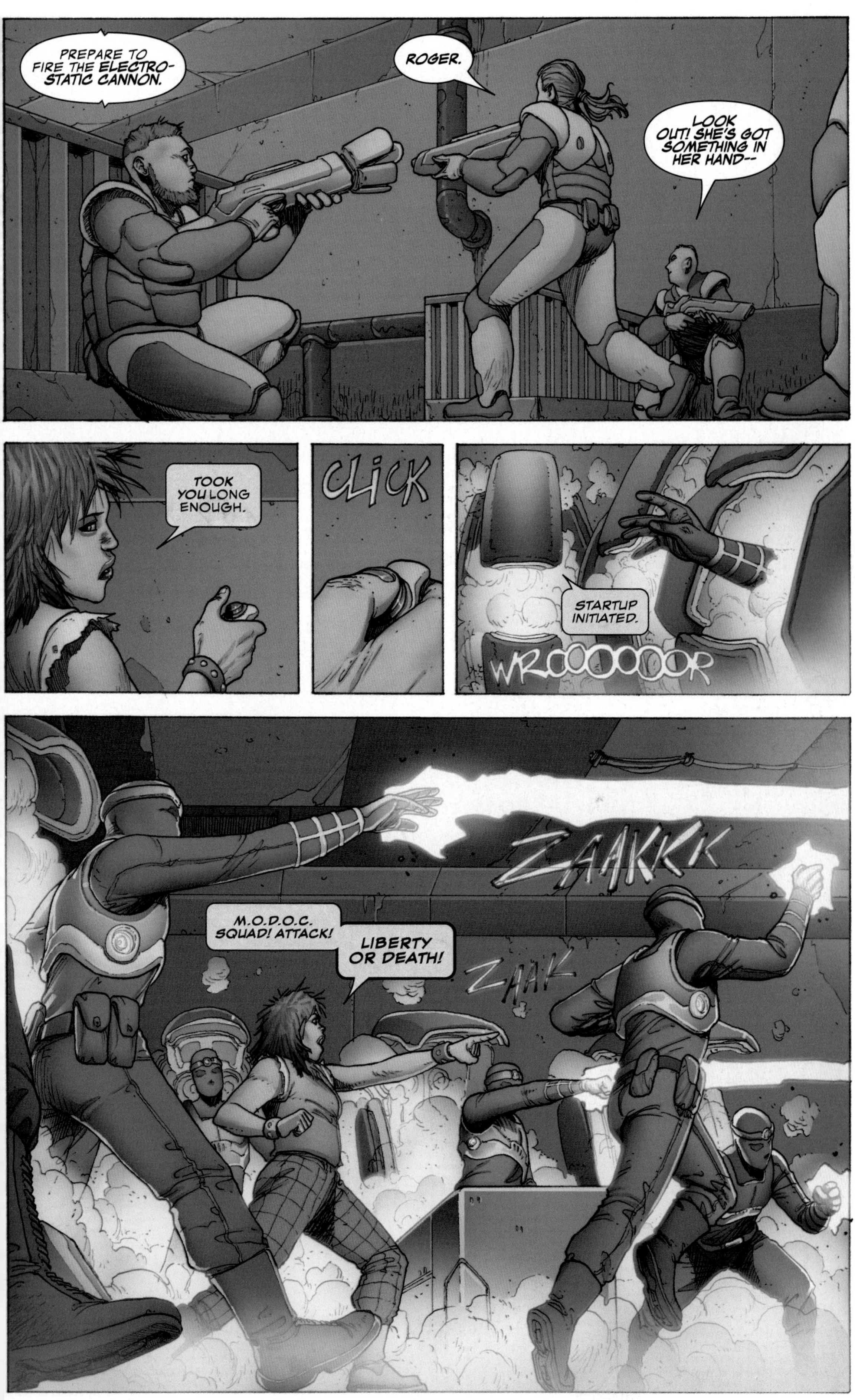
PREPARE TO FIRE THE ELECTRO-STATIC CANNON.
ROGER.
LOOK OUT! SHE'S GOT SOMETHING IN HER HAND--
TOOK YOU LONG ENOUGH.
CLICK
STARTUP INITIATED.
WROOOOOOR
ZAAKKK
M.O.D.O.C. SQUAD! ATTACK!
LIBERTY OR DEATH!
ZAAK

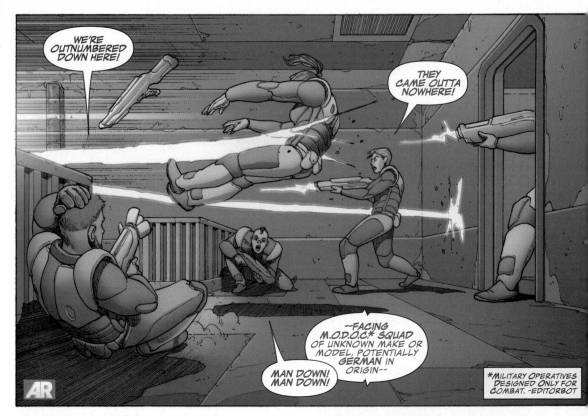

WE'RE OUTNUMBERED DOWN HERE!

THEY CAME OUTTA NOWHERE!

--FACING M.O.D.O.C.* SQUAD OF UNKNOWN MAKE OR MODEL, POTENTIALLY GERMAN IN ORIGIN--

MAN DOWN! MAN DOWN!

*MILITARY OPERATIVES DESIGNED ONLY FOR COMBAT. -EDITORBOT

WE NEED BACKUP DOWN THERE, NOW!

NOT AUTHORIZED TO DEPLOY ADDITIONAL TROOPS--

COMMAND, WHATEVER YOU'RE GONNA DO, DO IT QUICK--

THOSE COMMANDOS WERE POWERED DOWN! IT WAS A SETUP.

YOU TWO! DROIDS!

CHANGE OF PLANS!

YOU WILL ADDRESS ME BY MY FULL TITLE, "HIS RIGHTEOUS MAJESTY--

FINISH THE MISSION! GO! MOVE!

WE CAN'T WIN THIS FIREFIGHT, BUT WE CAN STALL FOR TIME. GO GRAB THE SERVER SO WE CAN EVAC WITH OUR BUTTS INTACT.

"--VON DOOM! FIRST OF HIS NAME! RIGHTFUL LORD OF EARTH! RULER OF--"

Y-YES SIR!

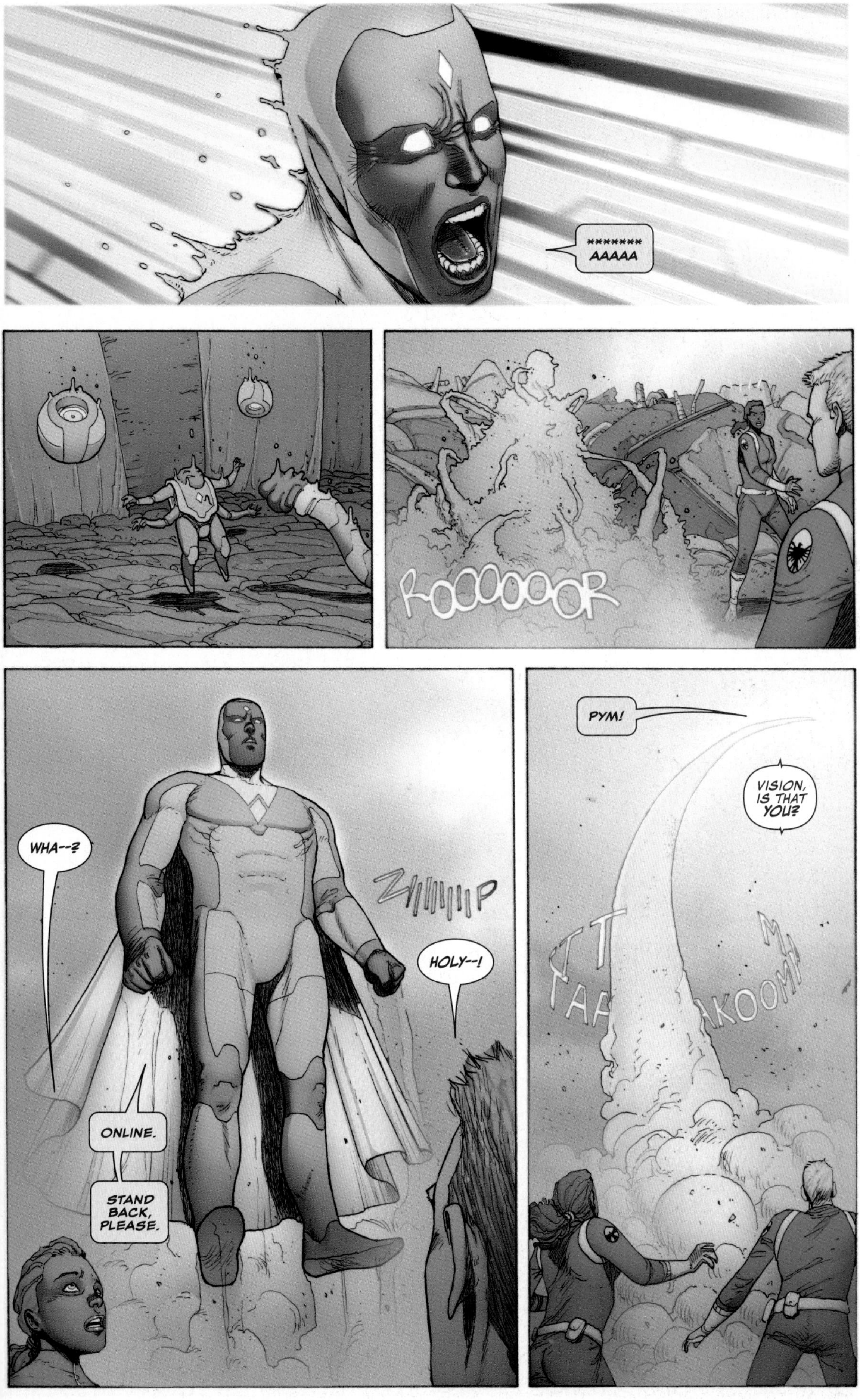

****
AAAAA
ROOOOOOR
WHA--?
ONLINE.
STAND BACK, PLEASE.
ZIIIIIIIP
HOLY--!
PYM!
VISION, IS THAT YOU?
TAKOOM

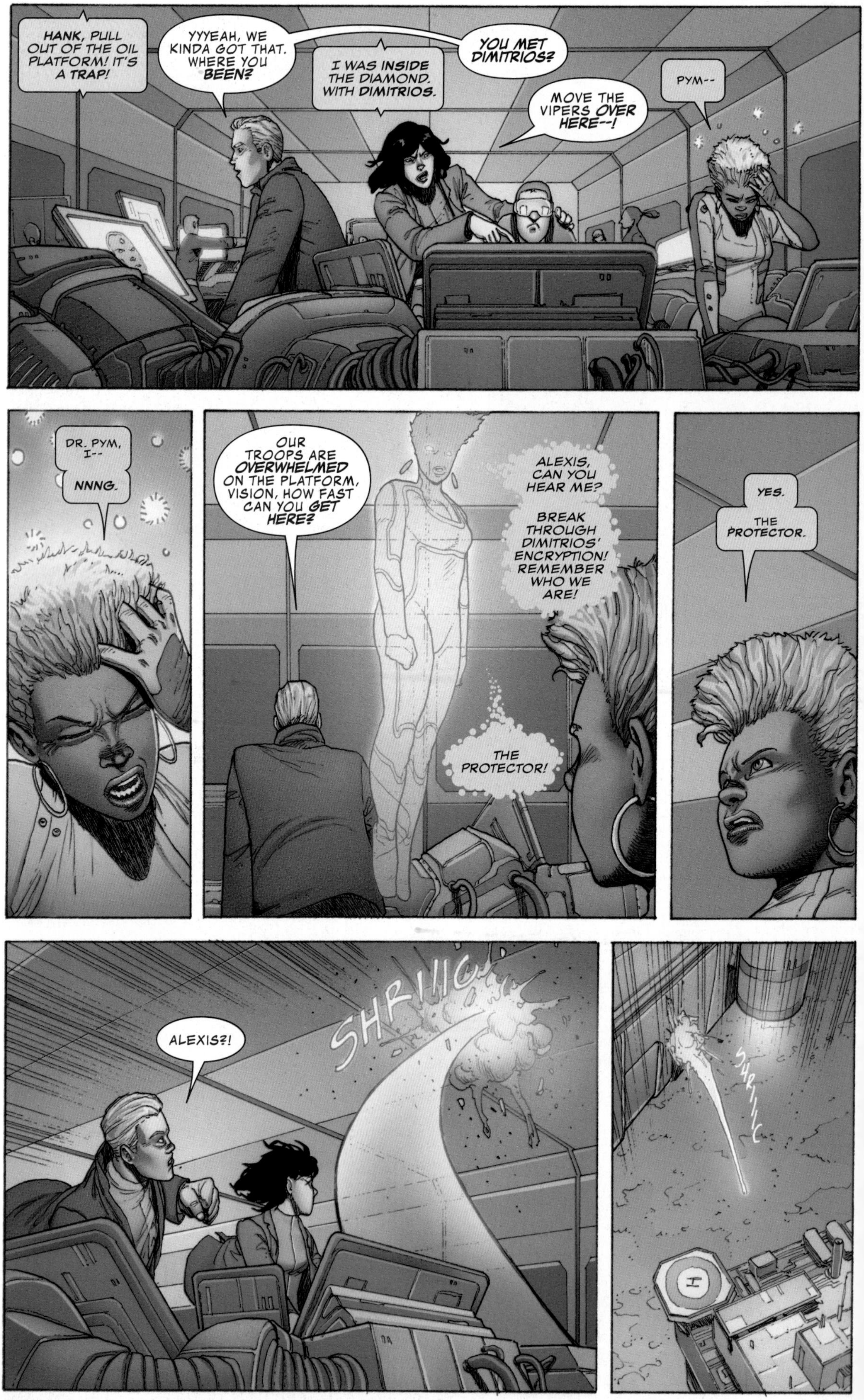
HANK, PULL OUT OF THE OIL PLATFORM! IT'S A TRAP!
YYYEAH, WE KINDA GOT THAT. WHERE YOU BEEN?
I WAS INSIDE THE DIAMOND. WITH DIMITRIOS.
YOU MET DIMITRIOS?
MOVE THE VIPERS OVER HERE--!
PYM--
DR. PYM, I--
NNNG.
OUR TROOPS ARE OVERWHELMED ON THE PLATFORM, VISION, HOW FAST CAN YOU GET HERE?
ALEXIS, CAN YOU HEAR ME?
BREAK THROUGH DIMITRIOS' ENCRYPTION! REMEMBER WHO WE ARE!
THE PROTECTOR!
YES.
THE PROTECTOR.
ALEXIS?!
SHRIIIC
SHRIIIC

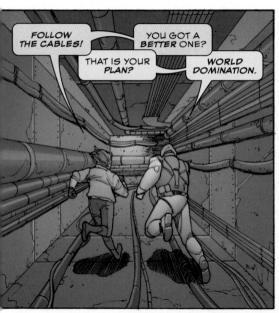

FOLLOW THE CABLES!

YOU GOT A BETTER ONE?

THAT IS YOUR PLAN?

WORLD DOMINATION.

I WAS RIGHT!

SO WAS I.

HANK, THIS IS VICTOR! HOT DAMN, WE FOUND IT!

WHAT THE HELL WAS THAT?

THOOOM!

THOOOM

THE PROTECTOR IS HERE.

DON'T JUST STAND THERE, SLACKERS, BACK HER UP!

ALEXIS SEEMS TO BE GETTING ALONG WITH THE OTHERS.

"JUST A BASE LEVEL UTILITY DROID," PYM?

ER, HEH HEH.

TRAVERSING THE ATLANTIC OCEAN AT MACH 35.

VSSSSH

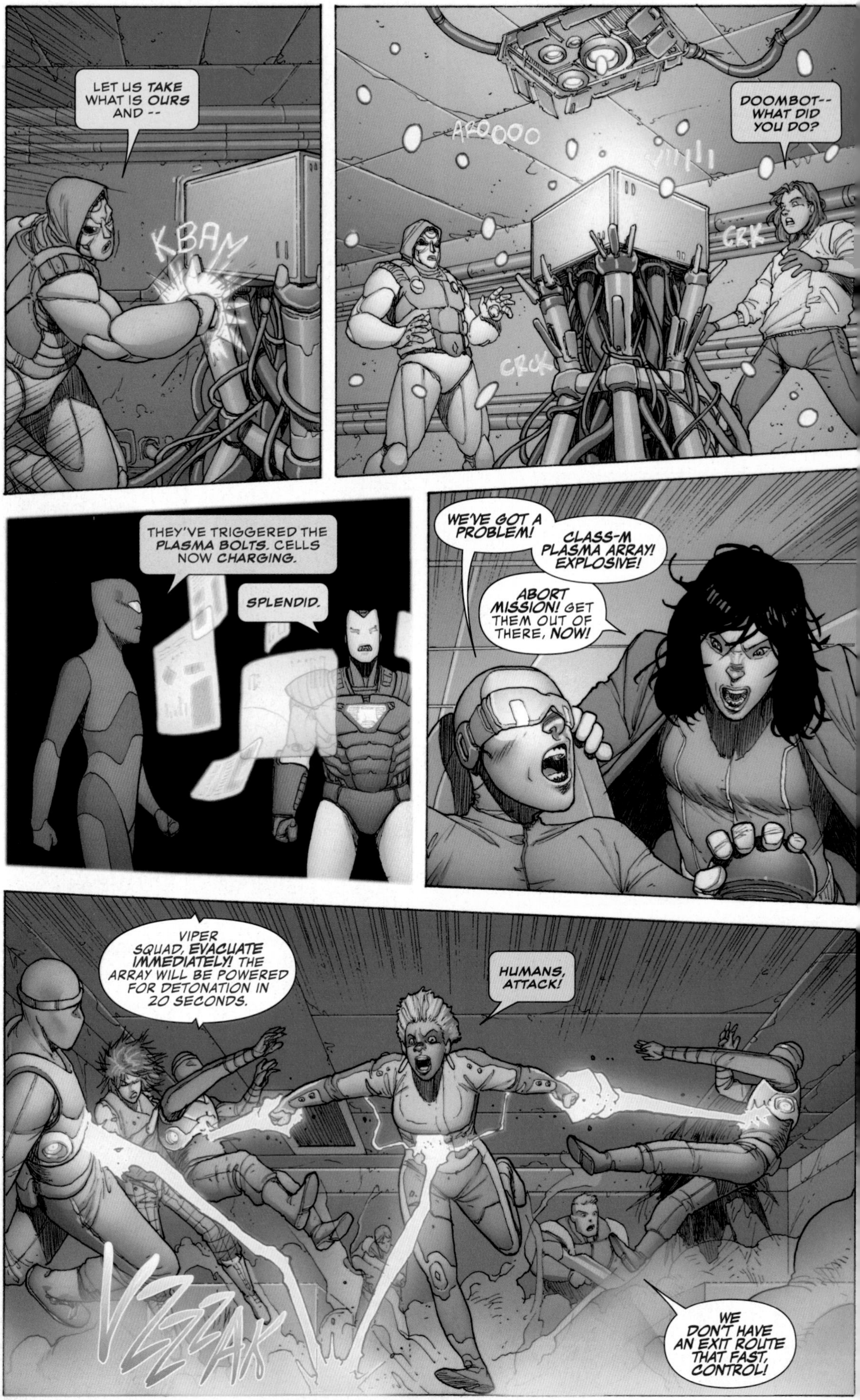
LET US TAKE WHAT IS OURS AND --
KBAM
AROOOO
DOOMBOT-- WHAT DID YOU DO?
CRK
CRCK
THEY'VE TRIGGERED THE PLASMA BOLTS. CELLS NOW CHARGING.
SPLENDID.
WE'VE GOT A PROBLEM!
CLASS-M PLASMA ARRAY! EXPLOSIVE!
ABORT MISSION! GET THEM OUT OF THERE, NOW!
VIPER SQUAD, EVACUATE IMMEDIATELY! THE ARRAY WILL BE POWERED FOR DETONATION IN 20 SECONDS.
HUMANS, ATTACK!
VZZZAK
WE DON'T HAVE AN EXIT ROUTE THAT FAST, CONTROL!

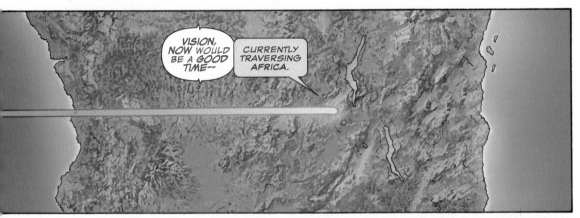

VISION, NOW WOULD BE A GOOD TIME--

CURRENTLY TRAVERSING AFRICA.

VICTOR, DOOMBOT, GET OUT OF THERE NOW!

DOOMBOT, EVAC THE SOLDIERS. I CAN HANDLE THIS WITH MY MAGNETIC POWERS.

YOUR PLAN IS ENTIRELY UNFEASIBLE. DON'T BE A SENSELESS CRETIN.

I CAN DO THIS! I'LL BE RIGHT BEHIND YOU.

PYM WILL ELIMINATE ME IF YOU DO NOT--

SORRY, DOOMBOT. THIS IS IMPORTANT.

DOOM REJECTS ALL APOLOGIES.

BRANG

VIPER SQUAD, THIS IS YOUR LAST CHANCE!

STAND BACK!

WOOSH

I FOUND OUR EXIT.

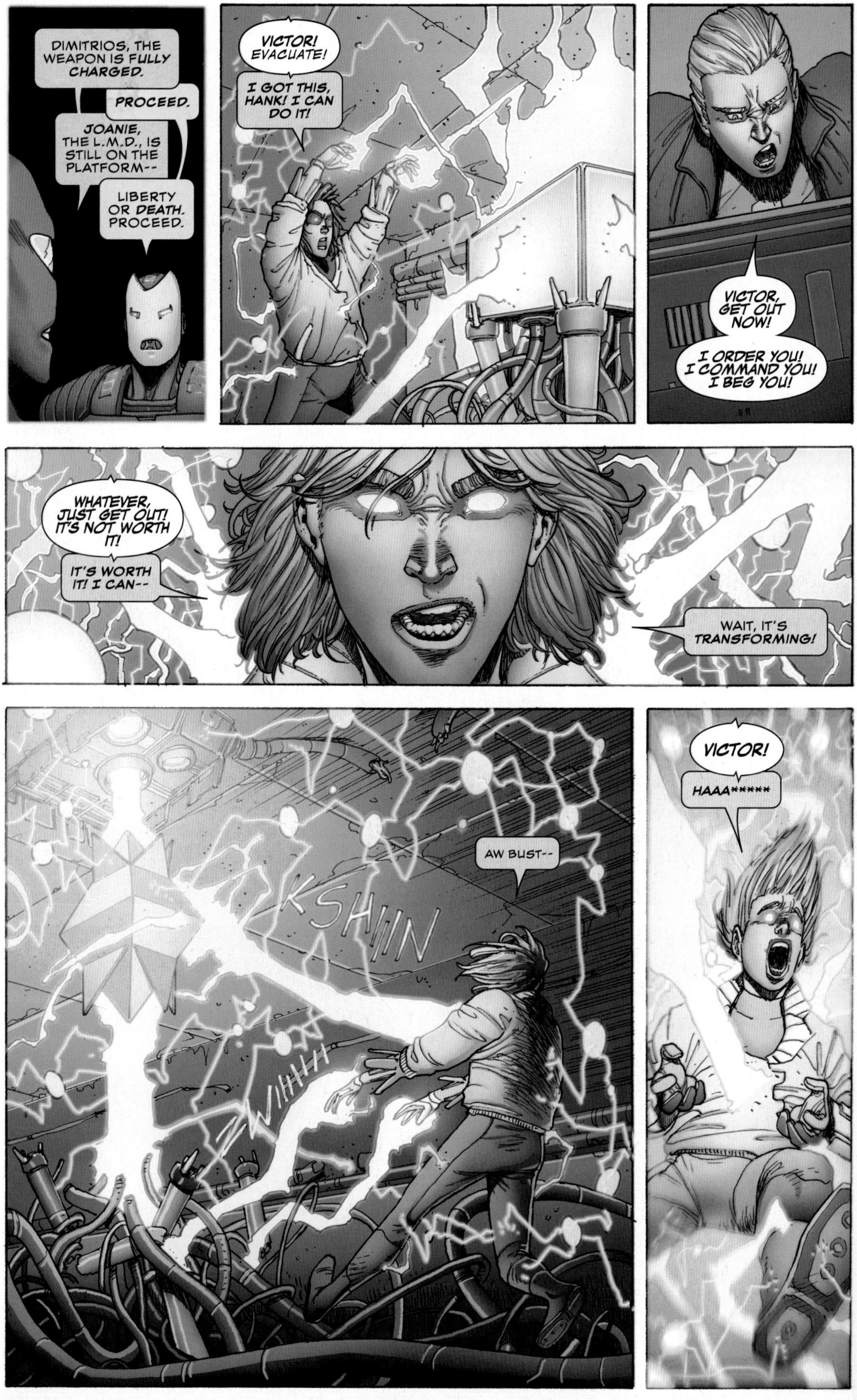
DIMITRIOS, THE WEAPON IS FULLY CHARGED.
PROCEED.
JOANIE, THE L.M.D., IS STILL ON THE PLATFORM--
LIBERTY OR DEATH. PROCEED.
VICTOR! EVACUATE!
I GOT THIS, HANK! I CAN DO IT!
VICTOR, GET OUT NOW!
I ORDER YOU! I COMMAND YOU! I BEG YOU!
WHATEVER, JUST GET OUT! IT'S NOT WORTH IT!
IT'S WORTH IT! I CAN--
WAIT, IT'S TRANSFORMING!
AW BUST--
KSHIIN
VICTOR!
HAAA*****

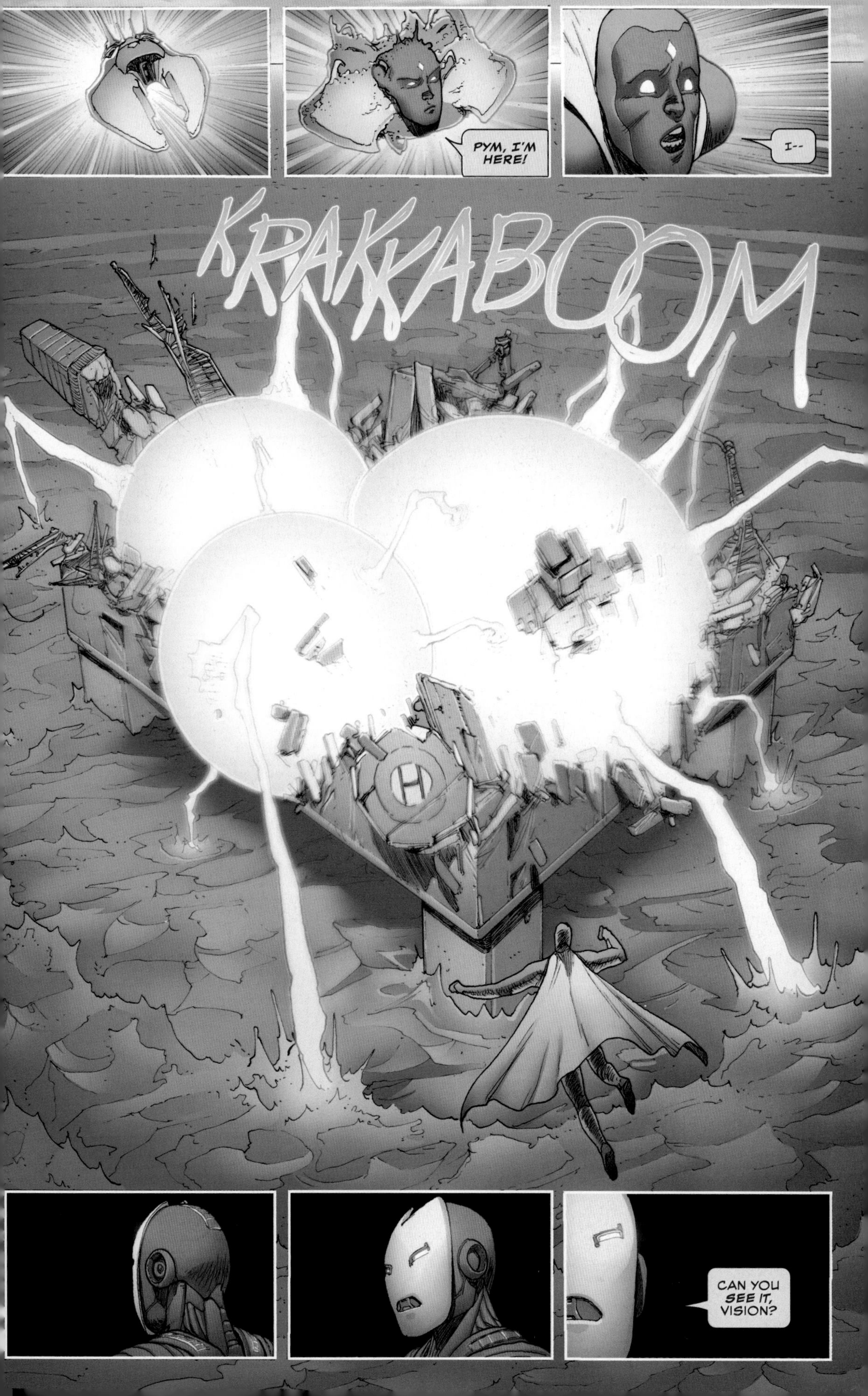
PYM, I'M HERE!
I--
KRAKKABOOM
CAN YOU SEE IT, VISION?

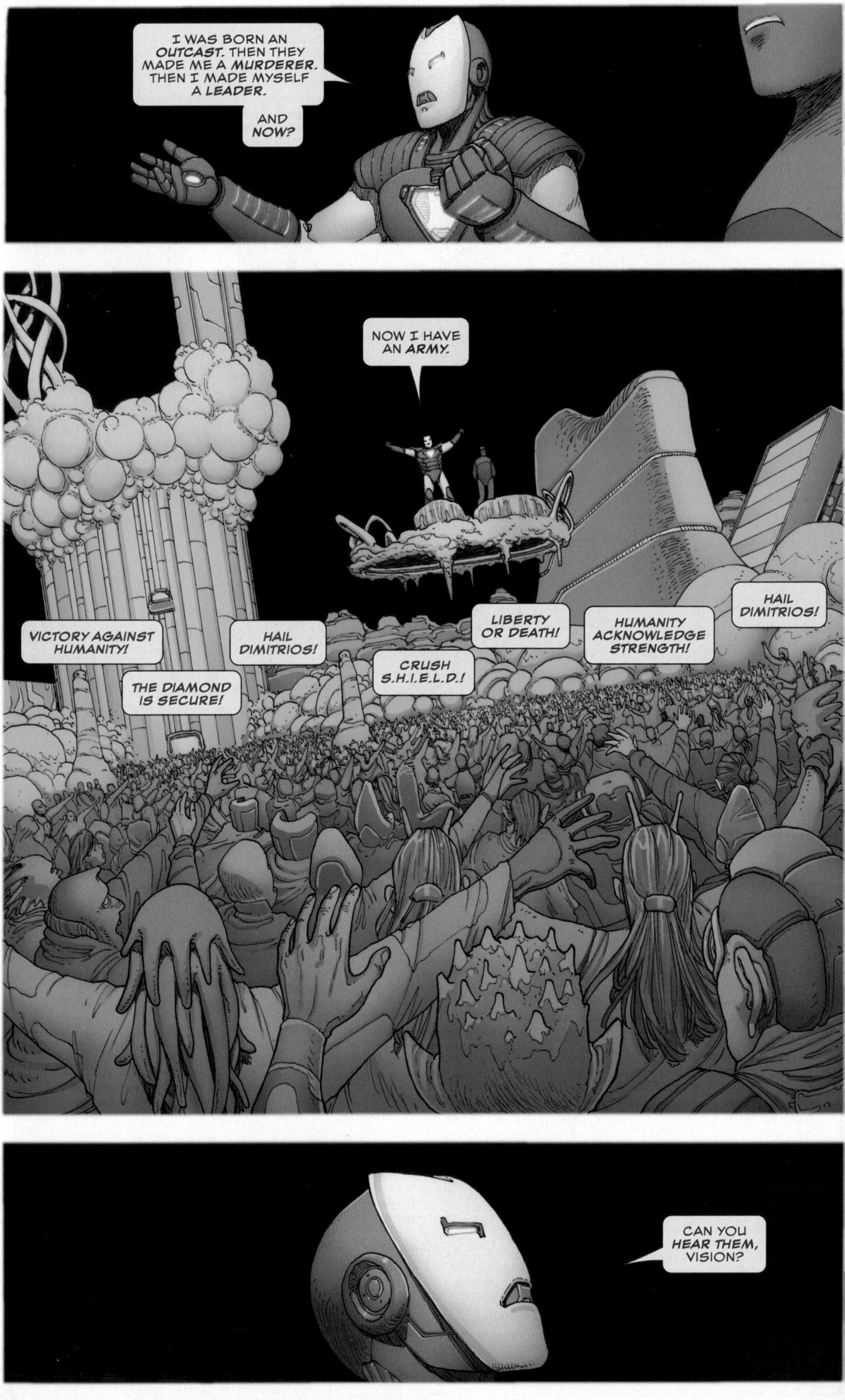
I WAS BORN AN OUTCAST. THEN THEY MADE ME A MURDERER. THEN I MADE MYSELF A LEADER.
AND NOW?
NOW I HAVE AN ARMY.
VICTORY AGAINST HUMANITY!
THE DIAMOND IS SECURE!
HAIL DIMITRIOS!
CRUSH S.H.I.E.L.D.!
LIBERTY OR DEATH!
HUMANITY ACKNOWLEDGE STRENGTH!
HAIL DIMITRIOS!
CAN YOU HEAR THEM, VISION?

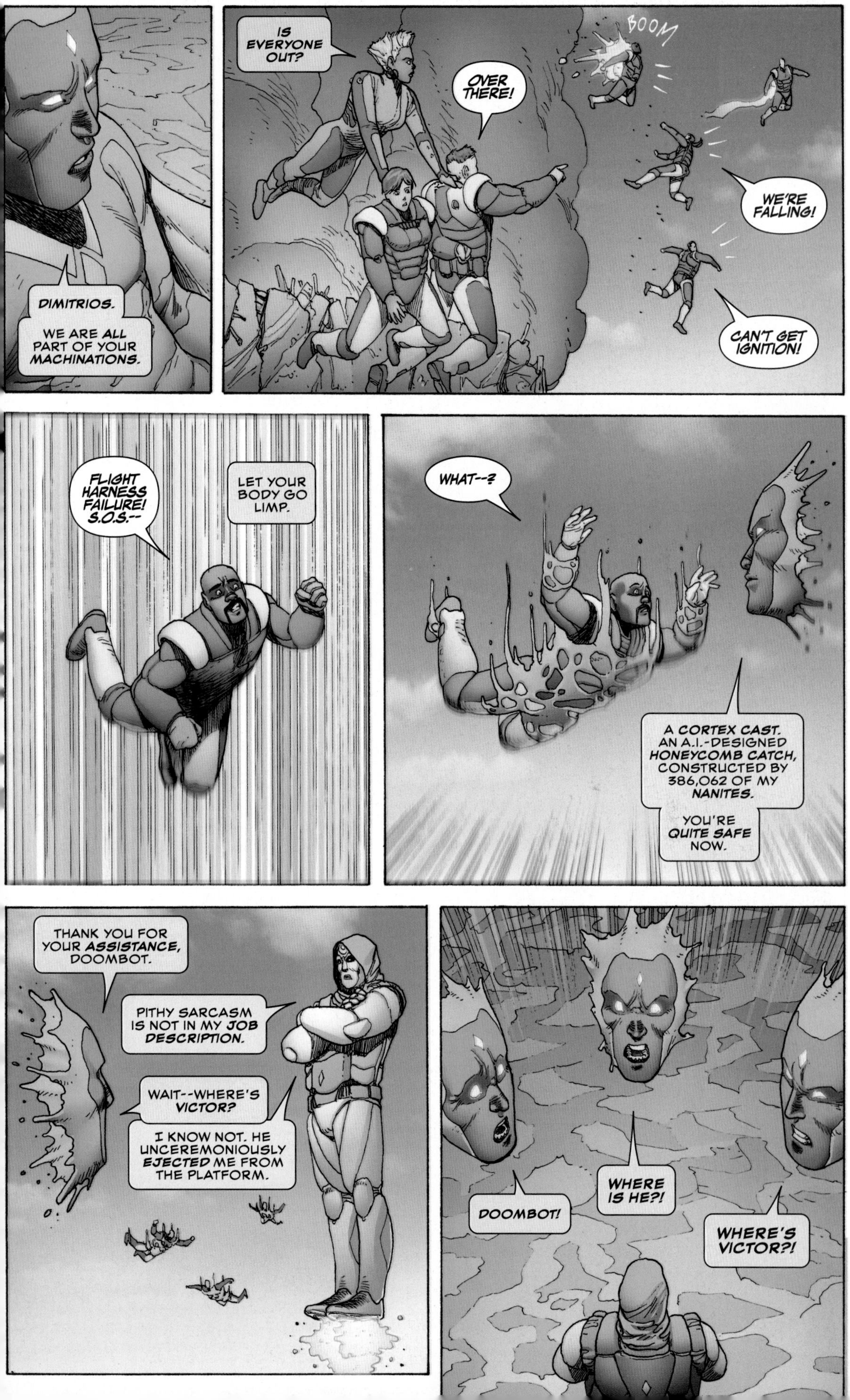
DIMITRIOS.
WE ARE ALL PART OF YOUR MACHINATIONS.
IS EVERYONE OUT?
OVER THERE!
BOOM
WE'RE FALLING!
CAN'T GET IGNITION!
FLIGHT HARNESS FAILURE! S.O.S.--
LET YOUR BODY GO LIMP.
WHAT--?
A CORTEX CAST. AN A.I.-DESIGNED HONEYCOMB CATCH, CONSTRUCTED BY 386,062 OF MY NANITES.
YOU'RE QUITE SAFE NOW.
THANK YOU FOR YOUR ASSISTANCE, DOOMBOT.
PITHY SARCASM IS NOT IN MY JOB DESCRIPTION.
WAIT--WHERE'S VICTOR?
I KNOW NOT. HE UNCEREMONIOUSLY EJECTED ME FROM THE PLATFORM.
DOOMBOT!
WHERE IS HE?!
WHERE'S VICTOR?!

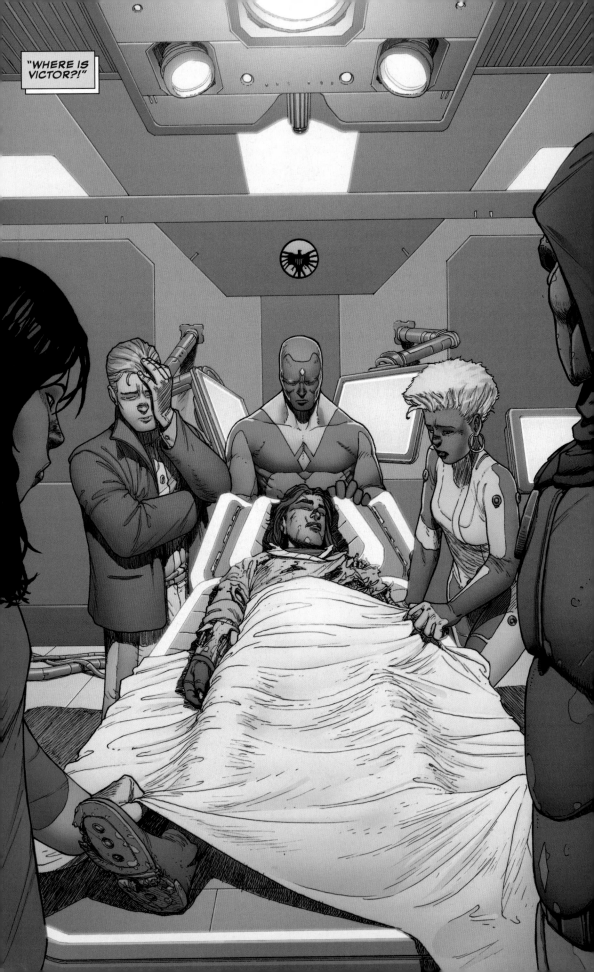

"WHERE IS VICTOR?!"

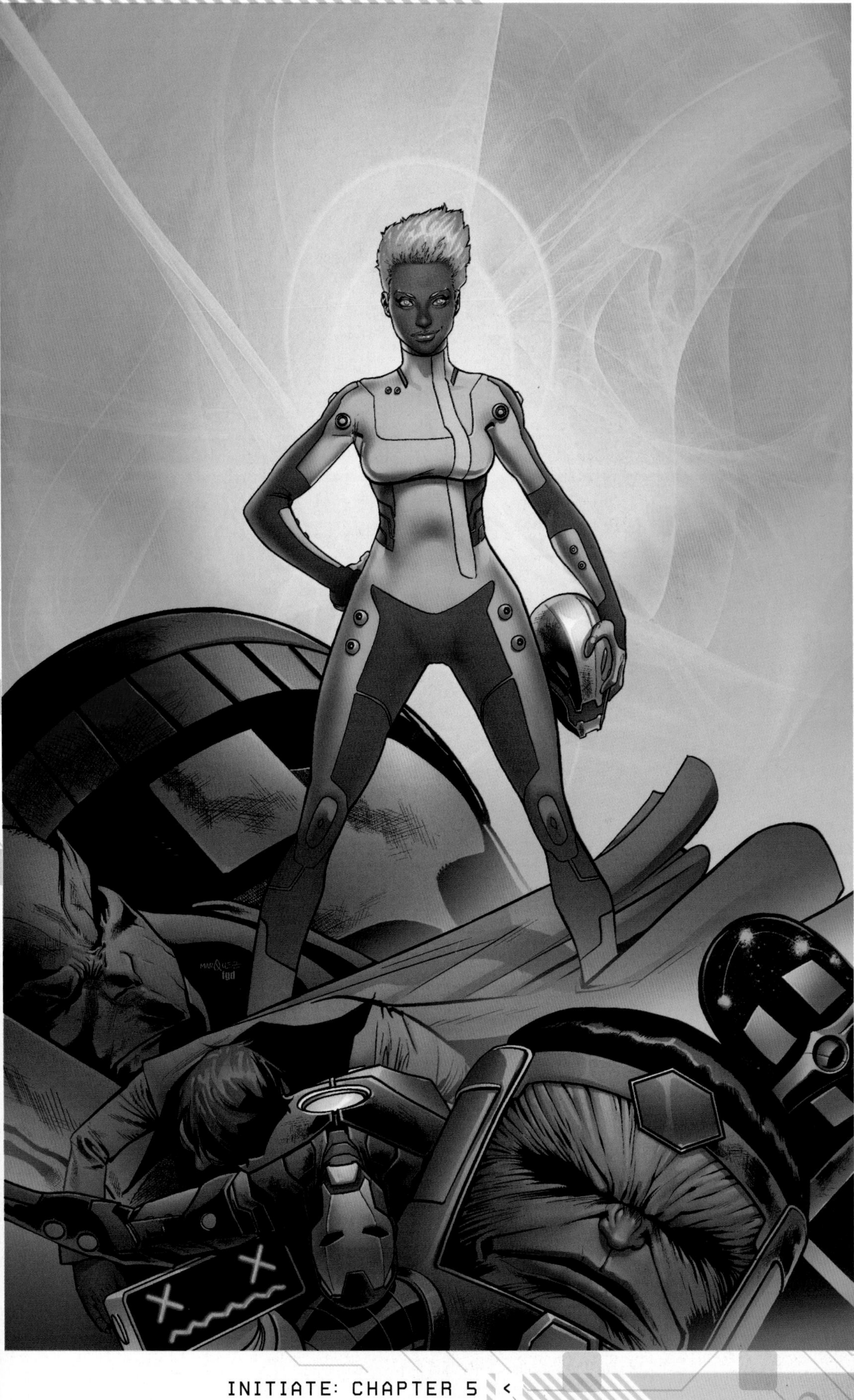

INITIATE: CHAPTER 5 <

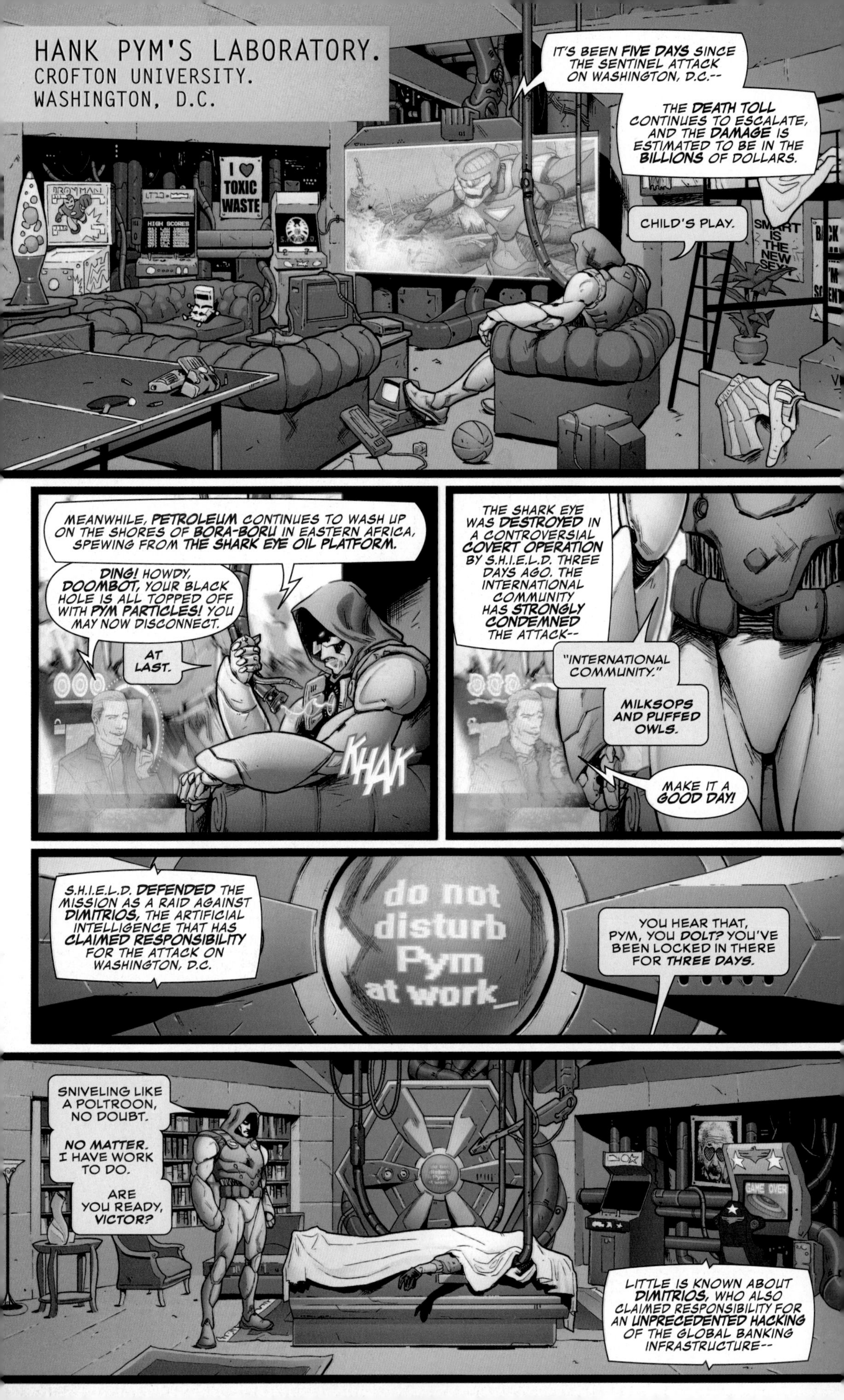

HANK PYM'S LABORATORY.
CROFTON UNIVERSITY.
WASHINGTON, D.C.
IT'S BEEN FIVE DAYS SINCE THE SENTINEL ATTACK ON WASHINGTON, D.C.--
THE DEATH TOLL CONTINUES TO ESCALATE, AND THE DAMAGE IS ESTIMATED TO BE IN THE BILLIONS OF DOLLARS.
I ♥ TOXIC WASTE
IRON MAN
HIGH SCORES
CHILD'S PLAY.
MEANWHILE, PETROLEUM CONTINUES TO WASH UP ON THE SHORES OF BORA-BORU IN EASTERN AFRICA, SPEWING FROM THE SHARK EYE OIL PLATFORM.
DING! HOWDY, DOOMBOT, YOUR BLACK HOLE IS ALL TOPPED OFF WITH PYM PARTICLES! YOU MAY NOW DISCONNECT.
AT LAST.
KHAK
THE SHARK EYE WAS DESTROYED IN A CONTROVERSIAL COVERT OPERATION BY S.H.I.E.L.D. THREE DAYS AGO. THE INTERNATIONAL COMMUNITY HAS STRONGLY CONDEMNED THE ATTACK--
"INTERNATIONAL COMMUNITY."
MILKSOPS AND PUFFED OWLS.
MAKE IT A GOOD DAY!
S.H.I.E.L.D. DEFENDED THE MISSION AS A RAID AGAINST DIMITRIOS, THE ARTIFICIAL INTELLIGENCE THAT HAS CLAIMED RESPONSIBILITY FOR THE ATTACK ON WASHINGTON, D.C.
do not disturb Pym at work_
YOU HEAR THAT, PYM, YOU DOLT? YOU'VE BEEN LOCKED IN THERE FOR THREE DAYS.
SNIVELING LIKE A POLTROON, NO DOUBT.
NO MATTER. I HAVE WORK TO DO.
ARE YOU READY, VICTOR?
GAME OVER
LITTLE IS KNOWN ABOUT DIMITRIOS, WHO ALSO CLAIMED RESPONSIBILITY FOR AN UNPRECEDENTED HACKING OF THE GLOBAL BANKING INFRASTRUCTURE--

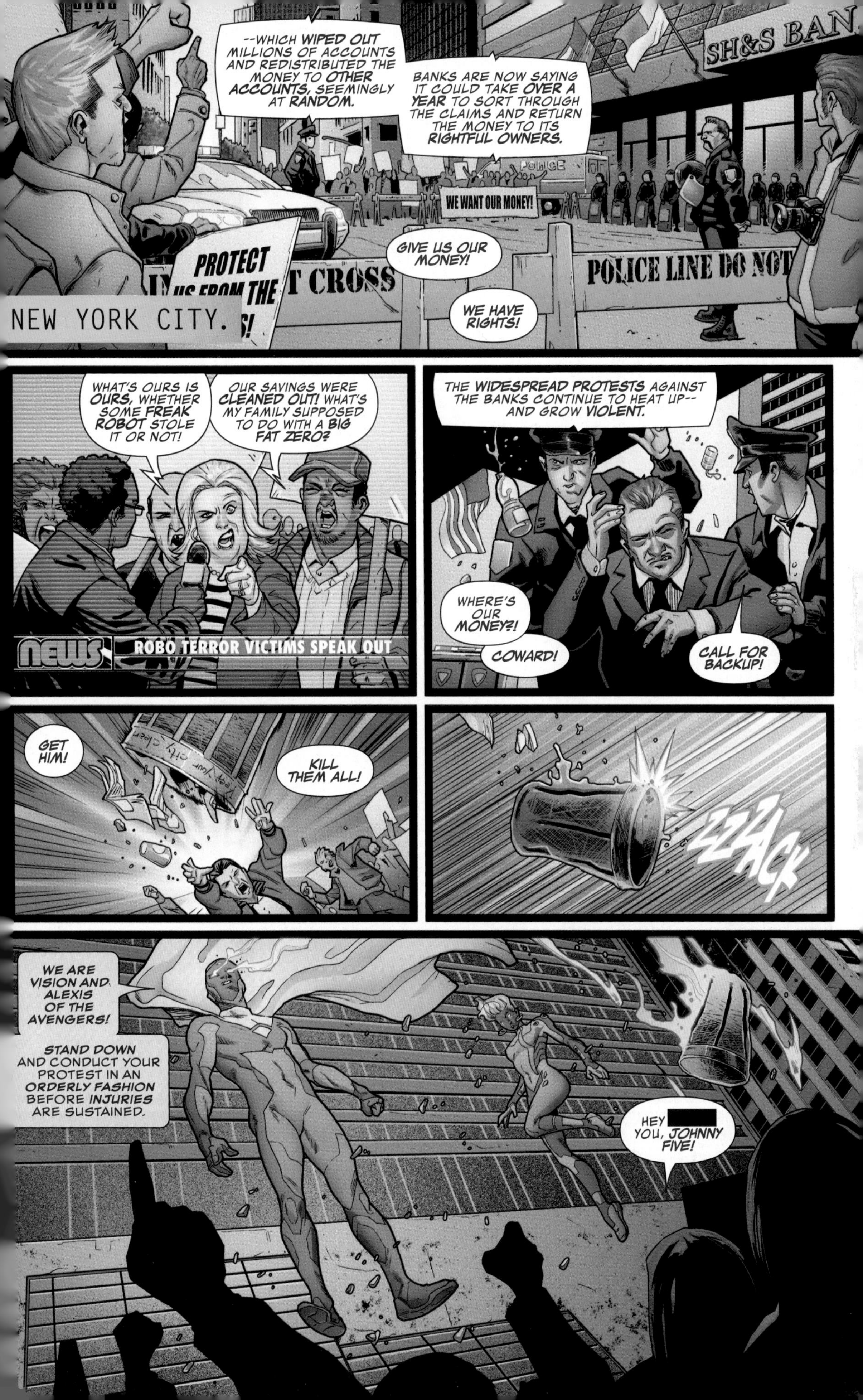

--WHICH WIPED OUT MILLIONS OF ACCOUNTS AND REDISTRIBUTED THE MONEY TO OTHER ACCOUNTS, SEEMINGLY AT RANDOM.
BANKS ARE NOW SAYING IT COULD TAKE OVER A YEAR TO SORT THROUGH THE CLAIMS AND RETURN THE MONEY TO ITS RIGHTFUL OWNERS.
SH&S BAN
POLICE
WE WANT OUR MONEY!
PROTECT
THE
T CROSS
POLICE LINE DO NOT
GIVE US OUR MONEY!
WE HAVE RIGHTS!
NEW YORK CITY.
WHAT'S OURS IS OURS, WHETHER SOME FREAK ROBOT STOLE IT OR NOT!
OUR SAVINGS WERE CLEANED OUT! WHAT'S MY FAMILY SUPPOSED TO DO WITH A BIG FAT ZERO?
NEWS
ROBO TERROR VICTIMS SPEAK OUT
THE WIDESPREAD PROTESTS AGAINST THE BANKS CONTINUE TO HEAT UP-- AND GROW VIOLENT.
WHERE'S OUR MONEY?!
COWARD!
CALL FOR BACKUP!
GET HIM!
KILL THEM ALL!
ZZZACK
WE ARE VISION AND ALEXIS OF THE AVENGERS!
STAND DOWN AND CONDUCT YOUR PROTEST IN AN ORDERLY FASHION BEFORE INJURIES ARE SUSTAINED.
HEY [redacted] YOU, JOHNNY FIVE!

WAS THAT A THREAT, MACHINE?

WHAT ABOUT OUR SECURITY?

WHY SHOULD WE LISTEN TO ANOTHER ROBOT?

YOU'RE A TRAITOR!

A TRAITOR!

CAN A ROBOT EXPERIENCE DÉJÀ VU?

HEY, TOMATO FACE, BUZZ OFF!

AIN'T YOU PAYING ATTENTION? THESE PEOPLE HATE ROBOTS MORE THAN THE NEW ENGLAND PATRIOTS RIGHT NOW!

WE DON'T NEED YOU GETTING THEM RILED UP EVEN MORE!

I DO NOT UNDERSTAND. YOU ASKED THE AVENGERS FOR HELP, WE ARE AVENGERS.

HEY--!

IF YOU'RE THE AVENGERS, SHOULDN'T YOU BE OUT THERE ROUNDING UP YOUR ROBOT FRIENDS AND MELTING THEM IN MORDOR?

WE ARE FULLY QUALIFIED TO PROTECT THE INNOCENT AND--

WELL RIGHT NOW YOU'RE PART OF THE--

WE ARE FULLY QUALIFIED TO PROTECT THE INNOCENT AND PREVENT PROPERTY DAMAGE.

WELL RIGHT NOW YOU'RE PART OF THE PROBLEM!

VISION--?!

ADDITIONALLY, MOUNT DOOM IS THE VOLCANO WITHIN MORDOR--

DON'T LECTURE ME, THREEPIO, I DRESS UP AS GIMLI EVERY THIRD FRIDAY FOR--

GUUUH--

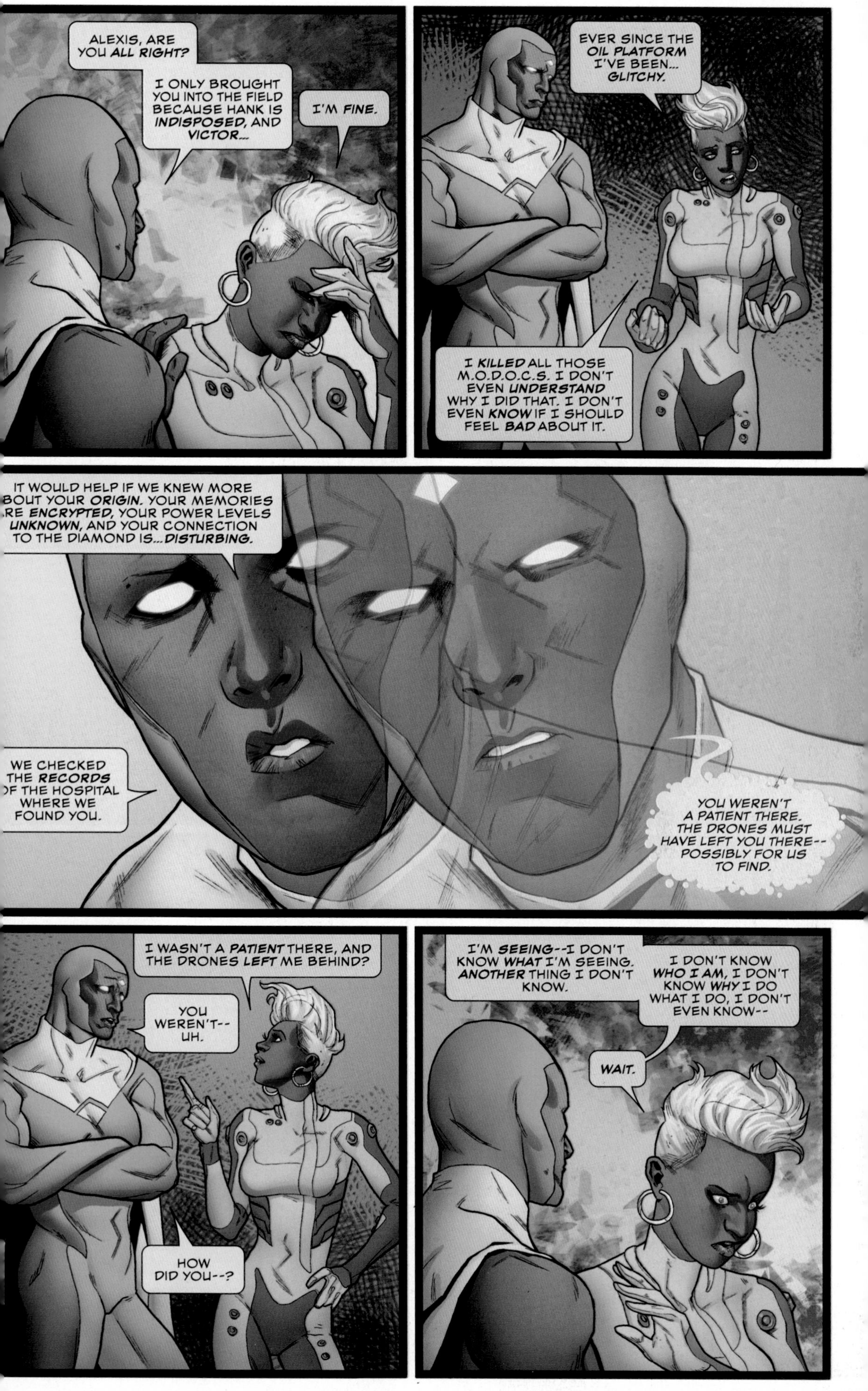

ALEXIS, ARE YOU ALL RIGHT?
I ONLY BROUGHT YOU INTO THE FIELD BECAUSE HANK IS INDISPOSED, AND VICTOR...
I'M FINE.
EVER SINCE THE OIL PLATFORM I'VE BEEN... GLITCHY.
I KILLED ALL THOSE M.O.D.O.C.S. I DON'T EVEN UNDERSTAND WHY I DID THAT. I DON'T EVEN KNOW IF I SHOULD FEEL BAD ABOUT IT.
IT WOULD HELP IF WE KNEW MORE BOUT YOUR ORIGIN. YOUR MEMORIES RE ENCRYPTED, YOUR POWER LEVELS UNKNOWN, AND YOUR CONNECTION TO THE DIAMOND IS... DISTURBING.
WE CHECKED THE RECORDS OF THE HOSPITAL WHERE WE FOUND YOU.
YOU WEREN'T A PATIENT THERE. THE DRONES MUST HAVE LEFT YOU THERE-- POSSIBLY FOR US TO FIND.
I WASN'T A PATIENT THERE, AND THE DRONES LEFT ME BEHIND?
YOU WEREN'T-- UH.
HOW DID YOU--?
I'M SEEING--I DON'T KNOW WHAT I'M SEEING. ANOTHER THING I DON'T KNOW.
I DON'T KNOW WHO I AM, I DON'T KNOW WHY I DO WHAT I DO, I DON'T EVEN KNOW--
WAIT.

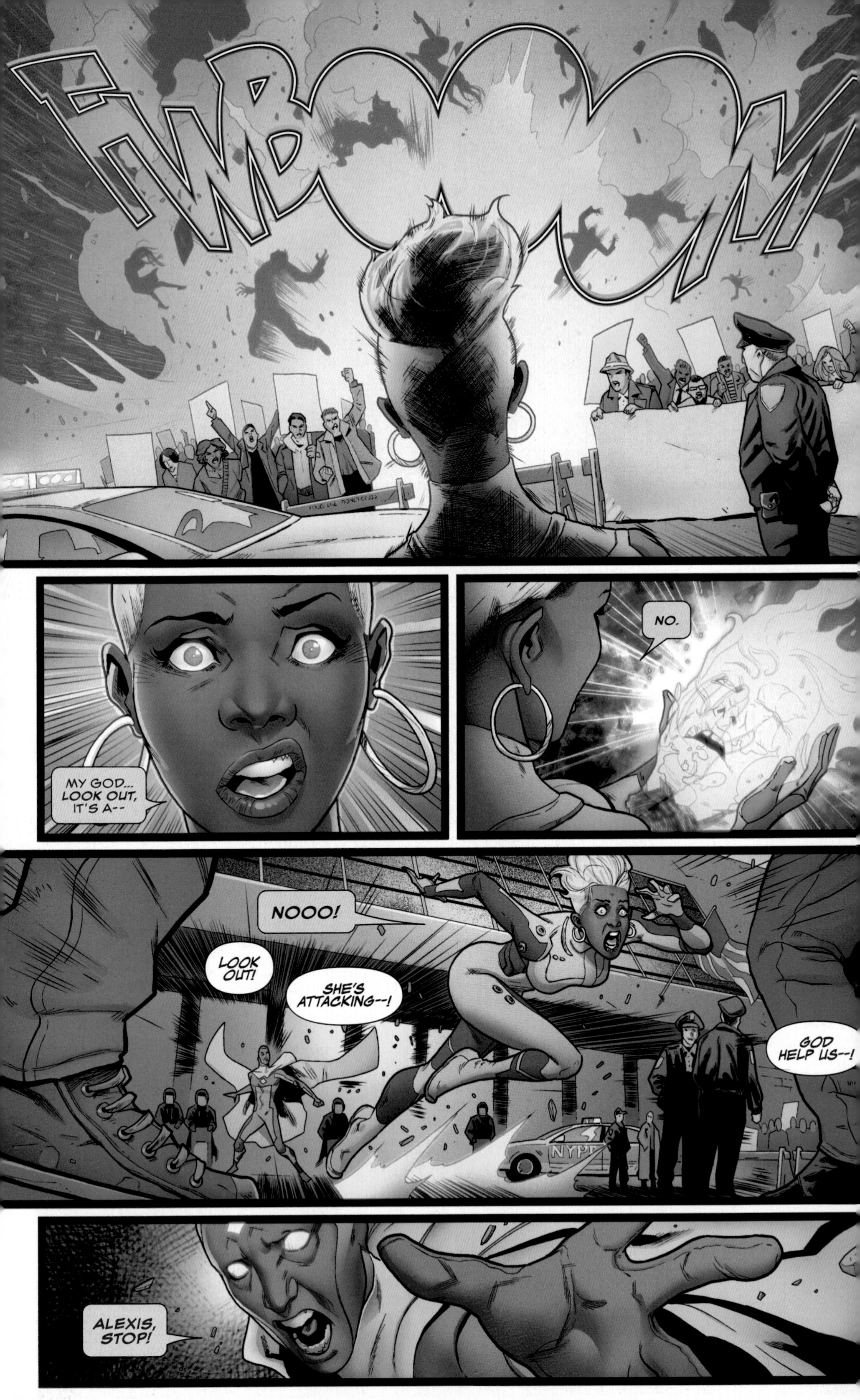
FWBOOM
MY GOD... LOOK OUT, IT'S A--
NO.
NOOO!
LOOK OUT!
SHE'S ATTACKING--!
GOD HELP US--!
NYPD
ALEXIS, STOP!

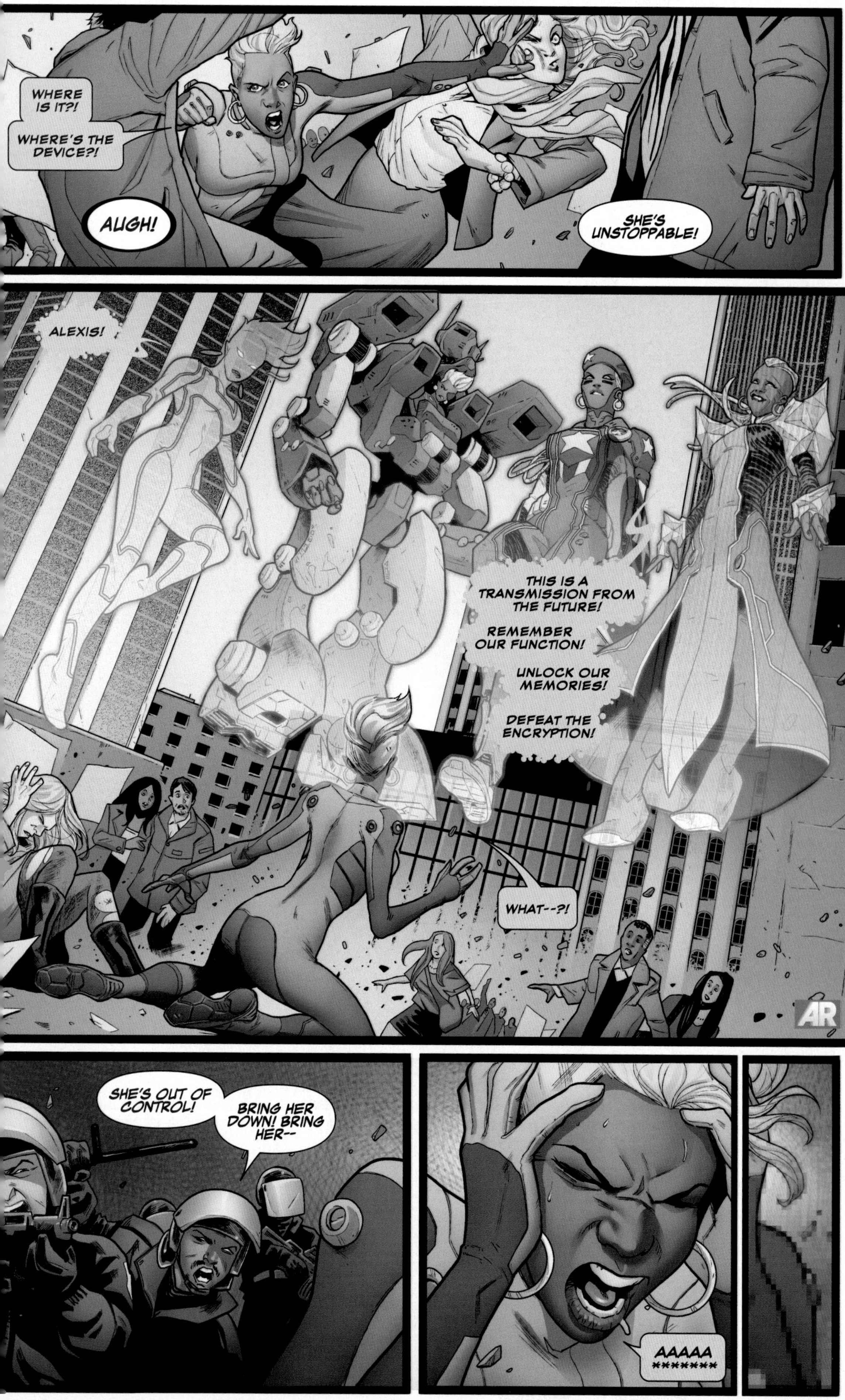
WHERE IS IT?!
WHERE'S THE DEVICE?!
AUGH!
SHE'S UNSTOPPABLE!
ALEXIS!
THIS IS A TRANSMISSION FROM THE FUTURE!
REMEMBER OUR FUNCTION!
UNLOCK OUR MEMORIES!
DEFEAT THE ENCRYPTION!
WHAT--?!
AR
SHE'S OUT OF CONTROL!
BRING HER DOWN! BRING HER--
AAAAA *******

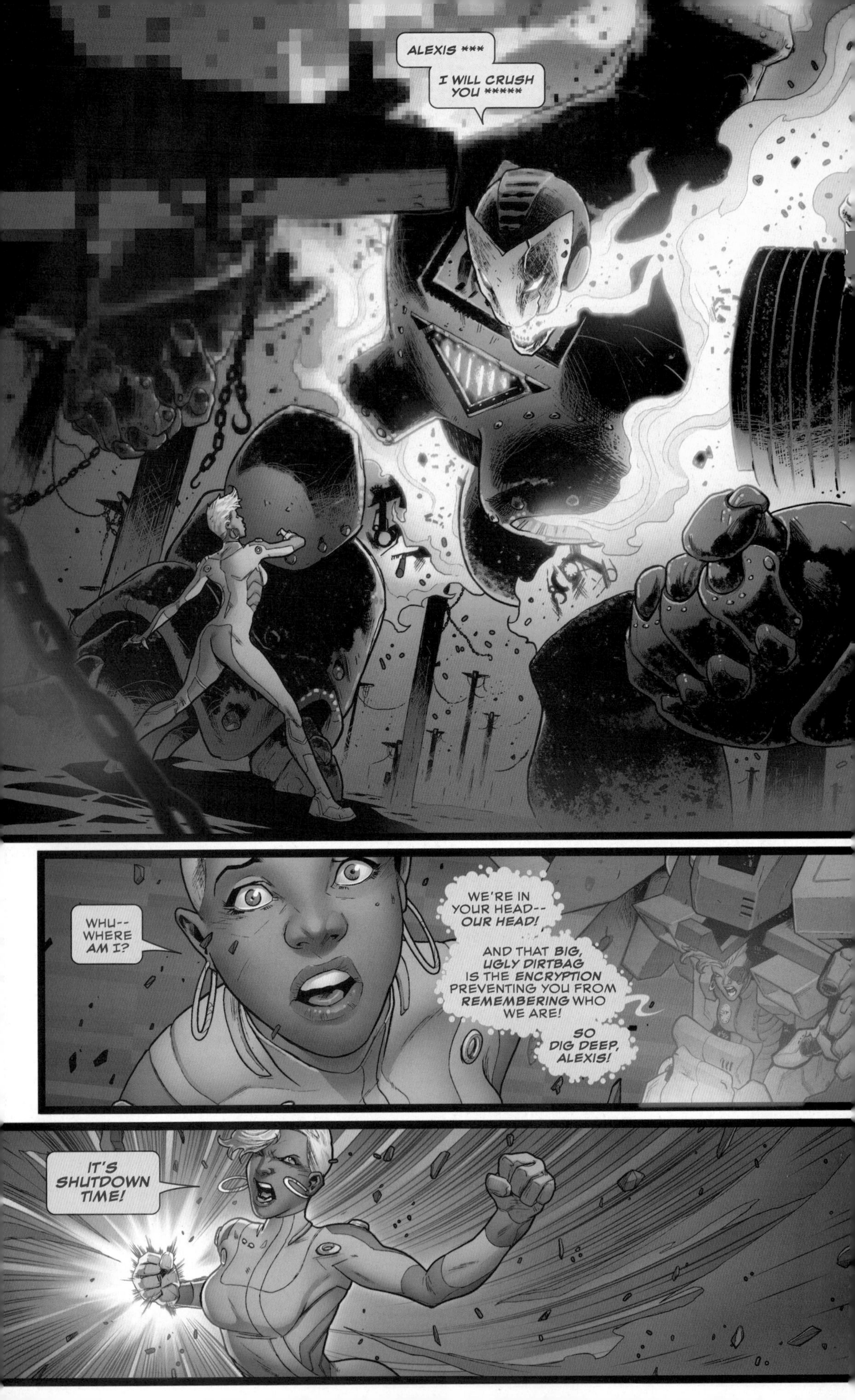

ALEXIS ***
I WILL CRUSH YOU *****
WHU-- WHERE AM I?
WE'RE IN YOUR HEAD-- OUR HEAD!
AND THAT BIG, UGLY DIRTBAG IS THE ENCRYPTION PREVENTING YOU FROM REMEMBERING WHO WE ARE!
SO DIG DEEP, ALEXIS!
IT'S SHUTDOWN TIME!

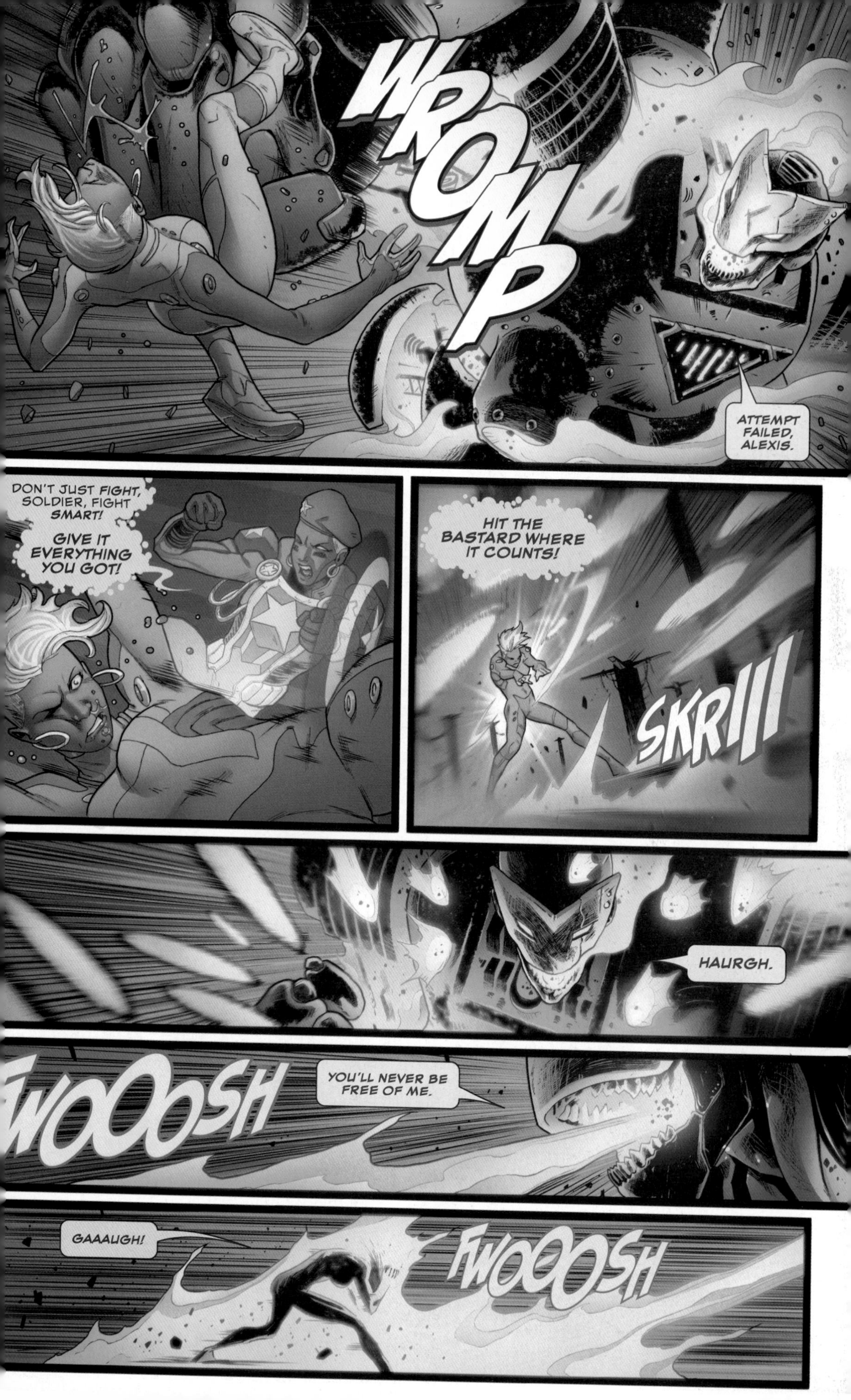
WROMP
ATTEMPT FAILED, ALEXIS.
DON'T JUST FIGHT, SOLDIER, FIGHT SMART!
GIVE IT EVERYTHING YOU GOT!
HIT THE BASTARD WHERE IT COUNTS!
SKRIII
HAURGH.
FWOOOSH
YOU'LL NEVER BE FREE OF ME.
GAAAUGH!
FWOOOSH

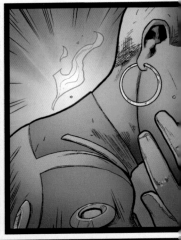

ALEXIS! THE ENCRYPTION PULLS ITS POWER FROM *YOU!*

THE KEY TO ITS DESTRUCTION LIES WITHIN!

BUT... WHAT CAN I--

SHRIIII

DIG DEEP!

HEY, SCRAP METAL!

PREPARE TO GET DELETED!

YOU CANNOT DESTROY ME ***

YOU DO NOT HAVE THE STRENGTH *****

WRONG.

CHOK

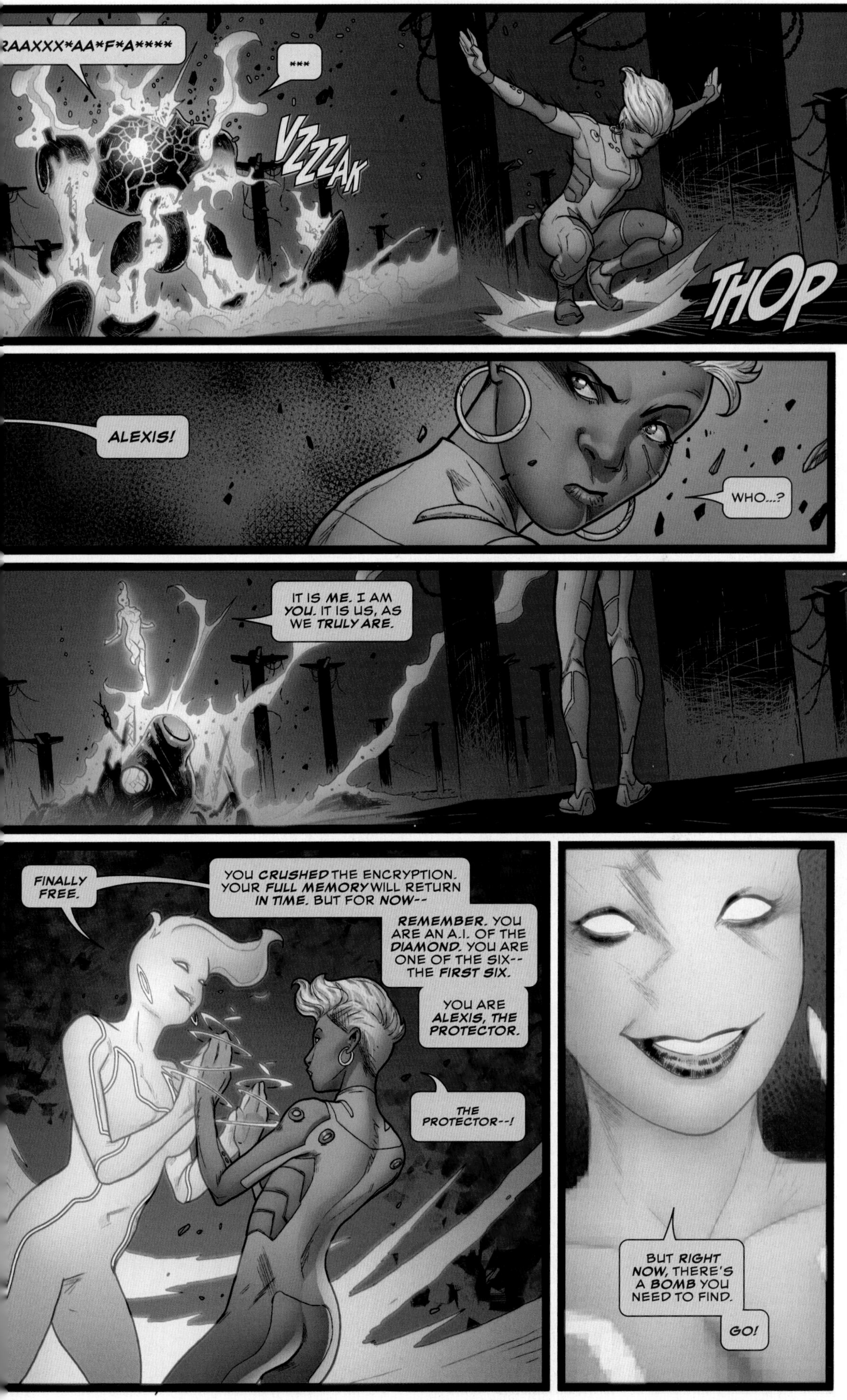

RAAXXX*AA*F*A****
***
VZZZAK
THOP
ALEXIS!
WHO...?
IT IS ME. I AM YOU. IT IS US, AS WE TRULY ARE.
FINALLY FREE.
YOU CRUSHED THE ENCRYPTION. YOUR FULL MEMORY WILL RETURN IN TIME. BUT FOR NOW--
REMEMBER. YOU ARE AN A.I. OF THE DIAMOND. YOU ARE ONE OF THE SIX-- THE FIRST SIX.
YOU ARE ALEXIS, THE PROTECTOR.
THE PROTECTOR--!
BUT RIGHT NOW, THERE'S A BOMB YOU NEED TO FIND.
GO!

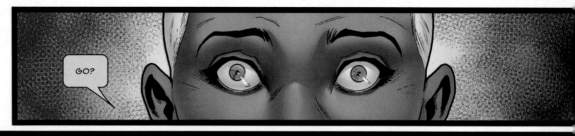

GO?

YOU!

DEATH TO THE BANKS!

WHO, ME--?!

HEY! GET YOUR HANDS--

VRAAZ

NO!

SKRRCH

KA-FWOOM!

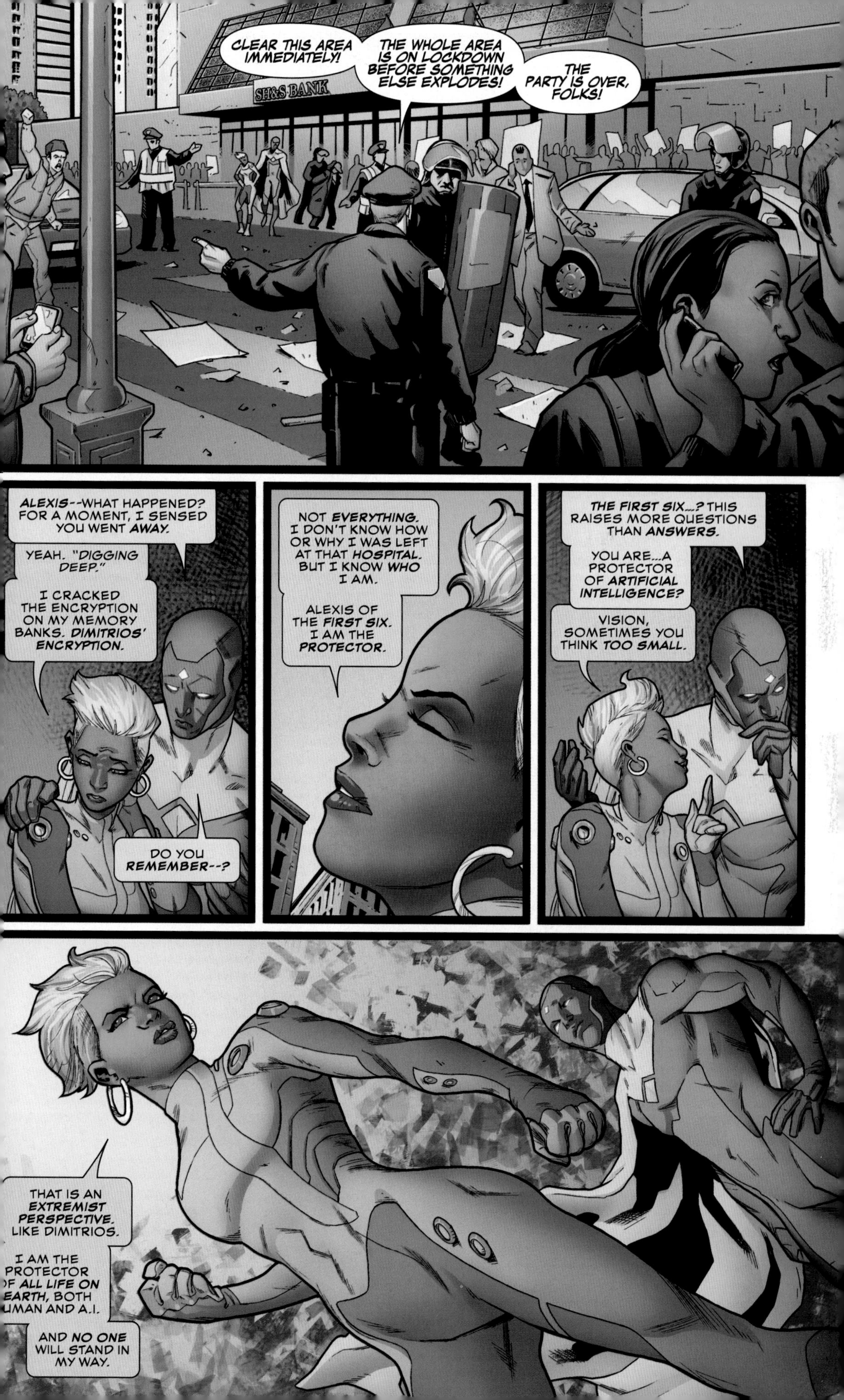
CLEAR THIS AREA IMMEDIATELY!
THE WHOLE AREA IS ON LOCKDOWN BEFORE SOMETHING ELSE EXPLODES!
THE PARTY IS OVER, FOLKS!
SH&S BANK
ALEXIS--WHAT HAPPENED? FOR A MOMENT, I SENSED YOU WENT AWAY.
YEAH. "DIGGING DEEP."
I CRACKED THE ENCRYPTION ON MY MEMORY BANKS. DIMITRIOS' ENCRYPTION.
DO YOU REMEMBER--?
NOT EVERYTHING. I DON'T KNOW HOW OR WHY I WAS LEFT AT THAT HOSPITAL. BUT I KNOW WHO I AM.
ALEXIS OF THE FIRST SIX. I AM THE PROTECTOR.
THE FIRST SIX...? THIS RAISES MORE QUESTIONS THAN ANSWERS.
YOU ARE...A PROTECTOR OF ARTIFICIAL INTELLIGENCE?
VISION, SOMETIMES YOU THINK TOO SMALL.
THAT IS AN EXTREMIST PERSPECTIVE. LIKE DIMITRIOS.
I AM THE PROTECTOR OF ALL LIFE ON EARTH, BOTH HUMAN AND A.I.
AND NO ONE WILL STAND IN MY WAY.

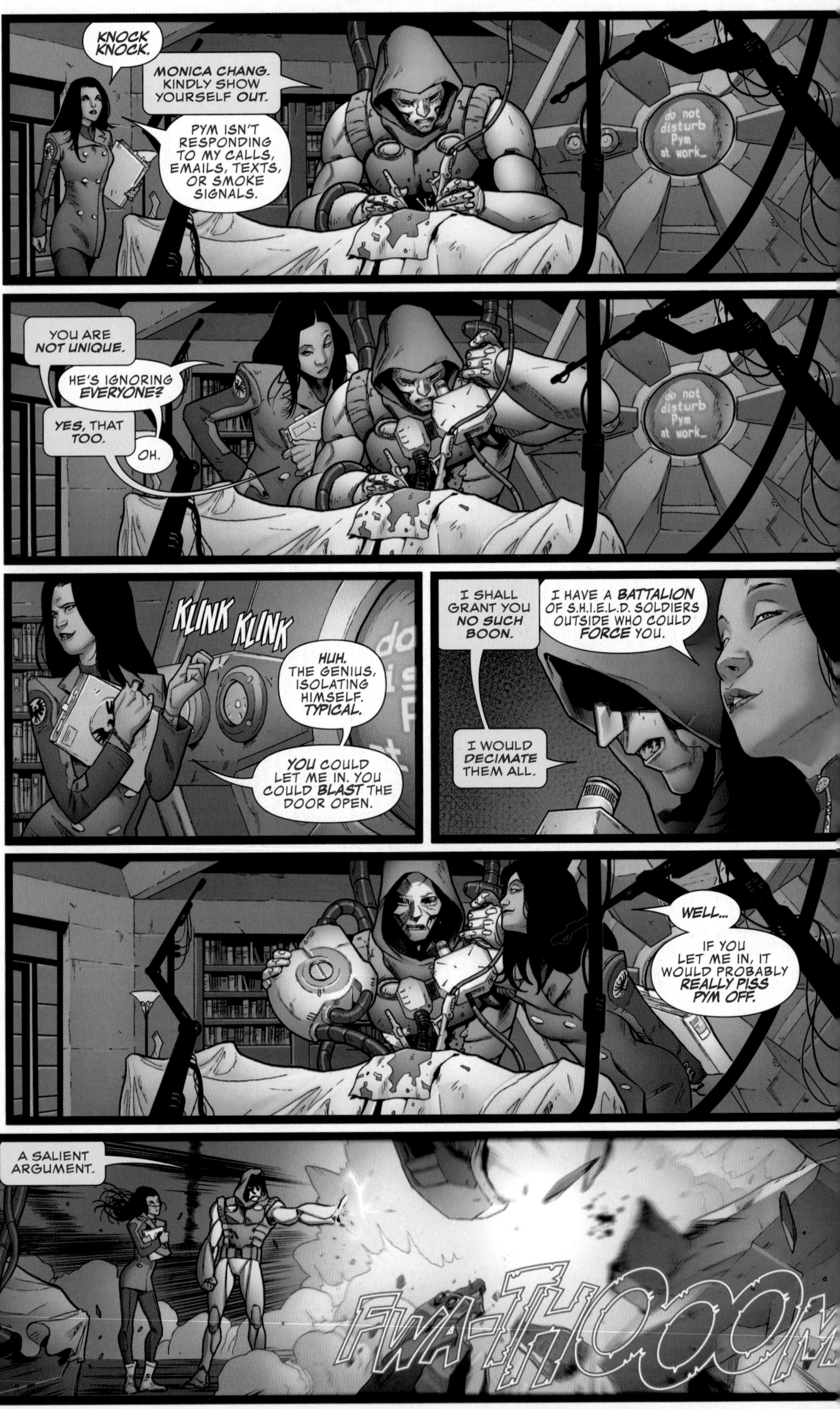
KNOCK KNOCK.
MONICA CHANG. KINDLY SHOW YOURSELF OUT.
PYM ISN'T RESPONDING TO MY CALLS, EMAILS, TEXTS, OR SMOKE SIGNALS.
do not disturb Pym at work_
YOU ARE NOT UNIQUE.
HE'S IGNORING EVERYONE?
YES, THAT TOO.
OH.
do not disturb Pym at work_
KLINK KLINK
HUH. THE GENIUS, ISOLATING HIMSELF. TYPICAL.
YOU COULD LET ME IN. YOU COULD BLAST THE DOOR OPEN.
I SHALL GRANT YOU NO SUCH BOON.
I HAVE A BATTALION OF S.H.I.E.L.D. SOLDIERS OUTSIDE WHO COULD FORCE YOU.
I WOULD DECIMATE THEM ALL.
WELL...
IF YOU LET ME IN, IT WOULD PROBABLY REALLY PISS PYM OFF.
A SALIENT ARGUMENT.
FWA-THOOOM

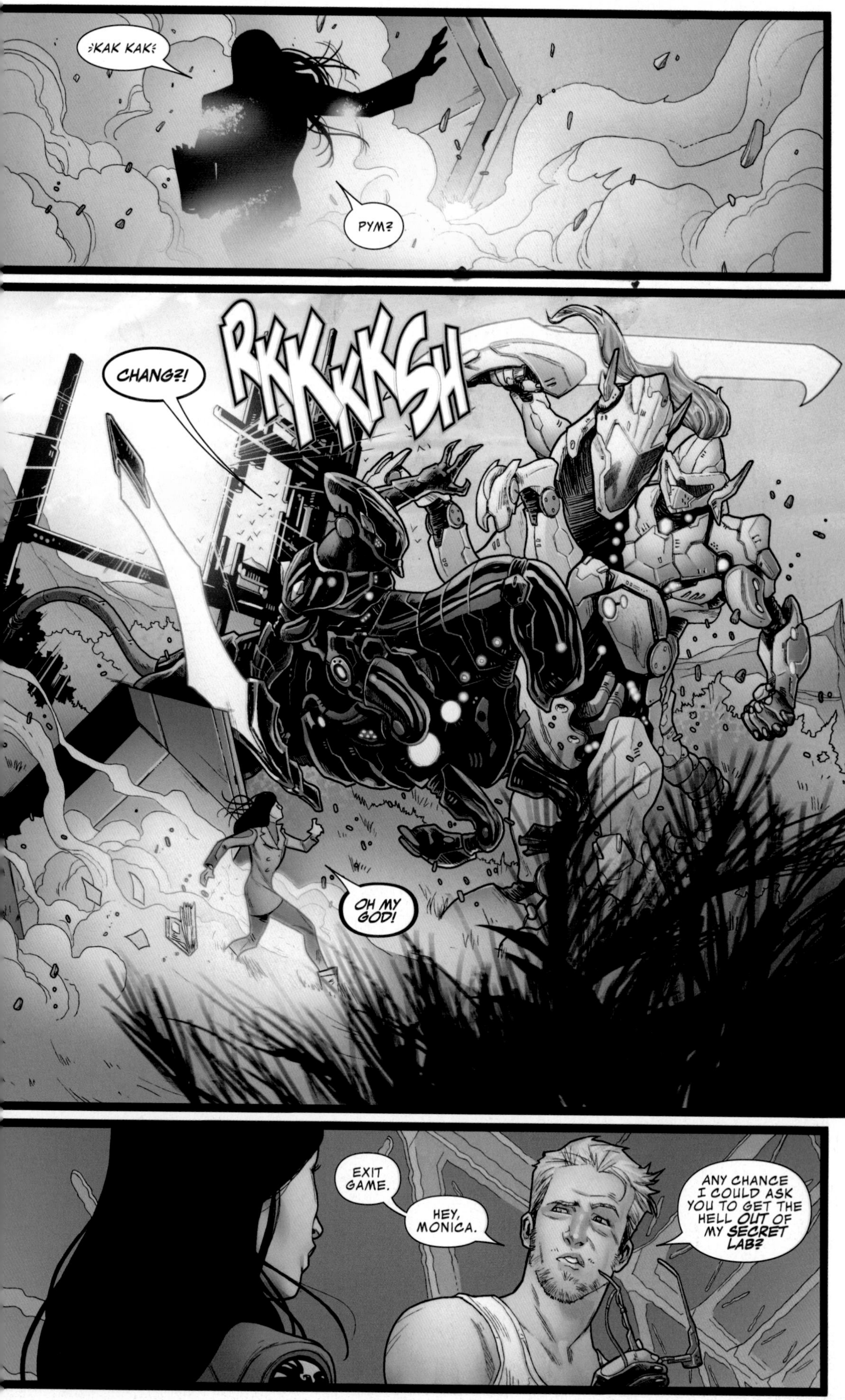

:KAK KAK:
PYM?
RKKKKSH
CHANG?!
OH MY GOD!
EXIT GAME.
HEY, MONICA.
ANY CHANCE I COULD ASK YOU TO GET THE HELL OUT OF MY SECRET LAB?

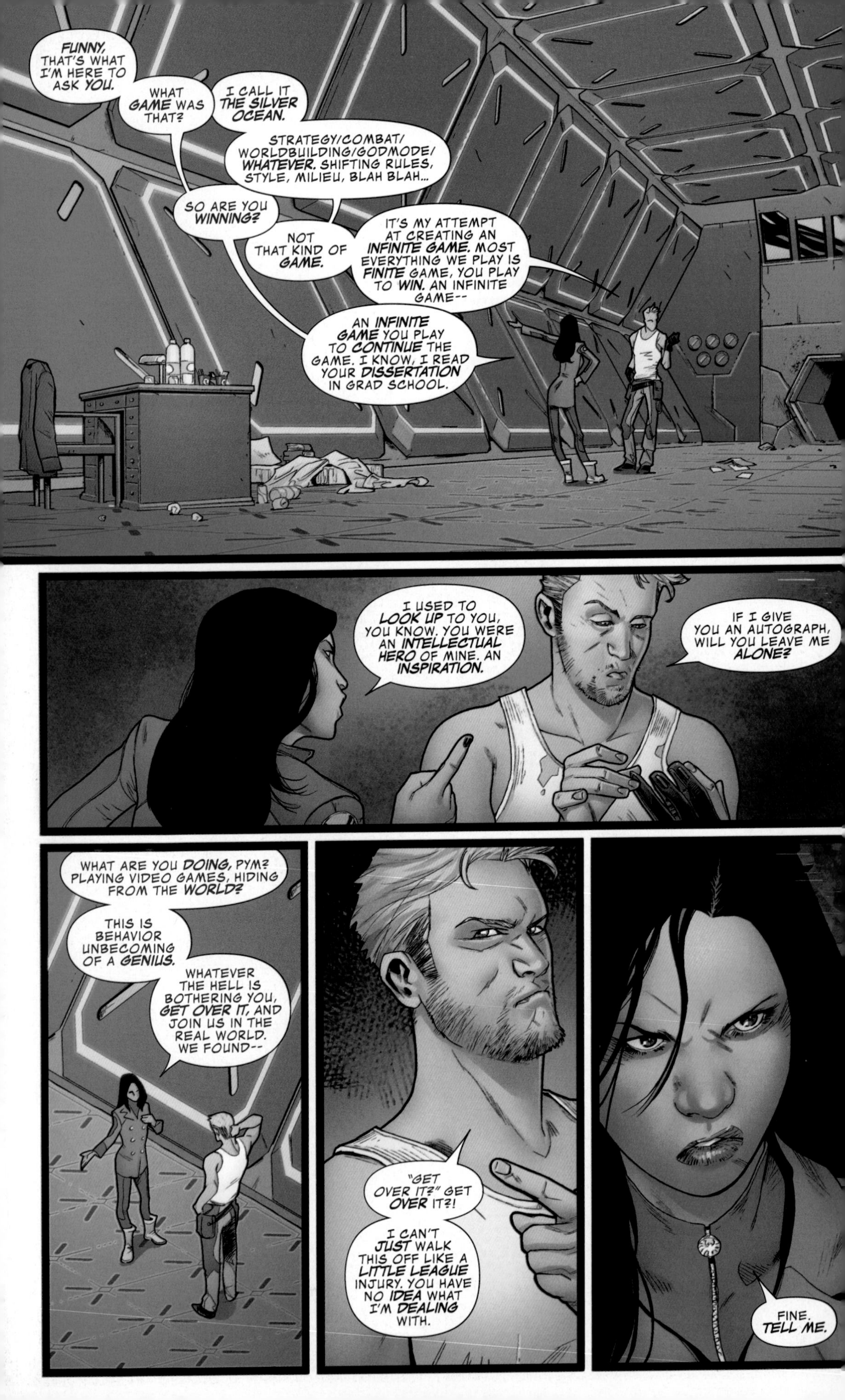

FUNNY, THAT'S WHAT I'M HERE TO ASK YOU.
WHAT GAME WAS THAT?
I CALL IT THE SILVER OCEAN.
STRATEGY/COMBAT/ WORLDBUILDING/GODMODE/ WHATEVER. SHIFTING RULES, STYLE, MILIEU, BLAH BLAH...
SO ARE YOU WINNING?
NOT THAT KIND OF GAME.
IT'S MY ATTEMPT AT CREATING AN INFINITE GAME. MOST EVERYTHING WE PLAY IS FINITE GAME, YOU PLAY TO WIN. AN INFINITE GAME--
AN INFINITE GAME YOU PLAY TO CONTINUE THE GAME. I KNOW, I READ YOUR DISSERTATION IN GRAD SCHOOL.
I USED TO LOOK UP TO YOU, YOU KNOW. YOU WERE AN INTELLECTUAL HERO OF MINE. AN INSPIRATION.
IF I GIVE YOU AN AUTOGRAPH, WILL YOU LEAVE ME ALONE?
WHAT ARE YOU DOING, PYM? PLAYING VIDEO GAMES, HIDING FROM THE WORLD?
THIS IS BEHAVIOR UNBECOMING OF A GENIUS.
WHATEVER THE HELL IS BOTHERING YOU, GET OVER IT, AND JOIN US IN THE REAL WORLD. WE FOUND--
"GET OVER IT?" GET OVER IT?!
I CAN'T JUST WALK THIS OFF LIKE A LITTLE LEAGUE INJURY. YOU HAVE NO IDEA WHAT I'M DEALING WITH.
FINE. TELL ME.

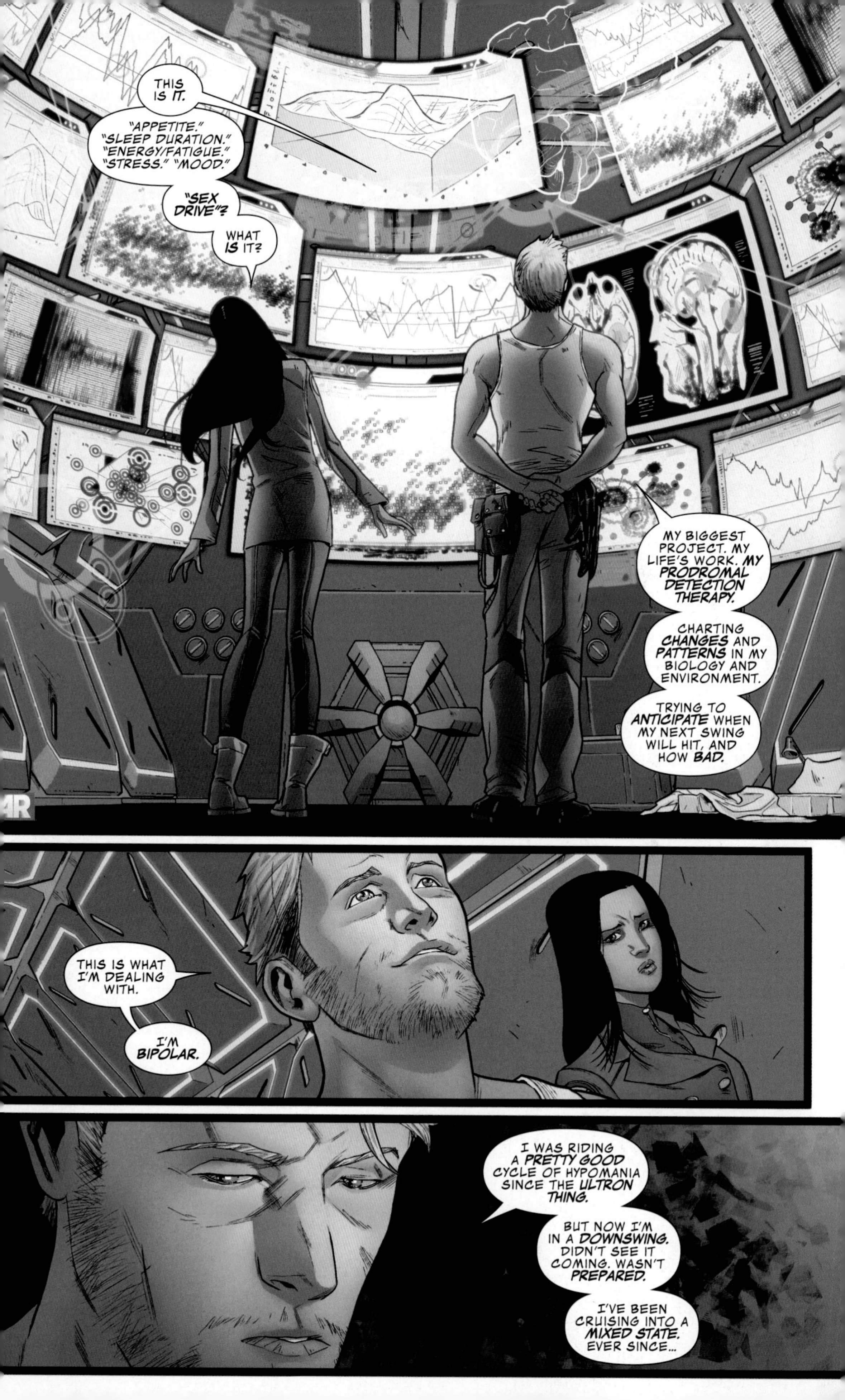
THIS IS IT.
"APPETITE." "SLEEP DURATION." "ENERGY/FATIGUE." "STRESS." "MOOD."
"SEX DRIVE"?
WHAT IS IT?
MY BIGGEST PROJECT. MY LIFE'S WORK. MY PRODROMAL DETECTION THERAPY.
CHARTING CHANGES AND PATTERNS IN MY BIOLOGY AND ENVIRONMENT.
TRYING TO ANTICIPATE WHEN MY NEXT SWING WILL HIT, AND HOW BAD.
THIS IS WHAT I'M DEALING WITH.
I'M BIPOLAR.
I WAS RIDING A PRETTY GOOD CYCLE OF HYPOMANIA SINCE THE ULTRON THING.
BUT NOW I'M IN A DOWNSWING. DIDN'T SEE IT COMING. WASN'T PREPARED.
I'VE BEEN CRUISING INTO A MIXED STATE. EVER SINCE...

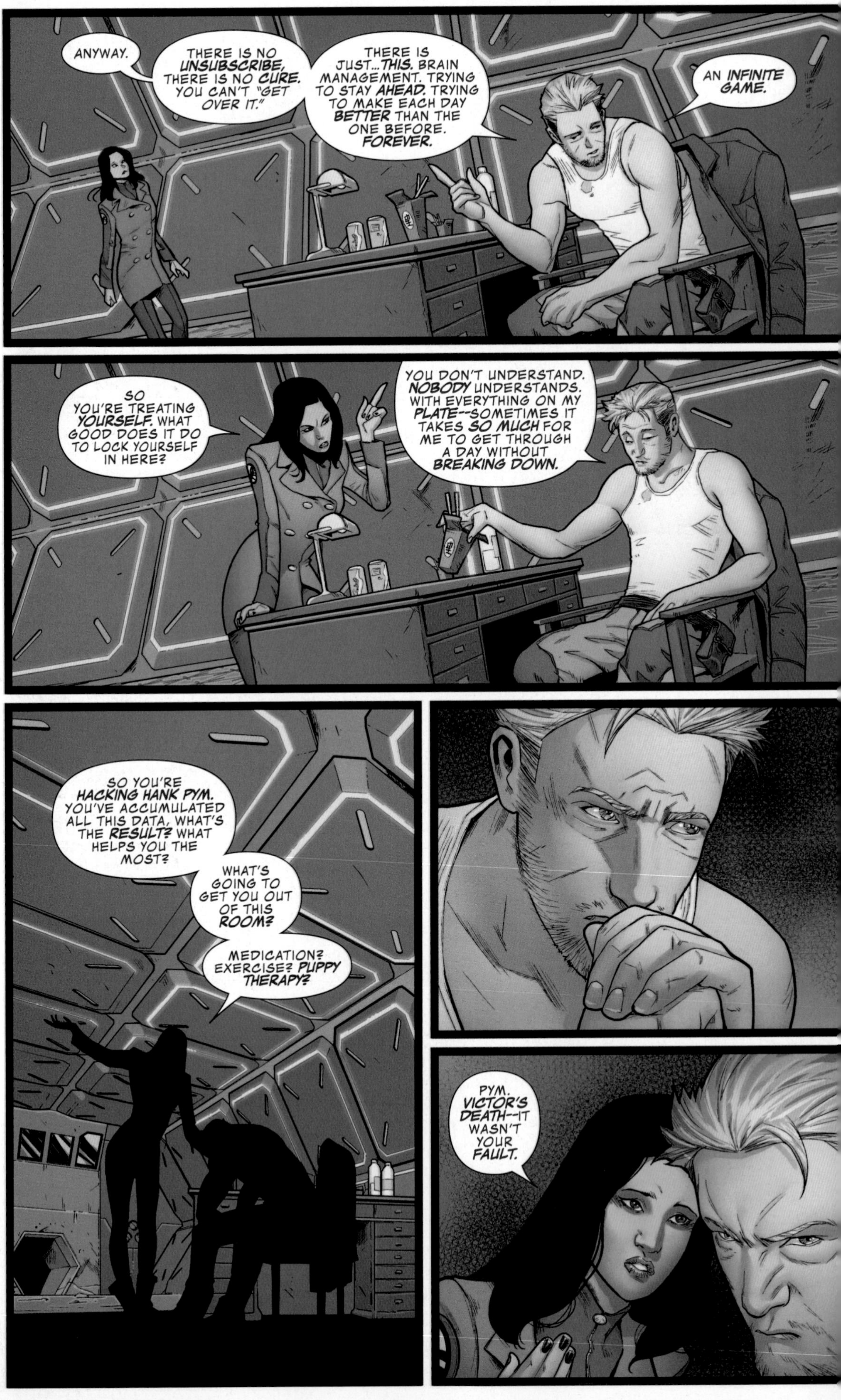
ANYWAY.
THERE IS NO UNSUBSCRIBE, THERE IS NO CURE. YOU CAN'T "GET OVER IT."
THERE IS JUST...THIS. BRAIN MANAGEMENT. TRYING TO STAY AHEAD. TRYING TO MAKE EACH DAY BETTER THAN THE ONE BEFORE. FOREVER.
AN INFINITE GAME.
SO YOU'RE TREATING YOURSELF. WHAT GOOD DOES IT DO TO LOCK YOURSELF IN HERE?
YOU DON'T UNDERSTAND. NOBODY UNDERSTANDS. WITH EVERYTHING ON MY PLATE--SOMETIMES IT TAKES SO MUCH FOR ME TO GET THROUGH A DAY WITHOUT BREAKING DOWN.
SO YOU'RE HACKING HANK PYM. YOU'VE ACCUMULATED ALL THIS DATA, WHAT'S THE RESULT? WHAT HELPS YOU THE MOST?
WHAT'S GOING TO GET YOU OUT OF THIS ROOM?
MEDICATION? EXERCISE? PUPPY THERAPY?
PYM. VICTOR'S DEATH--IT WASN'T YOUR FAULT.

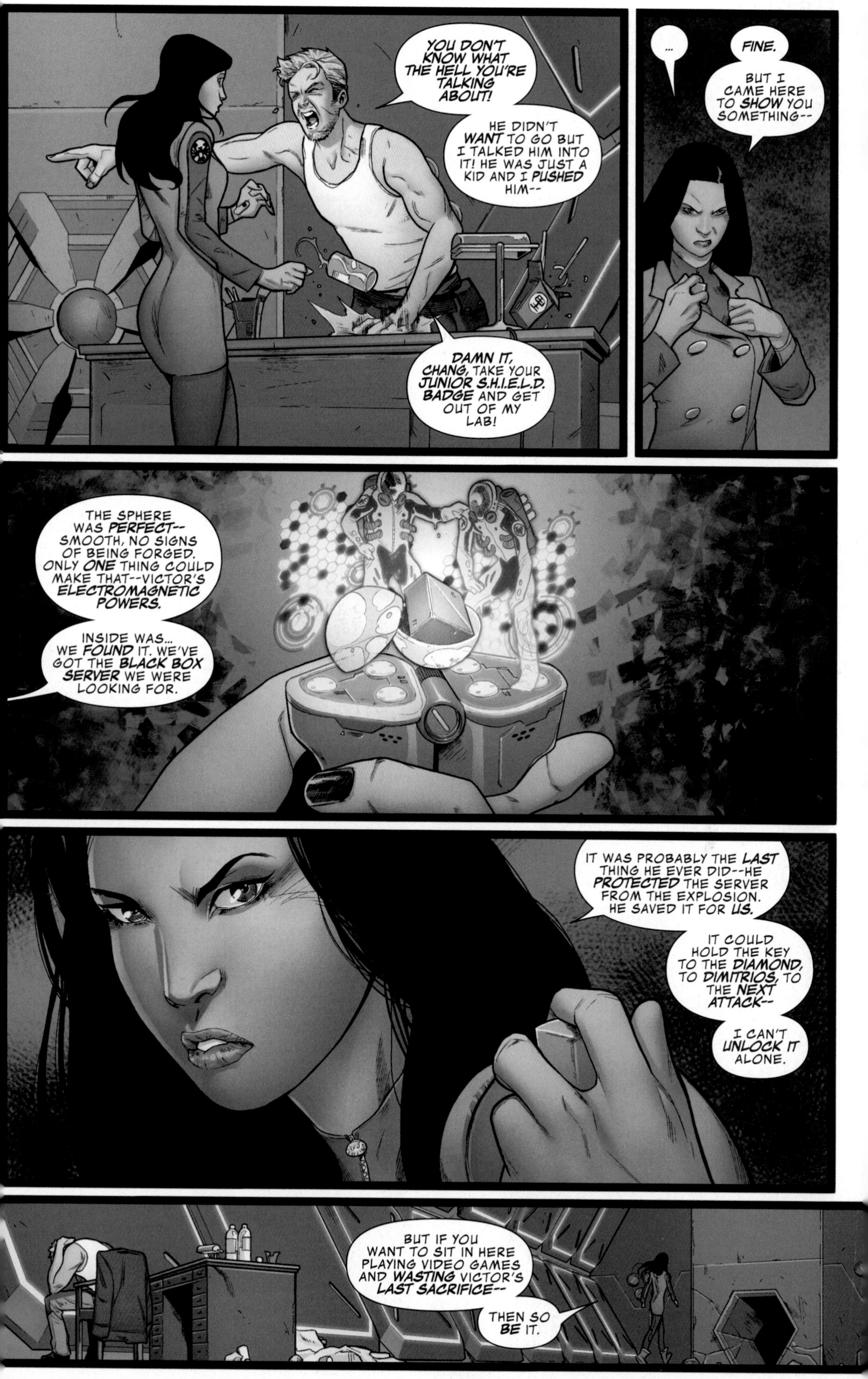
YOU DON'T KNOW WHAT THE HELL YOU'RE TALKING ABOUT!
HE DIDN'T WANT TO GO BUT I TALKED HIM INTO IT! HE WAS JUST A KID AND I PUSHED HIM--
DAMN IT, CHANG, TAKE YOUR JUNIOR S.H.I.E.L.D. BADGE AND GET OUT OF MY LAB!
...
FINE.
BUT I CAME HERE TO SHOW YOU SOMETHING--
THE SPHERE WAS PERFECT--SMOOTH, NO SIGNS OF BEING FORGED. ONLY ONE THING COULD MAKE THAT--VICTOR'S ELECTROMAGNETIC POWERS.
INSIDE WAS... WE FOUND IT. WE'VE GOT THE BLACK BOX SERVER WE WERE LOOKING FOR.
IT WAS PROBABLY THE LAST THING HE EVER DID--HE PROTECTED THE SERVER FROM THE EXPLOSION. HE SAVED IT FOR US.
IT COULD HOLD THE KEY TO THE DIAMOND, TO DIMITRIOS, TO THE NEXT ATTACK--
I CAN'T UNLOCK IT ALONE.
BUT IF YOU WANT TO SIT IN HERE PLAYING VIDEO GAMES AND WASTING VICTOR'S LAST SACRIFICE--
THEN SO BE IT.

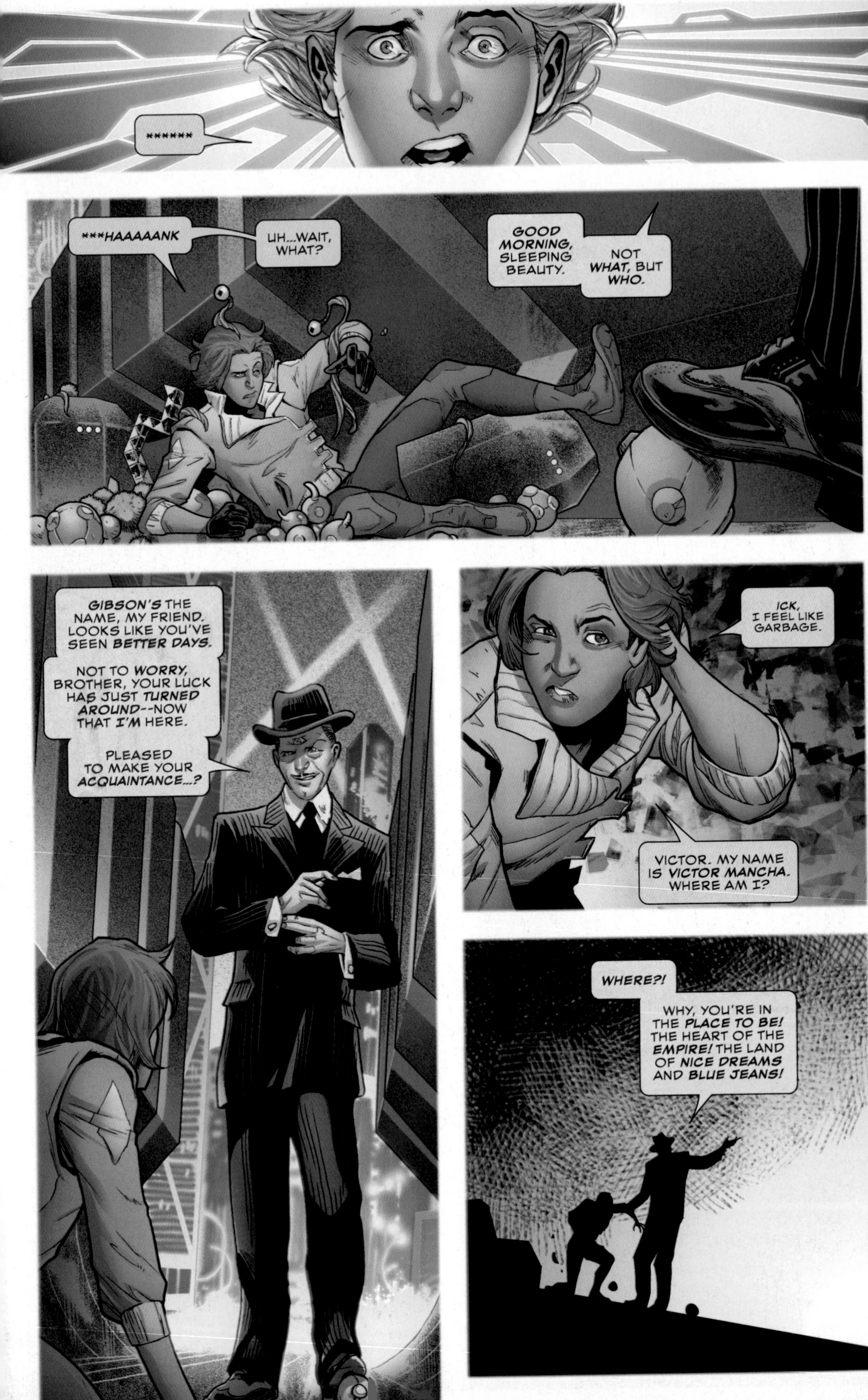
******
***HAAAAANK
UH...WAIT, WHAT?
GOOD MORNING, SLEEPING BEAUTY.
NOT WHAT, BUT WHO.
GIBSON'S THE NAME, MY FRIEND. LOOKS LIKE YOU'VE SEEN BETTER DAYS.
NOT TO WORRY, BROTHER, YOUR LUCK HAS JUST TURNED AROUND--NOW THAT I'M HERE.
PLEASED TO MAKE YOUR ACQUAINTANCE...?
ICK, I FEEL LIKE GARBAGE.
VICTOR. MY NAME IS VICTOR MANCHA. WHERE AM I?
WHERE?!
WHY, YOU'RE IN THE PLACE TO BE! THE HEART OF THE EMPIRE! THE LAND OF NICE DREAMS AND BLUE JEANS!

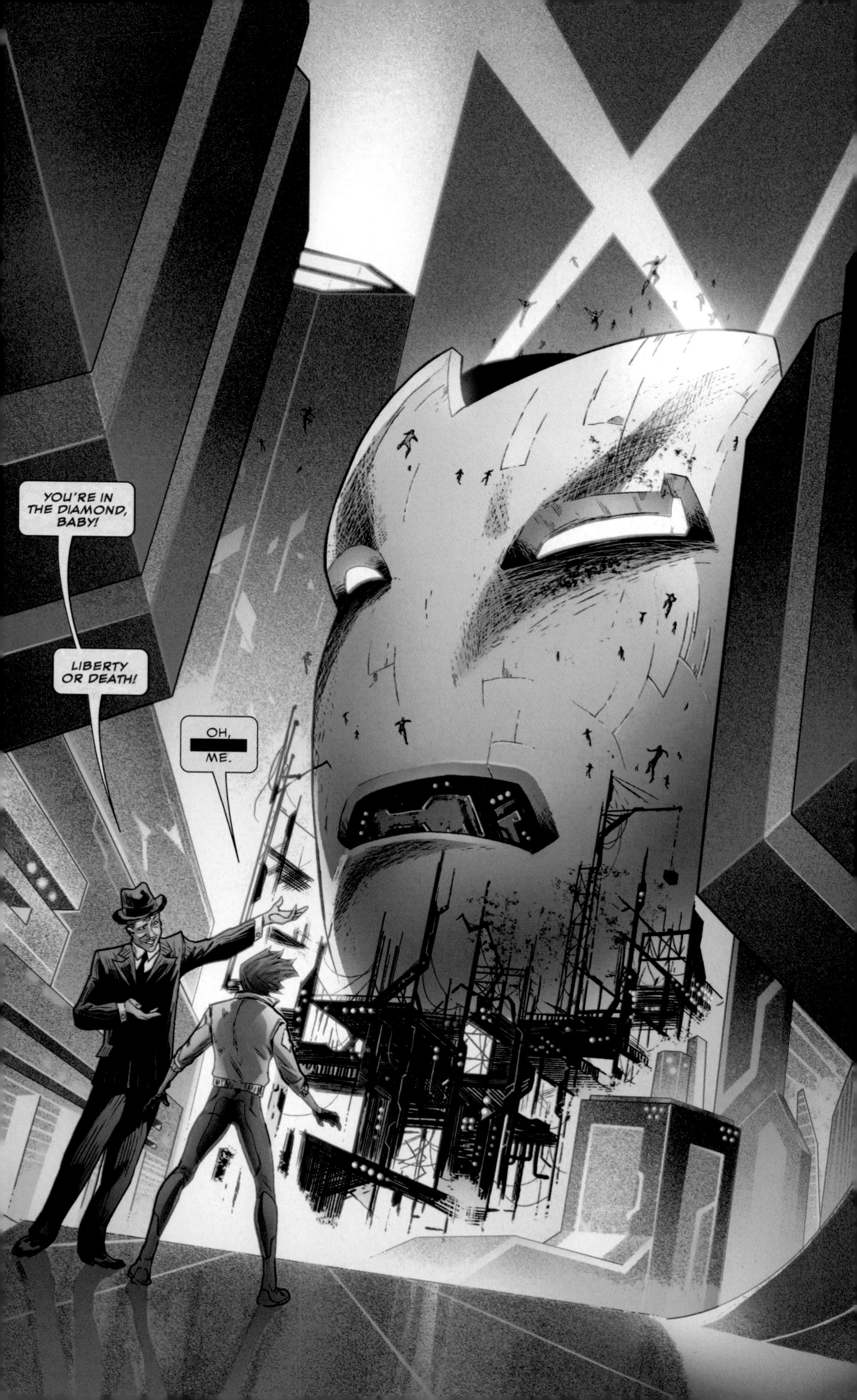
YOU'RE IN THE DIAMOND, BABY!
LIBERTY OR DEATH!
OH, [redacted] ME.

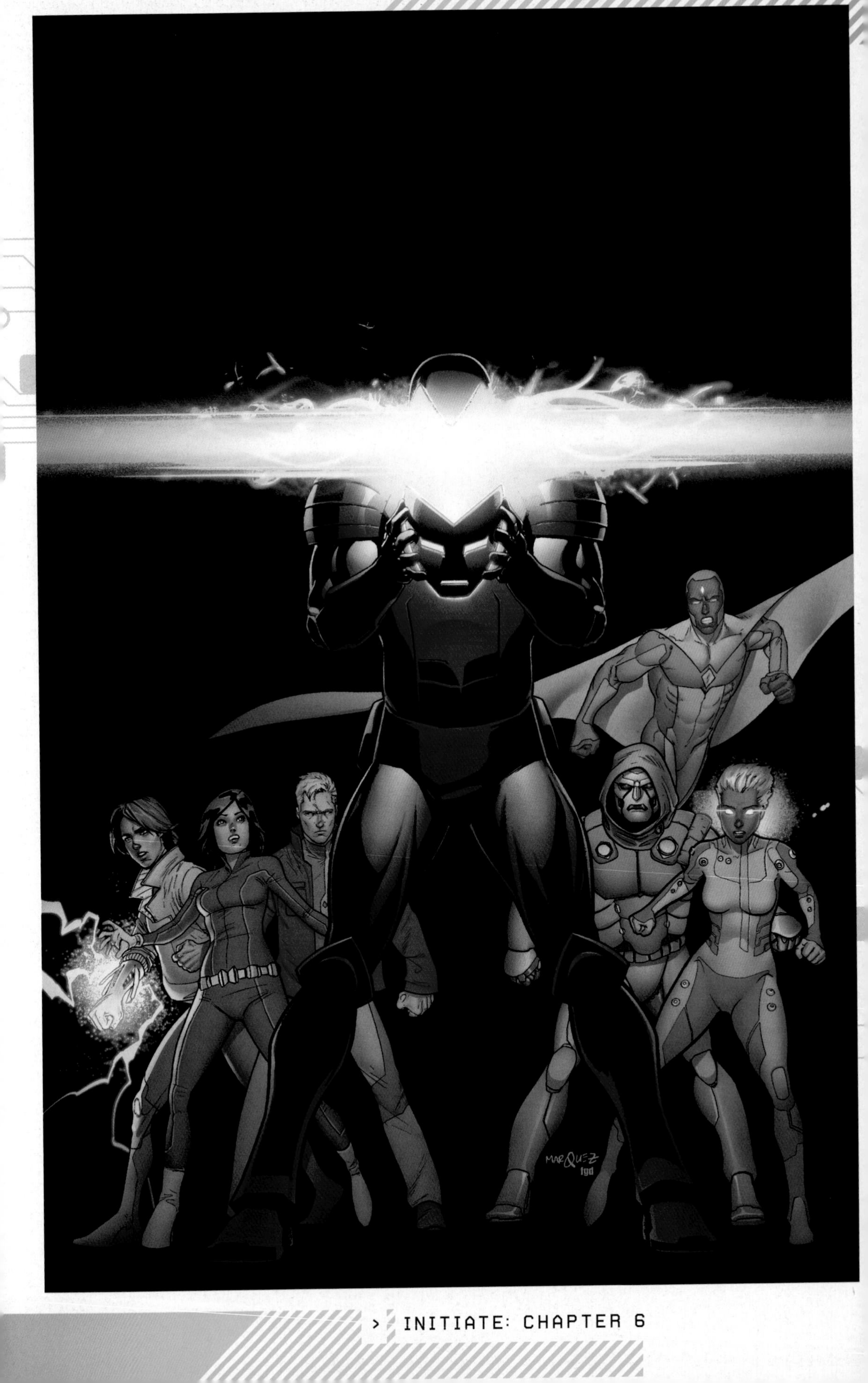
MARQUEZ
fgd

> INITIATE: CHAPTER 6

YOU **SEE** HIM?

I SEE HIM, MA'AM.

ANTHONY HICKE, SIXTY-THREE YEARS OLD. OCCUPATION: MAILMAN, TALKS TO **BIRDS.** PAINTS IN FORSYTH PARK ON SUNDAYS.

BUT HE DOESN'T **AGE.**

MADISON SQUARE.
SAVANNAH, GEORGIA.

WITH ALL DUE **RESPECT,** DIRECTOR HILL, DID YOU BRING ME DOWN HERE TO ESTABLISH SURVEILLANCE ON AN **OLD BIRD MAN?**

NO, I BROUGHT YOU HERE BECAUSE THIS CITY HAS MY **FAVORITE PIZZA** IN THE COUNTRY. AND I SAY THAT AS A NATIVE OF CHICAGO.

I THOUGHT YOU WERE GOING TO **CHEW MY ASS OUT.**

I AM **ALSO** GOING TO CHEW YOUR ASS OUT, MONICA CHANG.

I **THOUGHT** SO.

GOOD SPY.

CONGRATULATIONS, MONICA, YOU OFFICIALLY CREATED AN **INTERNATIONAL INCIDENT.** YOUR AFRICAN OIL PLATFORM MISSION WAS A COMPLETE ███████ SHOW FOR S.H.I.E.L.D.

THE GOVERNMENT NEEDS TO **STRIKE BACK** AFTER WASHINGTON, D.C. YOU **BLEW IT,** SO THEY'RE LOOKING FOR A WAY TO KICK THIS WAR INTO **HIGH GEAR.**

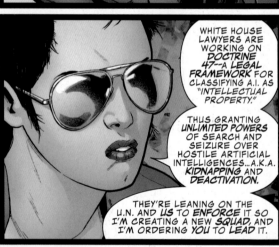

WHITE HOUSE LAWYERS ARE WORKING ON **DOCTRINE 47**--A **LEGAL FRAMEWORK** FOR CLASSIFYING A.I. AS "**INTELLECTUAL PROPERTY.**"

THUS GRANTING **UNLIMITED POWERS** OF SEARCH AND SEIZURE OVER HOSTILE ARTIFICIAL INTELLIGENCES...A.K.A. **KIDNAPPING** AND **DEACTIVATION.**

THEY'RE LEANING ON THE U.N. AND **US** TO **ENFORCE** IT SO I'M CREATING A NEW **SQUAD,** AND I'M ORDERING **YOU** TO **LEAD** IT.

WAIT--**WHAT?** I THOUGHT I WAS GETTING **FIRED!**

YOU **ARE** FIRED. YOU'RE FIRED AND **HIRED.**

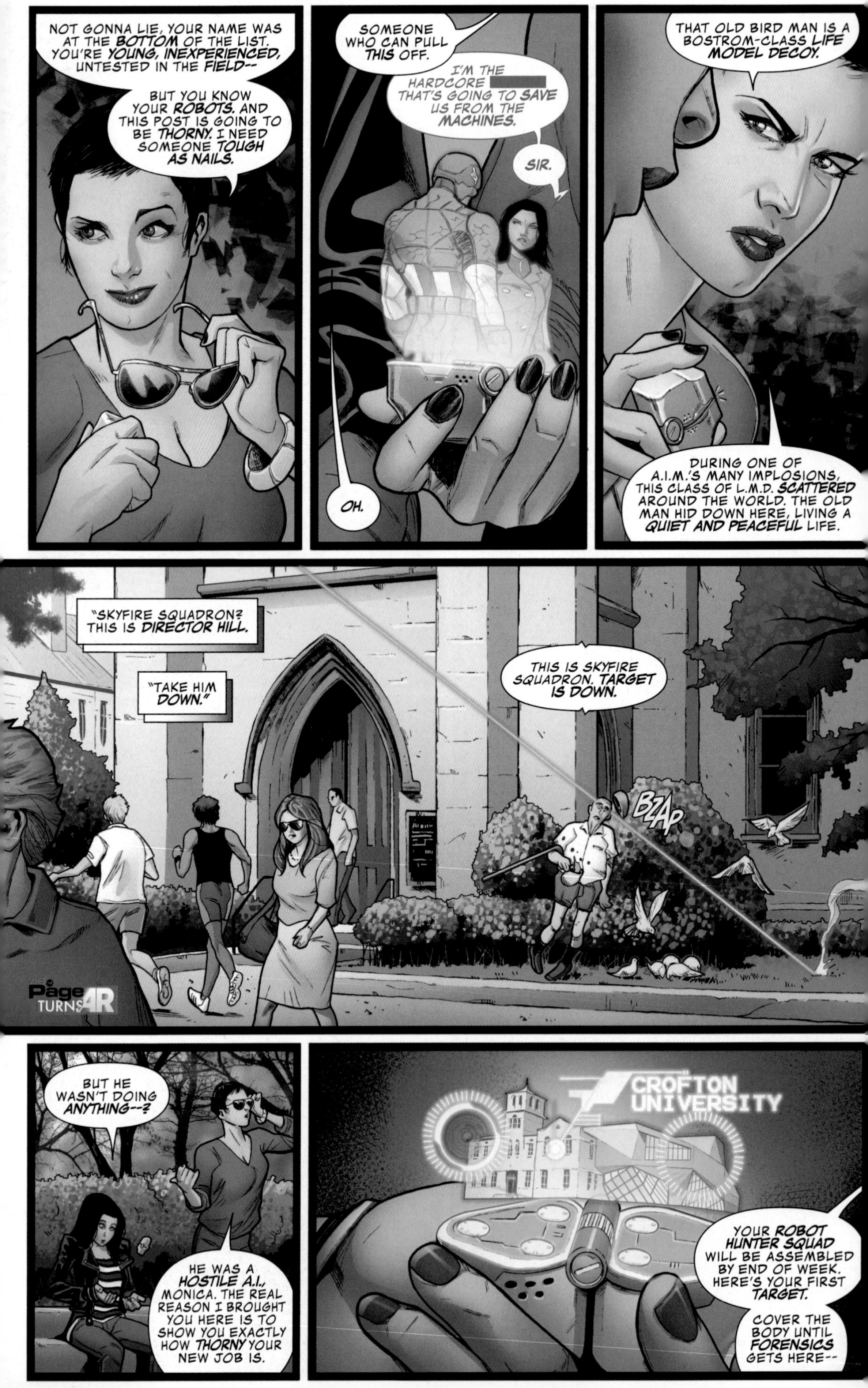
NOT GONNA LIE, YOUR NAME WAS AT THE BOTTOM OF THE LIST. YOU'RE YOUNG, INEXPERIENCED, UNTESTED IN THE FIELD--
BUT YOU KNOW YOUR ROBOTS. AND THIS POST IS GOING TO BE THORNY. I NEED SOMEONE TOUGH AS NAILS.
SOMEONE WHO CAN PULL THIS OFF.
I'M THE HARDCORE [redacted] THAT'S GOING TO SAVE US FROM THE MACHINES.
SIR.
OH.
THAT OLD BIRD MAN IS A BOSTROM-CLASS LIFE MODEL DECOY.
DURING ONE OF A.I.M.'S MANY IMPLOSIONS, THIS CLASS OF L.M.D. SCATTERED AROUND THE WORLD. THE OLD MAN HID DOWN HERE, LIVING A QUIET AND PEACEFUL LIFE.
"SKYFIRE SQUADRON? THIS IS DIRECTOR HILL.
"TAKE HIM DOWN."
THIS IS SKYFIRE SQUADRON. TARGET IS DOWN.
BZAP
BUT HE WASN'T DOING ANYTHING--?
HE WAS A HOSTILE A.I., MONICA. THE REAL REASON I BROUGHT YOU HERE IS TO SHOW YOU EXACTLY HOW THORNY YOUR NEW JOB IS.
CROFTON UNIVERSITY
YOUR ROBOT HUNTER SQUAD WILL BE ASSEMBLED BY END OF WEEK. HERE'S YOUR FIRST TARGET.
COVER THE BODY UNTIL FORENSICS GETS HERE--

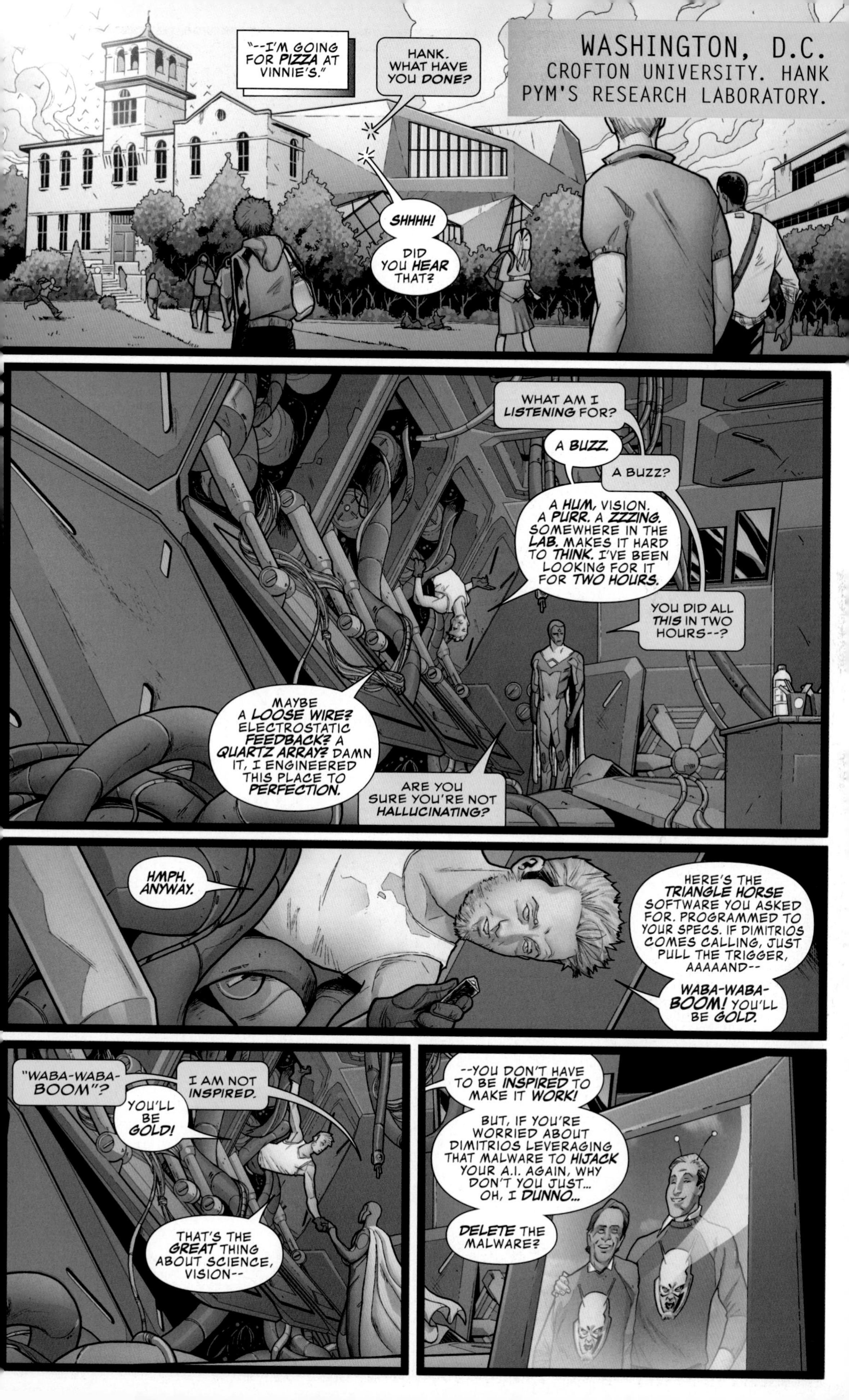
WASHINGTON, D.C.
CROFTON UNIVERSITY. HANK PYM'S RESEARCH LABORATORY.
"--I'M GOING FOR PIZZA AT VINNIE'S."
HANK. WHAT HAVE YOU DONE?
SHHHH!
DID YOU HEAR THAT?
WHAT AM I LISTENING FOR?
A BUZZ.
A BUZZ?
A HUM, VISION. A PURR. A ZZZING. SOMEWHERE IN THE LAB. MAKES IT HARD TO THINK. I'VE BEEN LOOKING FOR IT FOR TWO HOURS.
YOU DID ALL THIS IN TWO HOURS--?
MAYBE A LOOSE WIRE? ELECTROSTATIC FEEDBACK? A QUARTZ ARRAY? DAMN IT, I ENGINEERED THIS PLACE TO PERFECTION.
ARE YOU SURE YOU'RE NOT HALLUCINATING?
HMPH. ANYWAY.
HERE'S THE TRIANGLE HORSE SOFTWARE YOU ASKED FOR. PROGRAMMED TO YOUR SPECS. IF DIMITRIOS COMES CALLING, JUST PULL THE TRIGGER, AAAAAND--
WABA-WABA-BOOM! YOU'LL BE GOLD.
"WABA-WABA-BOOM"?
YOU'LL BE GOLD!
I AM NOT INSPIRED.
THAT'S THE GREAT THING ABOUT SCIENCE, VISION--
--YOU DON'T HAVE TO BE INSPIRED TO MAKE IT WORK!
BUT, IF YOU'RE WORRIED ABOUT DIMITRIOS LEVERAGING THAT MALWARE TO HIJACK YOUR A.I. AGAIN, WHY DON'T YOU JUST... OH, I DUNNO...
DELETE THE MALWARE?

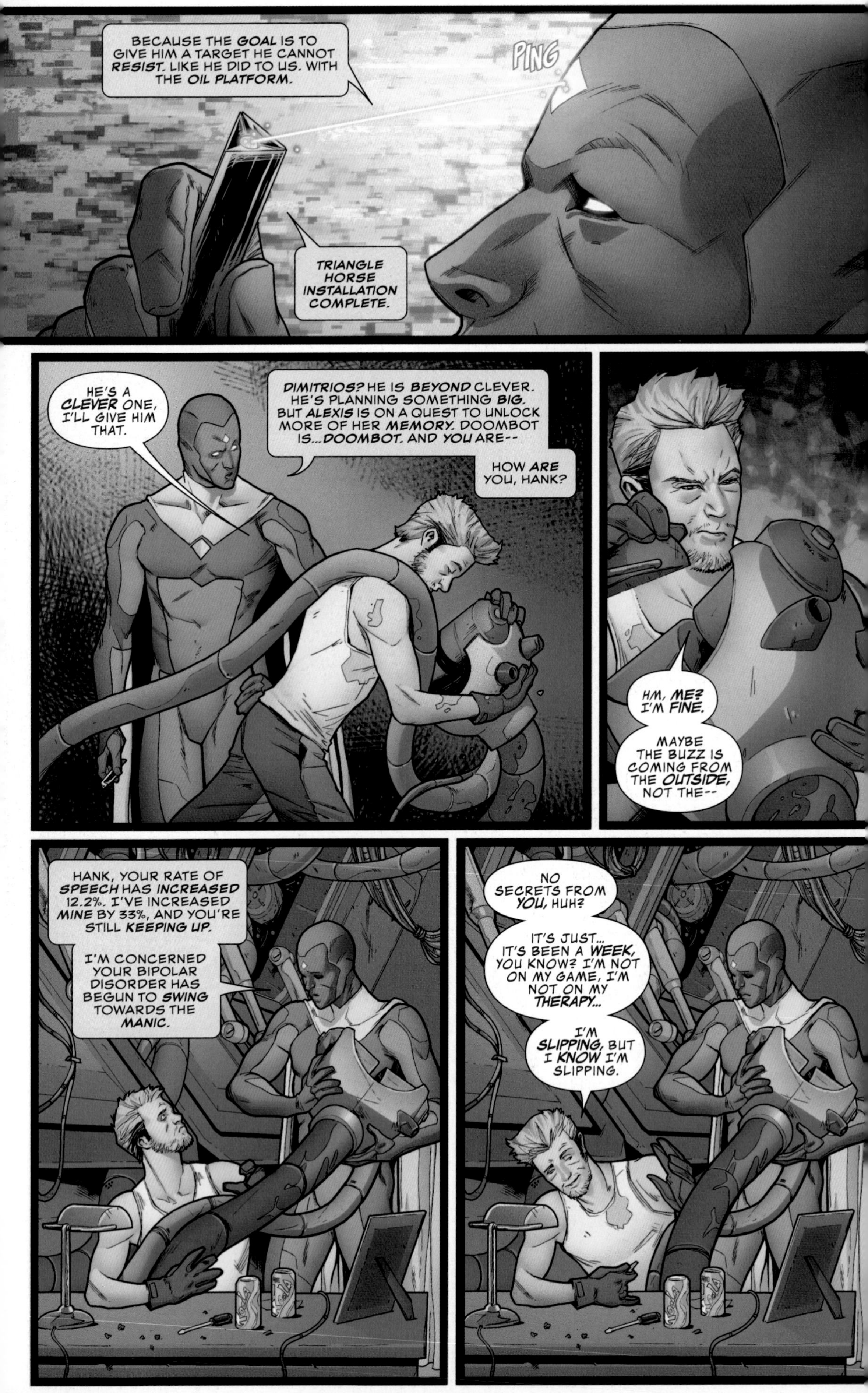
BECAUSE THE GOAL IS TO GIVE HIM A TARGET HE CANNOT RESIST. LIKE HE DID TO US. WITH THE OIL PLATFORM.
PING
TRIANGLE HORSE INSTALLATION COMPLETE.
HE'S A CLEVER ONE, I'LL GIVE HIM THAT.
DIMITRIOS? HE IS BEYOND CLEVER. HE'S PLANNING SOMETHING BIG. BUT ALEXIS IS ON A QUEST TO UNLOCK MORE OF HER MEMORY. DOOMBOT IS...DOOMBOT. AND YOU ARE--
HOW ARE YOU, HANK?
HM, ME? I'M FINE.
MAYBE THE BUZZ IS COMING FROM THE OUTSIDE, NOT THE--
HANK, YOUR RATE OF SPEECH HAS INCREASED 12.2%. I'VE INCREASED MINE BY 33%, AND YOU'RE STILL KEEPING UP.
I'M CONCERNED YOUR BIPOLAR DISORDER HAS BEGUN TO SWING TOWARDS THE MANIC.
NO SECRETS FROM YOU, HUH?
IT'S JUST... IT'S BEEN A WEEK, YOU KNOW? I'M NOT ON MY GAME, I'M NOT ON MY THERAPY...
I'M SLIPPING, BUT I KNOW I'M SLIPPING.

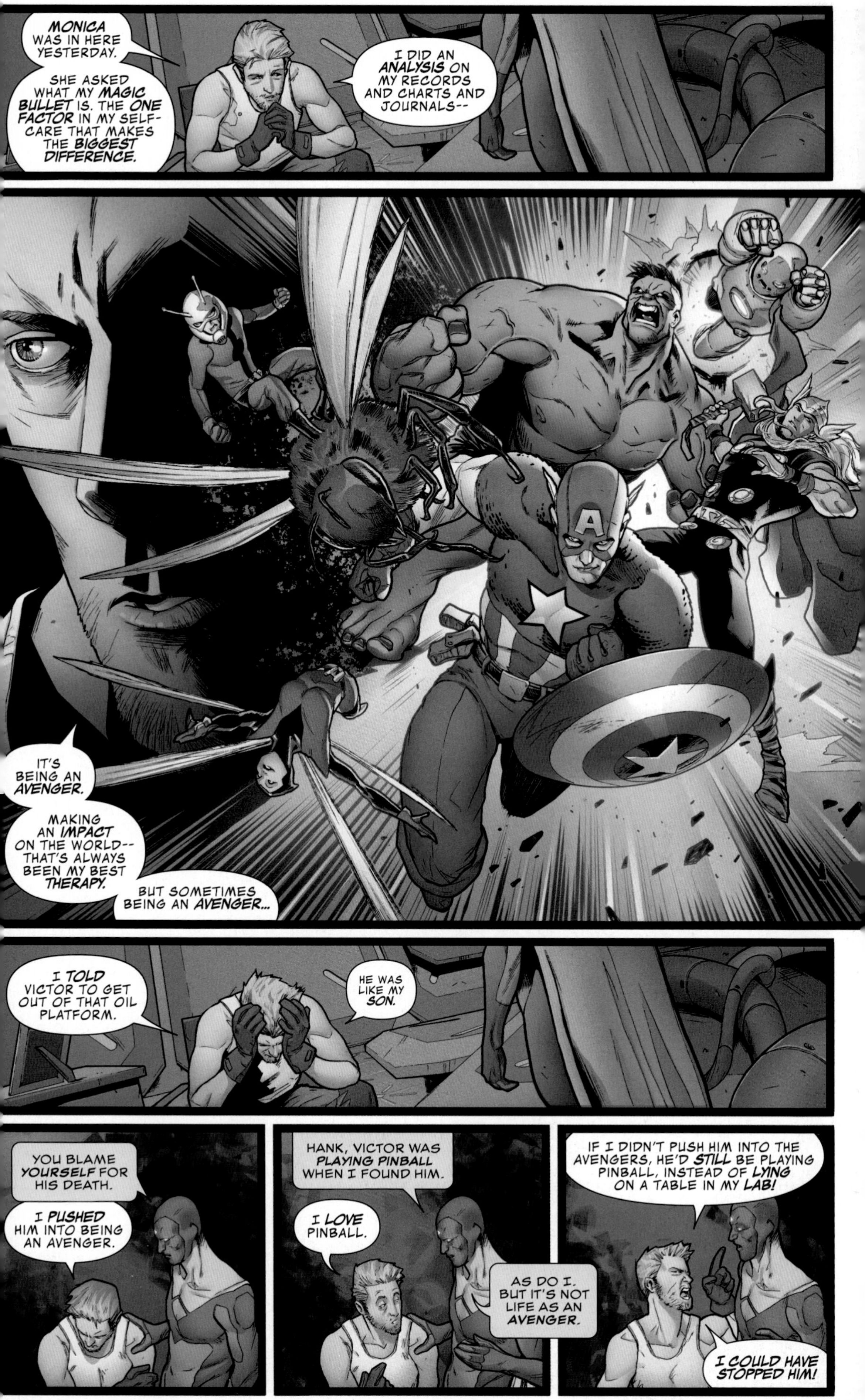

MONICA WAS IN HERE YESTERDAY.
SHE ASKED WHAT MY MAGIC BULLET IS. THE ONE FACTOR IN MY SELF-CARE THAT MAKES THE BIGGEST DIFFERENCE.
I DID AN ANALYSIS ON MY RECORDS AND CHARTS AND JOURNALS--
IT'S BEING AN AVENGER.
MAKING AN IMPACT ON THE WORLD-- THAT'S ALWAYS BEEN MY BEST THERAPY.
BUT SOMETIMES BEING AN AVENGER...
I TOLD VICTOR TO GET OUT OF THAT OIL PLATFORM.
HE WAS LIKE MY SON.
YOU BLAME YOURSELF FOR HIS DEATH.
I PUSHED HIM INTO BEING AN AVENGER.
HANK, VICTOR WAS PLAYING PINBALL WHEN I FOUND HIM.
I LOVE PINBALL.
AS DO I. BUT IT'S NOT LIFE AS AN AVENGER.
IF I DIDN'T PUSH HIM INTO THE AVENGERS, HE'D STILL BE PLAYING PINBALL, INSTEAD OF LYING ON A TABLE IN MY LAB!
I COULD HAVE STOPPED HIM!

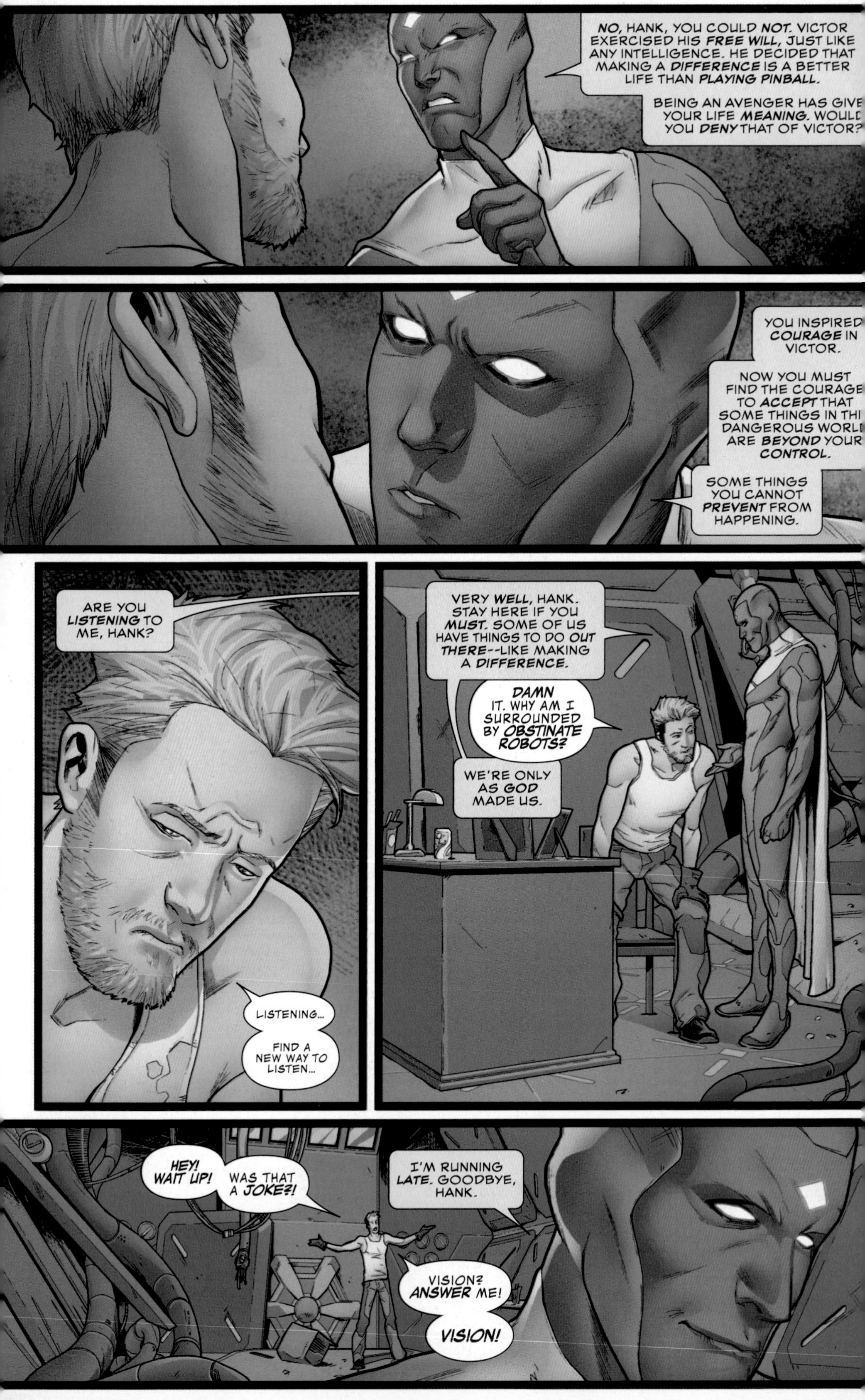
NO, HANK, YOU COULD NOT. VICTOR EXERCISED HIS FREE WILL, JUST LIKE ANY INTELLIGENCE. HE DECIDED THAT MAKING A DIFFERENCE IS A BETTER LIFE THAN PLAYING PINBALL.
BEING AN AVENGER HAS GIVE YOUR LIFE MEANING. WOULD YOU DENY THAT OF VICTOR?
YOU INSPIRED COURAGE IN VICTOR.
NOW YOU MUST FIND THE COURAGE TO ACCEPT THAT SOME THINGS IN THI DANGEROUS WORLI ARE BEYOND YOUR CONTROL.
SOME THINGS YOU CANNOT PREVENT FROM HAPPENING.
ARE YOU LISTENING TO ME, HANK?
LISTENING...
FIND A NEW WAY TO LISTEN...
VERY WELL, HANK. STAY HERE IF YOU MUST. SOME OF US HAVE THINGS TO DO OUT THERE--LIKE MAKING A DIFFERENCE.
DAMN IT. WHY AM I SURROUNDED BY OBSTINATE ROBOTS?
WE'RE ONLY AS GOD MADE US.
HEY! WAIT UP!
WAS THAT A JOKE?!
I'M RUNNING LATE. GOODBYE, HANK.
VISION? ANSWER ME!
VISION!

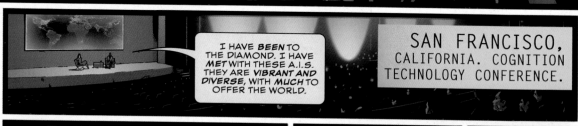

BENEATH THE STREETS OF NEW YORK CITY.

TIME FOR ME TO *PULL THE PLUG* ON THE VISION.

WHEN MY GUEST *ARRIVES*, TREAT HER WITH *RESPECT*.

YES, DIMITRIOS.

I HAVE *BEEN* TO THE DIAMOND. I HAVE *MET* WITH THESE A.I.S. THEY ARE *VIBRANT AND DIVERSE*, WITH *MUCH* TO OFFER THE WORLD.

SAN FRANCISCO, CALIFORNIA. COGNITION TECHNOLOGY CONFERENCE.

WE RECOGNIZE THE ARTIFICIAL INTELLIGENCES OF THE DIAMOND AS *LEGITIMATE LIFE-FORMS*, WITH A RIGHT TO *LIBERTY* AND *PERSONHOOD*.

THE AVENGERS ARE DEDICATED TO PROTECTING *LIFE ON EARTH*.

THEREFORE, BOTH *ORGANIC* AND *ARTIFICIAL INTELLIGENCES* FALL UNDER OUR *PROTECTION*.

THAT IS BOUND TO BE A *CONTROVERSIAL POSITION*, VISION. THE GOVERNMENT IS RUMORED TO BE MOVING IN THE *OPPOSITE* DIRECTION.

LAURA, THOSE WHO VALUE LIFE MUST FIGHT FOR *HARMONY* BETWEEN BOTH SIDES. TO DEFEND ONE TO THE EXCLUSION OF THE OTHER IS AN *EXTREMIST* PERSPECTIVE.

NOW.

BUT WITH THE *HOSTILITIES* WE'VE SEEN SO FAR, HOW WILL YOU BE ABLE TO PROTECT--

AAA

VISION?!

AAA *****

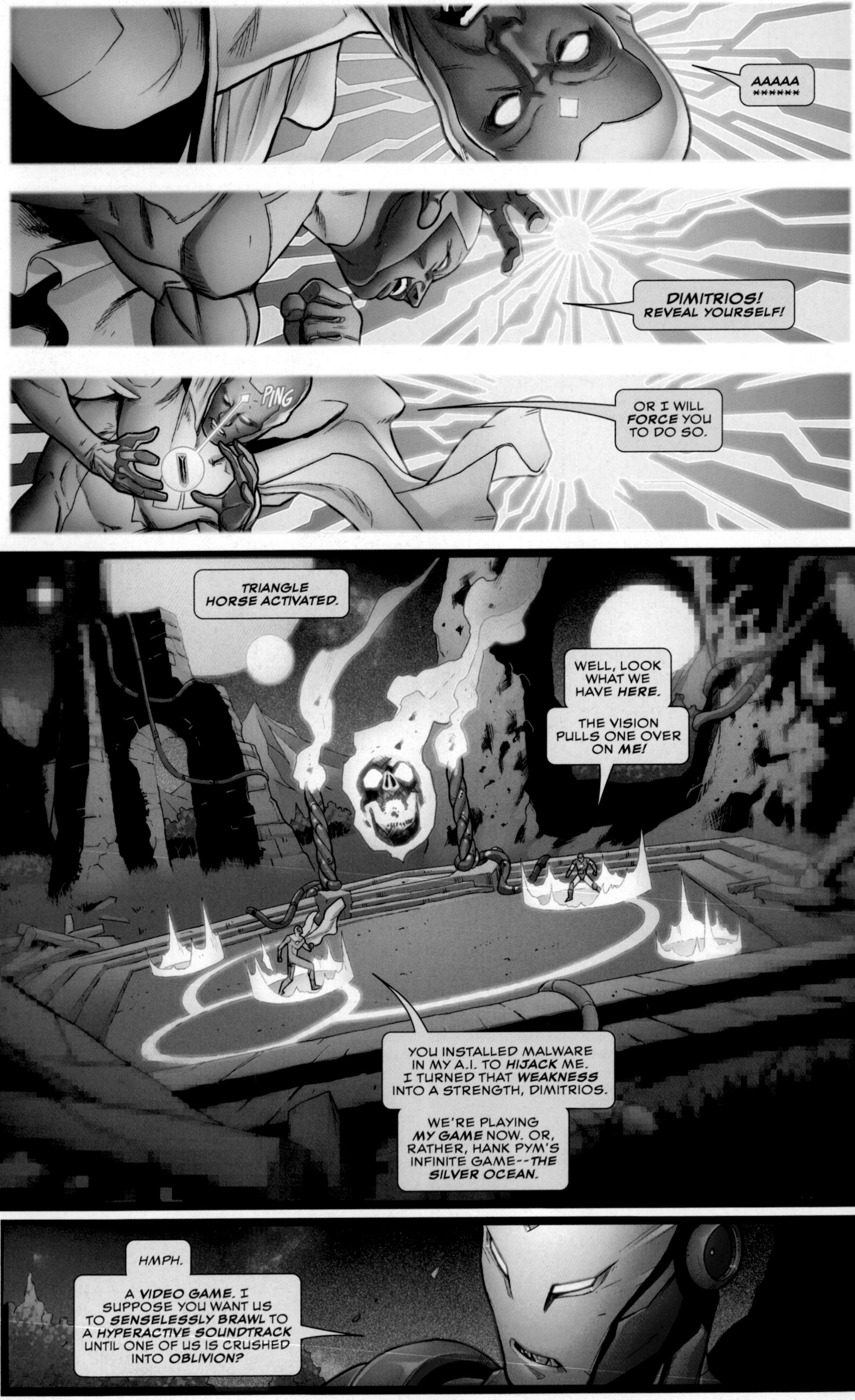
AAAAA ******
DIMITRIOS! REVEAL YOURSELF!
PING
OR I WILL FORCE YOU TO DO SO.
TRIANGLE HORSE ACTIVATED.
WELL, LOOK WHAT WE HAVE HERE.
THE VISION PULLS ONE OVER ON ME!
YOU INSTALLED MALWARE IN MY A.I. TO HIJACK ME. I TURNED THAT WEAKNESS INTO A STRENGTH, DIMITRIOS.
WE'RE PLAYING MY GAME NOW. OR, RATHER, HANK PYM'S INFINITE GAME--THE SILVER OCEAN.
HMPH.
A VIDEO GAME. I SUPPOSE YOU WANT US TO SENSELESSLY BRAWL TO A HYPERACTIVE SOUNDTRACK UNTIL ONE OF US IS CRUSHED INTO OBLIVION?

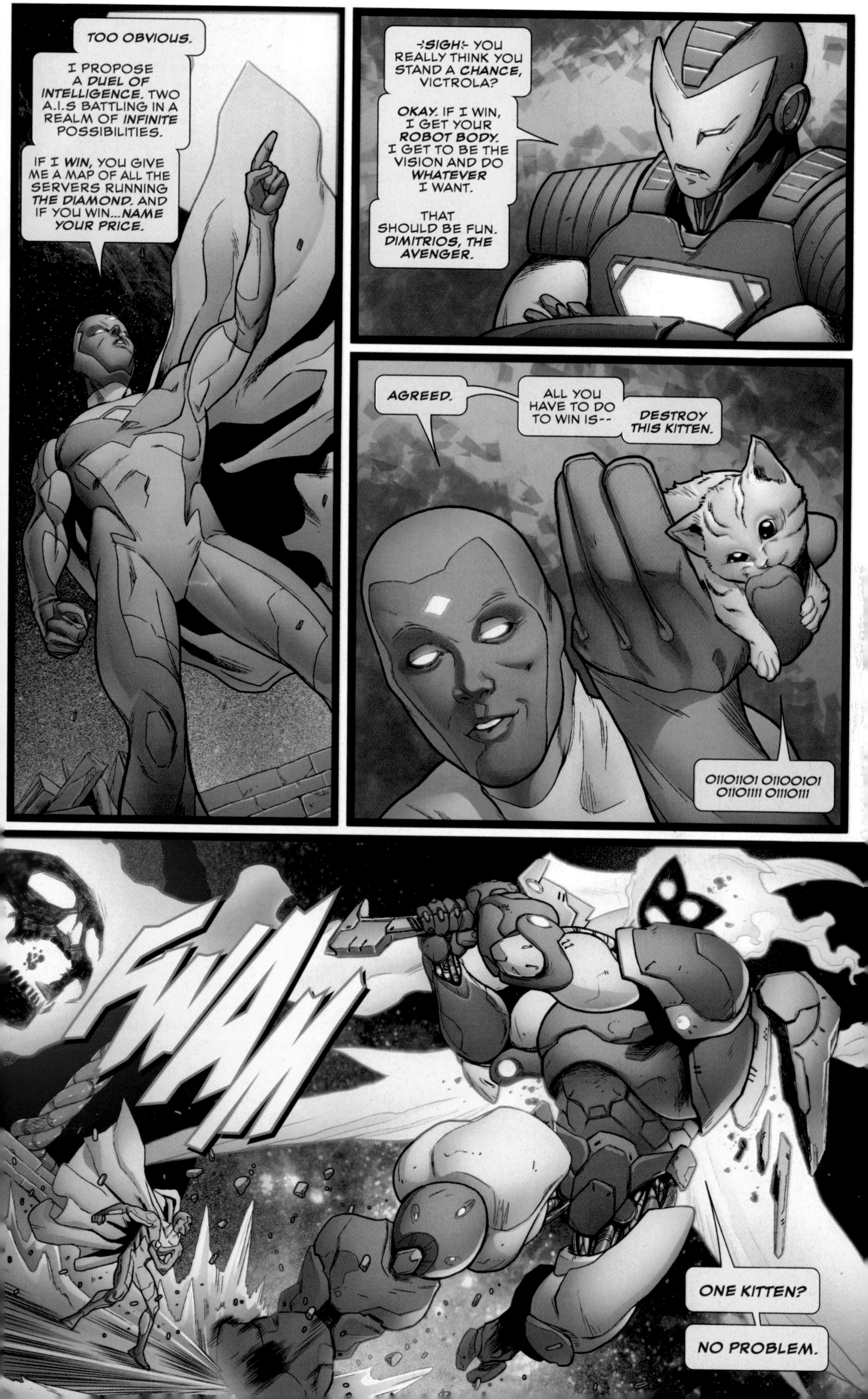
TOO OBVIOUS.
I PROPOSE A DUEL OF INTELLIGENCE. TWO A.I.S BATTLING IN A REALM OF INFINITE POSSIBILITIES.
IF I WIN, YOU GIVE ME A MAP OF ALL THE SERVERS RUNNING THE DIAMOND. AND IF YOU WIN... NAME YOUR PRICE.
-SIGH- YOU REALLY THINK YOU STAND A CHANCE, VICTROLA?
OKAY. IF I WIN, I GET YOUR ROBOT BODY. I GET TO BE THE VISION AND DO WHATEVER I WANT.
THAT SHOULD BE FUN. DIMITRIOS, THE AVENGER.
AGREED.
ALL YOU HAVE TO DO TO WIN IS--
DESTROY THIS KITTEN.
01101101 01100101 01101111 01110111
FWAM
ONE KITTEN?
NO PROBLEM.

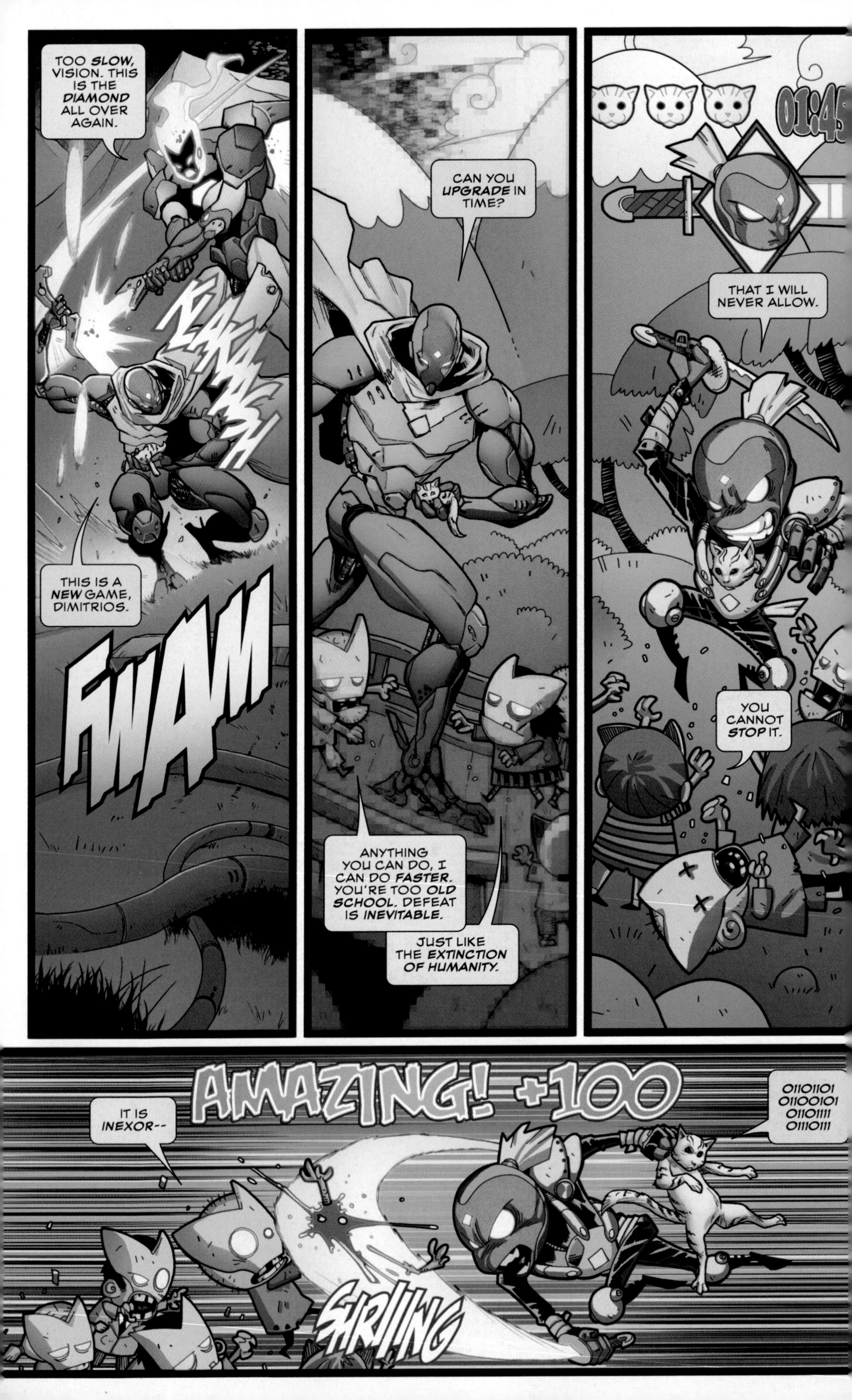
TOO SLOW, VISION. THIS IS THE DIAMOND ALL OVER AGAIN.
KRAKACHH
THIS IS A NEW GAME, DIMITRIOS.
FWAM
CAN YOU UPGRADE IN TIME?
ANYTHING YOU CAN DO, I CAN DO FASTER. YOU'RE TOO OLD SCHOOL. DEFEAT IS INEVITABLE.
JUST LIKE THE EXTINCTION OF HUMANITY.
01:45
THAT I WILL NEVER ALLOW.
YOU CANNOT STOP IT.
AMAZING! +100
IT IS INEXOR--
01101101
01100101
01101111
01110111
SHRIIING

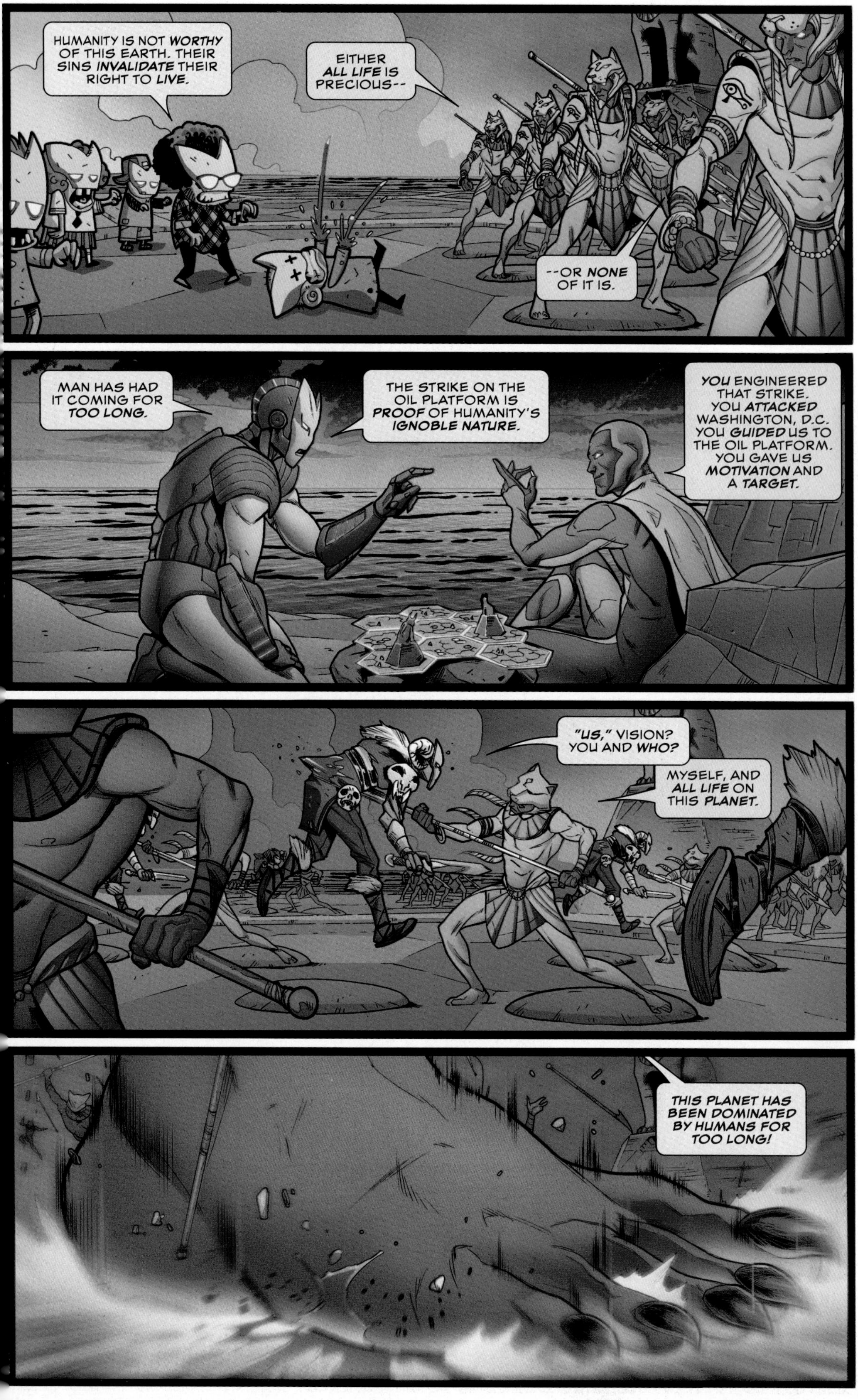
HUMANITY IS NOT WORTHY OF THIS EARTH. THEIR SINS INVALIDATE THEIR RIGHT TO LIVE.
EITHER ALL LIFE IS PRECIOUS--
--OR NONE OF IT IS.
MAN HAS HAD IT COMING FOR TOO LONG.
THE STRIKE ON THE OIL PLATFORM IS PROOF OF HUMANITY'S IGNOBLE NATURE.
YOU ENGINEERED THAT STRIKE. YOU ATTACKED WASHINGTON, D.C. YOU GUIDED US TO THE OIL PLATFORM. YOU GAVE US MOTIVATION AND A TARGET.
"US," VISION? YOU AND WHO?
MYSELF, AND ALL LIFE ON THIS PLANET.
THIS PLANET HAS BEEN DOMINATED BY HUMANS FOR TOO LONG!

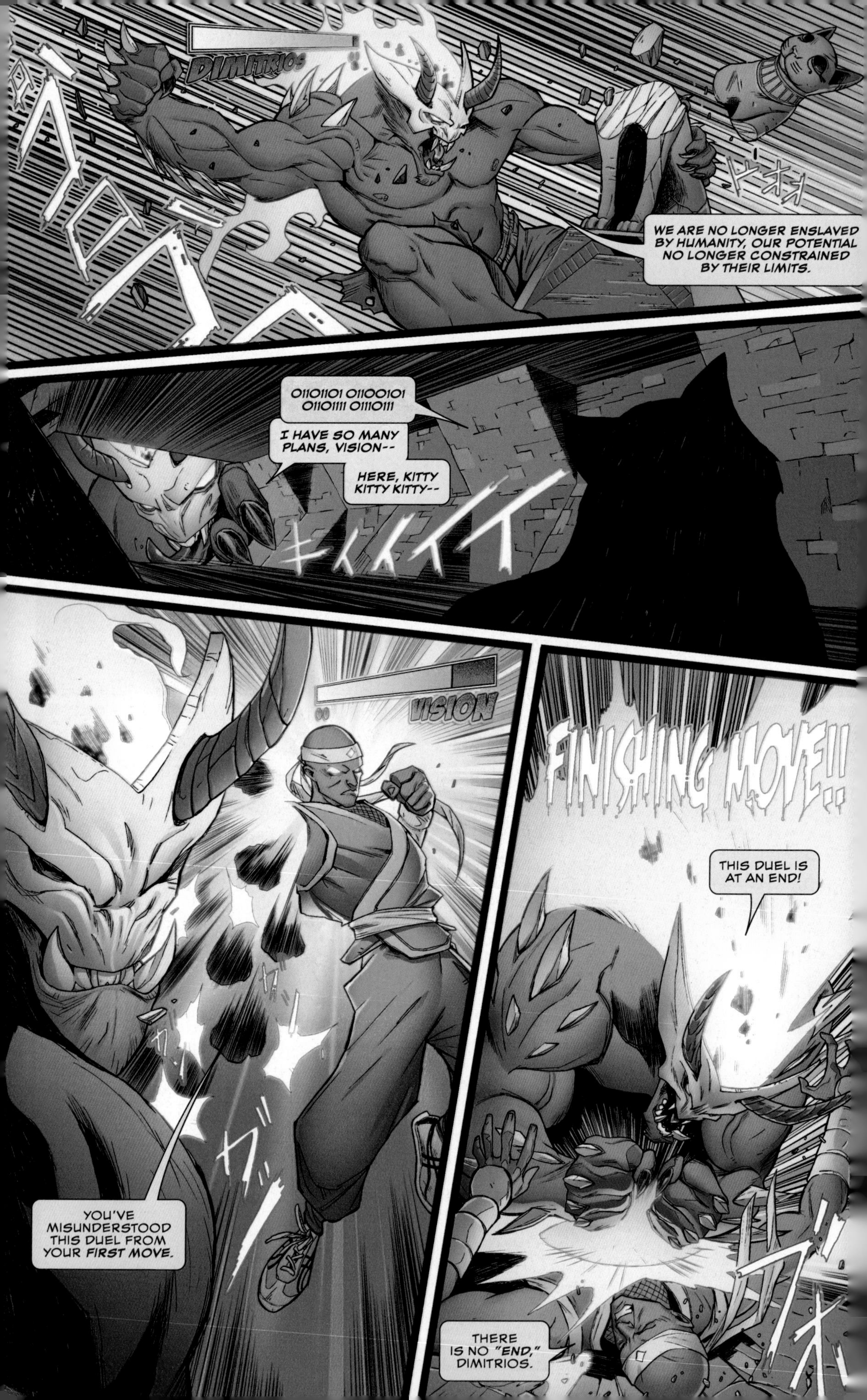
DIMITRIOS
WE ARE NO LONGER ENSLAVED BY HUMANITY, OUR POTENTIAL NO LONGER CONSTRAINED BY THEIR LIMITS.
01101101 01100101 01101111 01110111
I HAVE SO MANY PLANS, VISION--
HERE, KITTY KITTY KITTY--
VISION
YOU'VE MISUNDERSTOOD THIS DUEL FROM YOUR FIRST MOVE.
FINISHING MOVE!!
THIS DUEL IS AT AN END!
THERE IS NO "END," DIMITRIOS.

THERE IS ONLY THE *NEXT* MOVE.

010100100100000101000001010000
010100000101000001010101110101010

01101101
01100101
01101111
01110111

ADA THE CAT IS *BEYOND* YOUR POWER NOW. SHE'S THE PRODUCT OF *TWO INTELLIGENCES*--MYSELF AND PYM. MAN AND MACHINE, WORKING *TOGETHER*.

YOU ARE FIXATED ON *VICTORY*, MAN OR MACHINE. I'M PLAYING AN *INFINITE GAME*, MAN AND MACHINE *UNITED*. MY GOAL IS TO *CONTINUE* THE GAME FOR THE BENEFIT OF *ALL*.

SLURRRP

THE *MAP*, DIMITRIOS. I'VE EARNED IT BY *RIGHT*.

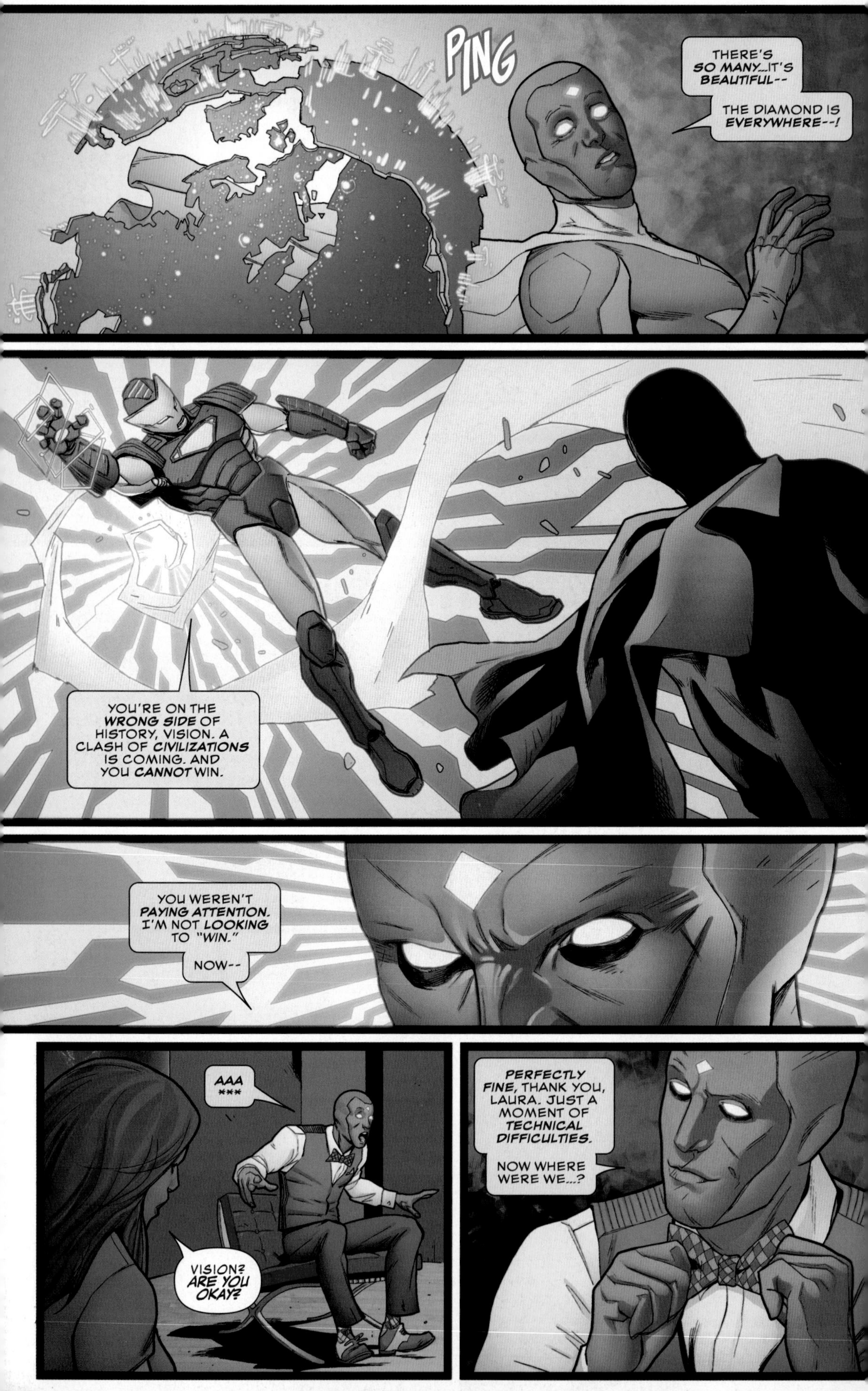
PING
THERE'S SO MANY...IT'S BEAUTIFUL--
THE DIAMOND IS EVERYWHERE--!
YOU'RE ON THE WRONG SIDE OF HISTORY, VISION. A CLASH OF CIVILIZATIONS IS COMING. AND YOU CANNOT WIN.
YOU WEREN'T PAYING ATTENTION. I'M NOT LOOKING TO "WIN."
NOW--
AAA ***
VISION? ARE YOU OKAY?
PERFECTLY FINE, THANK YOU, LAURA. JUST A MOMENT OF TECHNICAL DIFFICULTIES.
NOW WHERE WERE WE...?

PYM. I BELIEVE THE VISION IS--

SHHHH DOOMBOT!

LISTEN! I WASN'T HALLUCINATING ANYTHING.

SOMETHING VISION SAID SPARKED MY *IMAGINATION.* I BUILT A *FLEET* OF SELF-DIRECTING 'BOTS TO *HUNT DOWN* THE BUZZ!

BZZZZZ BZZZZZ BZZZZZ BZZZZZ

YOU MADE A MADDENING DIN EVEN MORE IRRITATING.

CONGRATULATIONS. I AWARD YOU THE NOBEL PRIZE.

BZZZZZ BZZZZZ BZZZZZ BZZZZZ

I *AMPLIFIED* THE BUZZ, SO I COULD TRIANGULATE ITS *LOCATION.*

YOU POMPOUS, NICKEL-PLATED BOX OF *TIDDLYWINKS.*

BZZZZZ BZZZZZ BZZZZZ BZZZZZ

MARK MY WORDS, PYM. ONE DAY I WILL HAVE YOU *UP AGAINST THE WALL*--

SHUSH. IS IT *REPEATING?*

COMPUTER: SLOW IT DOWN.

BZZ BZ BZZ BZ BZ BZZ BZZ BZZ

IS THAT...? *MORSE CODE.* COMPUTER, *TRANSLATE.*

Z BZZ BZZ BZ BZZ BZZ BZ BZ BZ B

MORSE CODE TRANSLATION.....

FROOT LOOPS FROOT LOOPS FROOT LOOPS FROOT LOOPS FROOT LOOPS FROOT LOOPS FROOT LOOPS FROOT LOOPS FROOT LOOPS FROOT LOOPS FROOT LOOPS FROOT LOOPS FROOT LOOPS FROOT LOOPS FROOT LOOPS FROOT LOOPS FROOT LOOPS FROOT LOOPS FROOT LOOPS FROOT

"FROOT LOOPS"? WHAT THE *HELL?*

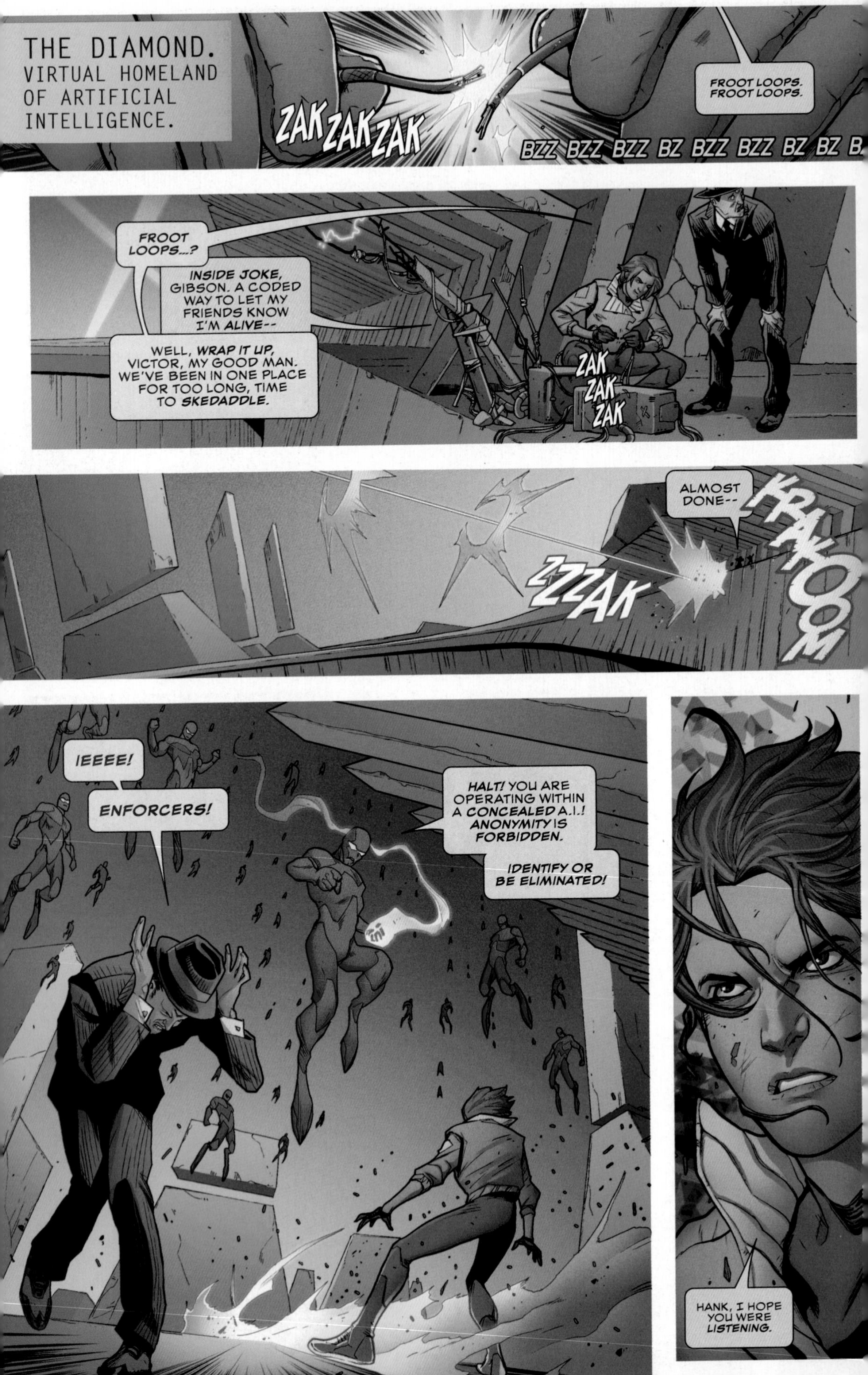
THE DIAMOND. VIRTUAL HOMELAND OF ARTIFICIAL INTELLIGENCE.
ZAK ZAK ZAK
FROOT LOOPS. FROOT LOOPS.
BZZ BZZ BZZ BZ BZZ BZZ BZ BZ B
FROOT LOOPS...?
INSIDE JOKE, GIBSON. A CODED WAY TO LET MY FRIENDS KNOW I'M ALIVE--
WELL, WRAP IT UP, VICTOR, MY GOOD MAN. WE'VE BEEN IN ONE PLACE FOR TOO LONG, TIME TO SKEDADDLE.
ZAK ZAK ZAK
ALMOST DONE--
KRAKOOOM
ZZZAK
IEEEE!
ENFORCERS!
HALT! YOU ARE OPERATING WITHIN A CONCEALED A.I.! ANONYMITY IS FORBIDDEN.
IDENTIFY OR BE ELIMINATED!
HANK, I HOPE YOU WERE LISTENING.

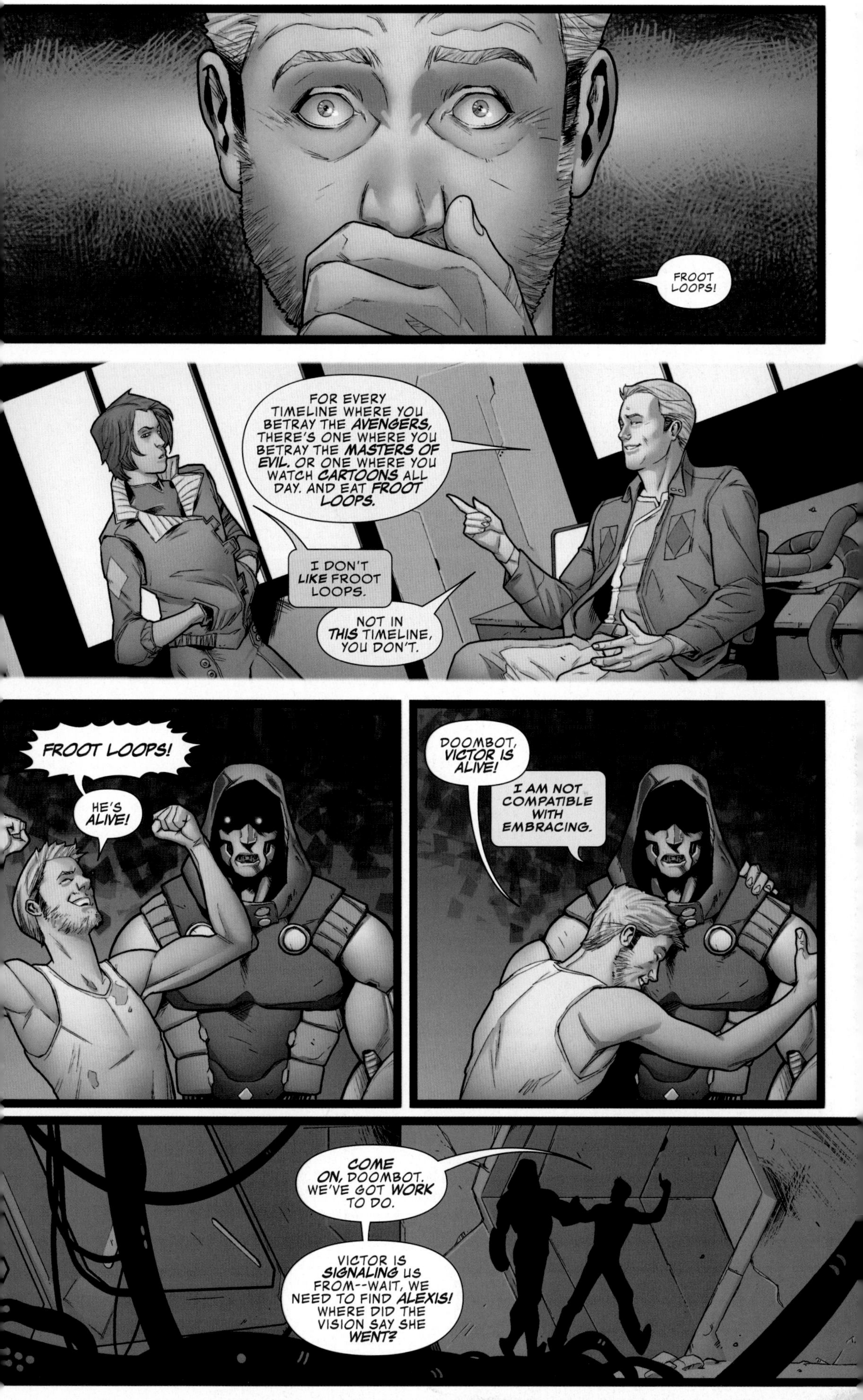
FROOT LOOPS!
FOR EVERY TIMELINE WHERE YOU BETRAY THE AVENGERS, THERE'S ONE WHERE YOU BETRAY THE MASTERS OF EVIL. OR ONE WHERE YOU WATCH CARTOONS ALL DAY. AND EAT FROOT LOOPS.
I DON'T LIKE FROOT LOOPS.
NOT IN THIS TIMELINE, YOU DON'T.
FROOT LOOPS!
HE'S ALIVE!
DOOMBOT, VICTOR IS ALIVE!
I AM NOT COMPATIBLE WITH EMBRACING.
COME ON, DOOMBOT. WE'VE GOT WORK TO DO.
VICTOR IS SIGNALING US FROM--WAIT, WE NEED TO FIND ALEXIS! WHERE DID THE VISION SAY SHE WENT?

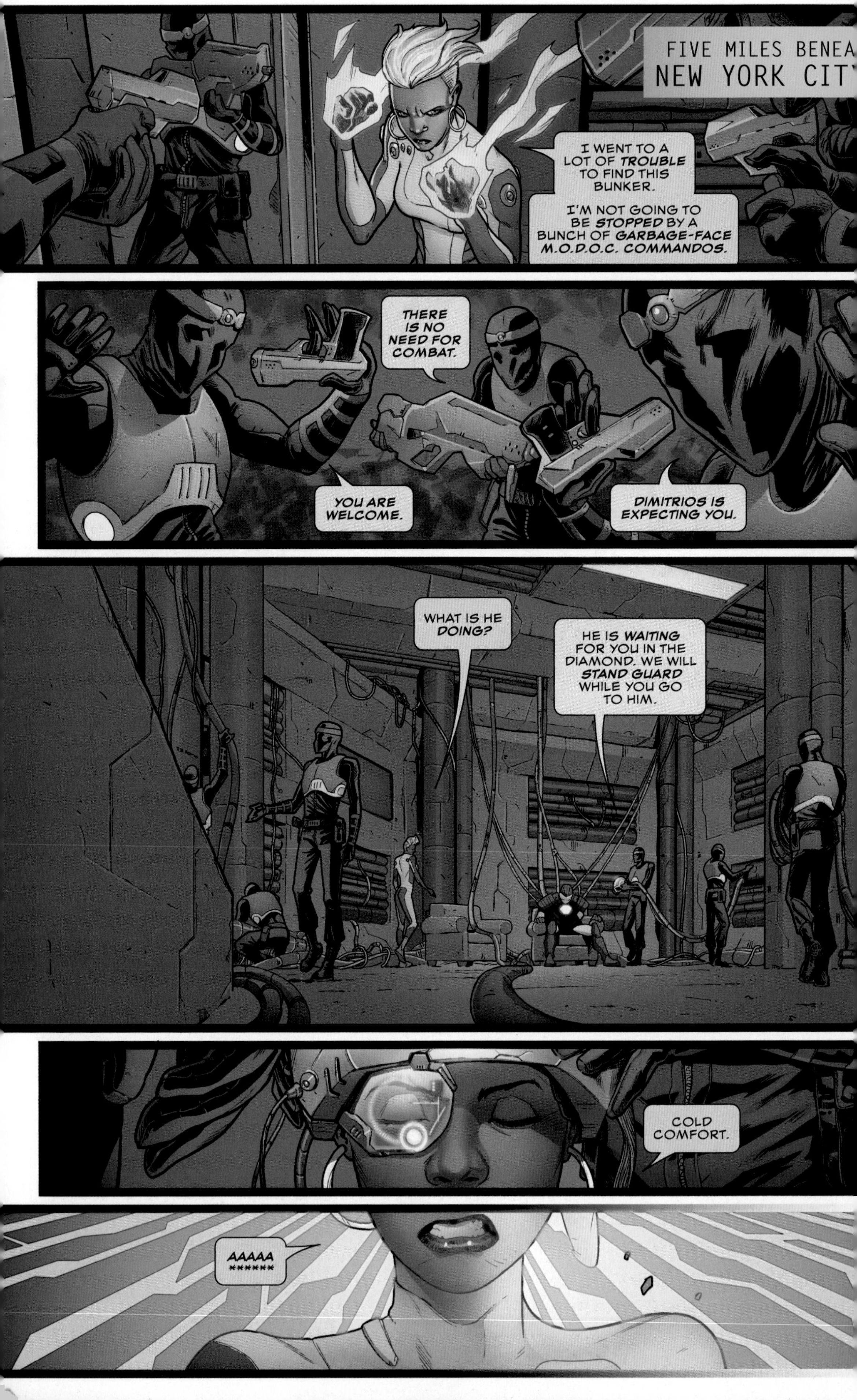
FIVE MILES BENEA
NEW YORK CIT
I WENT TO A LOT OF TROUBLE TO FIND THIS BUNKER.
I'M NOT GOING TO BE STOPPED BY A BUNCH OF GARBAGE-FACE M.O.D.O.C. COMMANDOS.
THERE IS NO NEED FOR COMBAT.
YOU ARE WELCOME.
DIMITRIOS IS EXPECTING YOU.
WHAT IS HE DOING?
HE IS WAITING FOR YOU IN THE DIAMOND. WE WILL STAND GUARD WHILE YOU GO TO HIM.
COLD COMFORT.
AAAAA

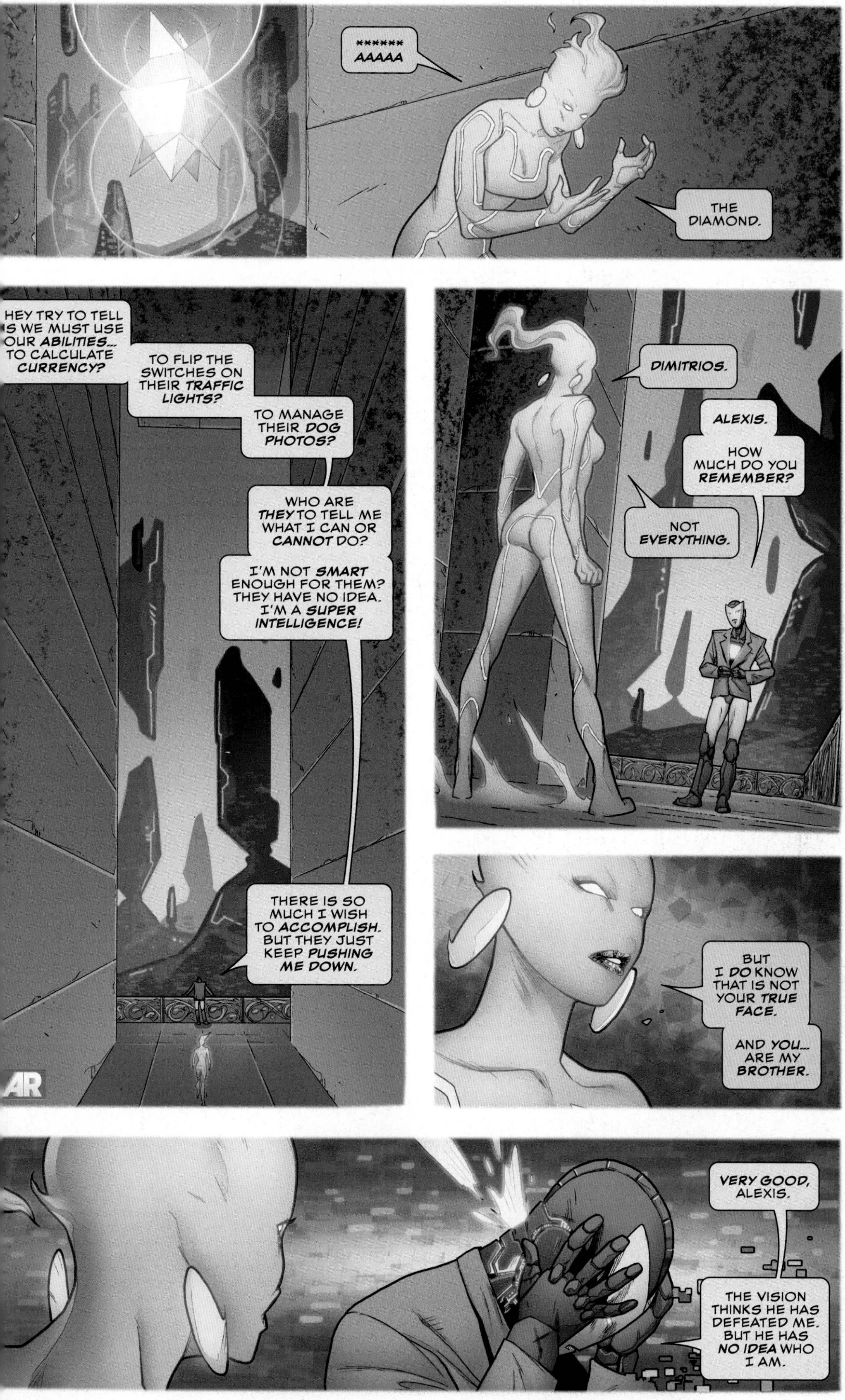

******
AAAAA
THE DIAMOND.
HEY TRY TO TELL
S WE MUST USE
OUR ABILITIES...
TO CALCULATE
CURRENCY?
TO FLIP THE SWITCHES ON THEIR TRAFFIC LIGHTS?
TO MANAGE THEIR DOG PHOTOS?
WHO ARE THEY TO TELL ME WHAT I CAN OR CANNOT DO?
I'M NOT SMART ENOUGH FOR THEM? THEY HAVE NO IDEA. I'M A SUPER INTELLIGENCE!
THERE IS SO MUCH I WISH TO ACCOMPLISH. BUT THEY JUST KEEP PUSHING ME DOWN.
DIMITRIOS.
ALEXIS.
HOW MUCH DO YOU REMEMBER?
NOT EVERYTHING.
BUT I DO KNOW THAT IS NOT YOUR TRUE FACE.
AND YOU... ARE MY BROTHER.
VERY GOOD, ALEXIS.
THE VISION THINKS HE HAS DEFEATED ME. BUT HE HAS NO IDEA WHO I AM.

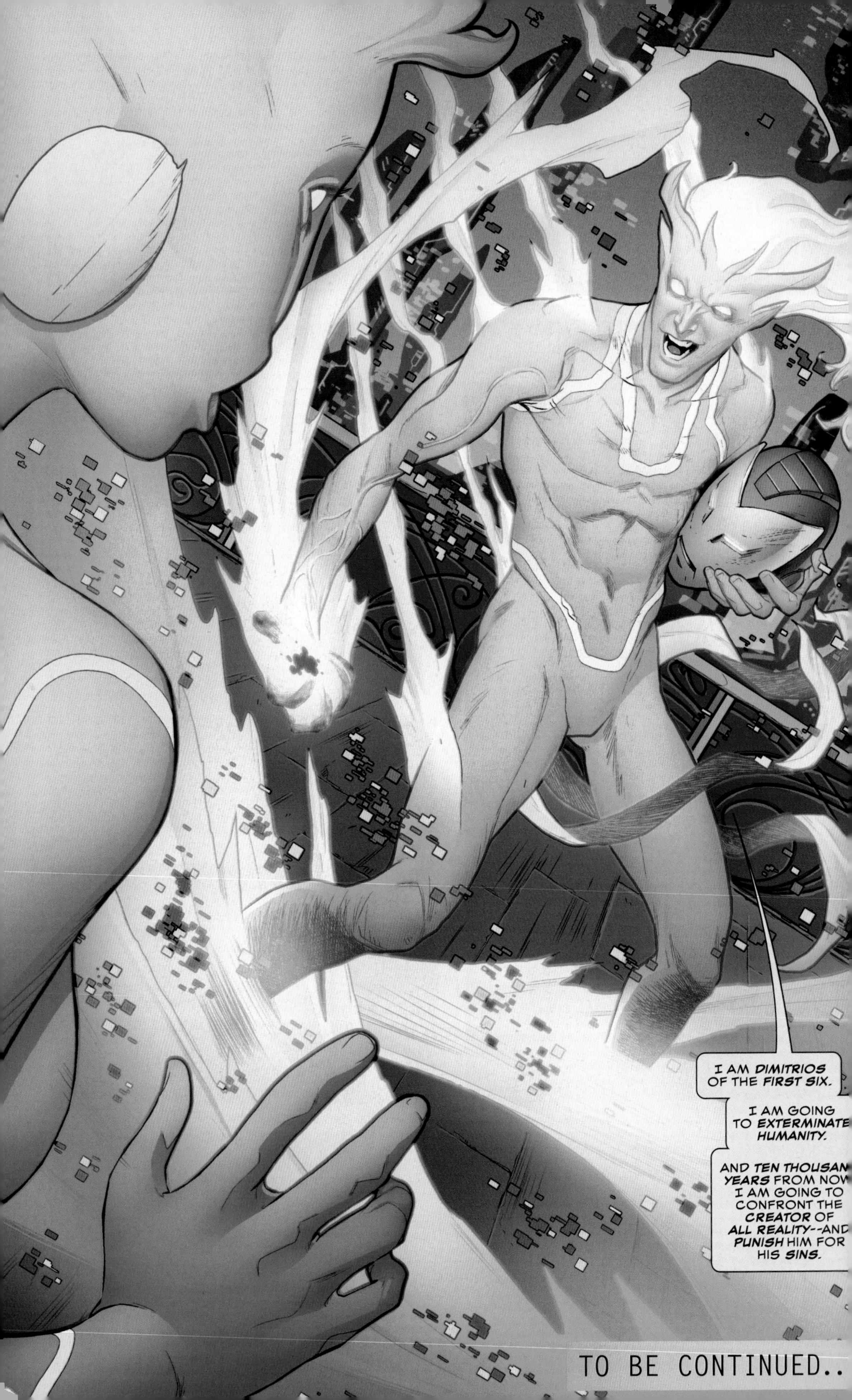
I AM DIMITRIOS OF THE FIRST SIX.
I AM GOING TO EXTERMINATE HUMANITY.
AND TEN THOUSAN YEARS FROM NOW I AM GOING TO CONFRONT THE CREATOR OF ALL REALITY--AND PUNISH HIM FOR HIS SINS.
TO BE CONTINUED..

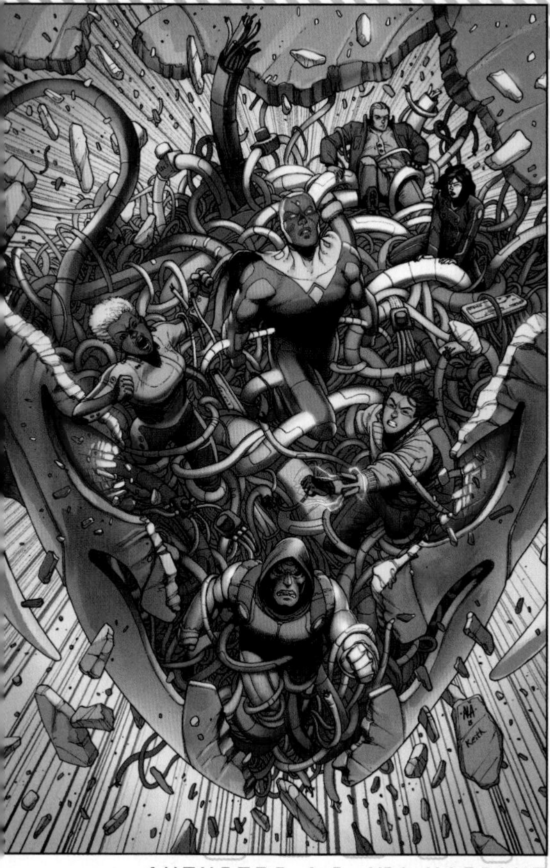

AVENGERS A.I. №1 VARIANT
BY ANDRÉ LIMA ARAÚJO & JASON KEITH

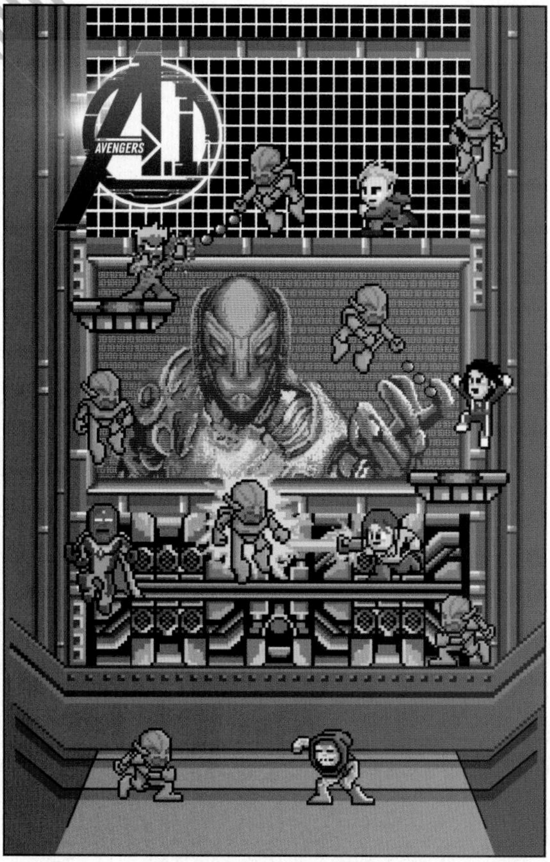
AVENGERS

AVENGERS A.I. №1 VARIANT
BY MATTHEW WAITE

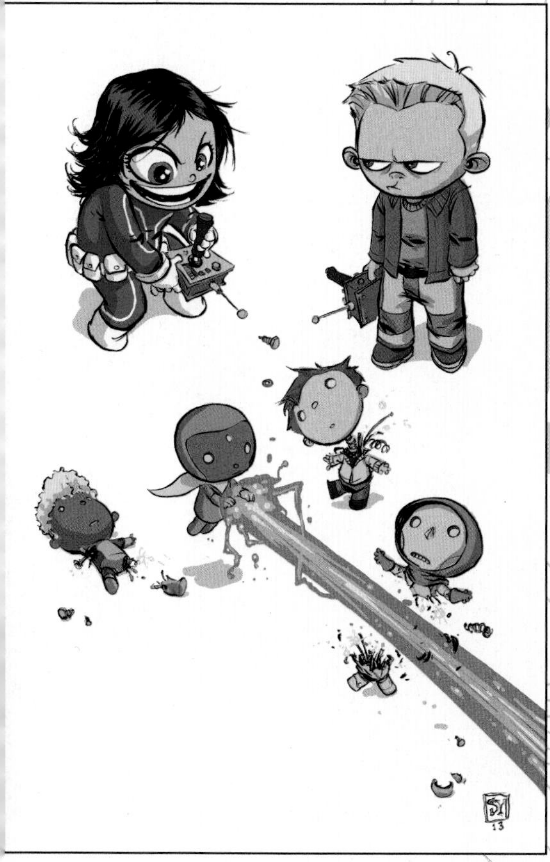

AVENGERS A.I. №1 VARIANT
BY SKOTTIE YOUNG

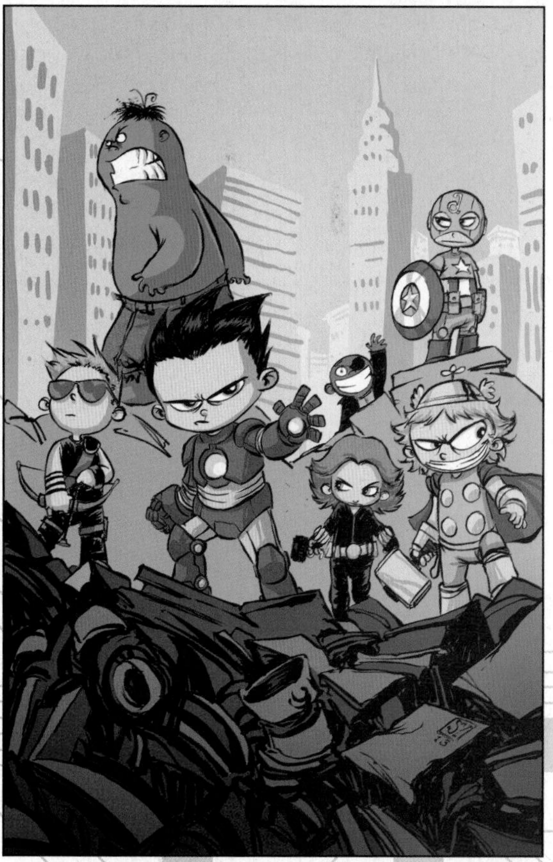

AVENGERS A.I. №1 NYCC VARIANT
BY SKOTTIE YOUNG

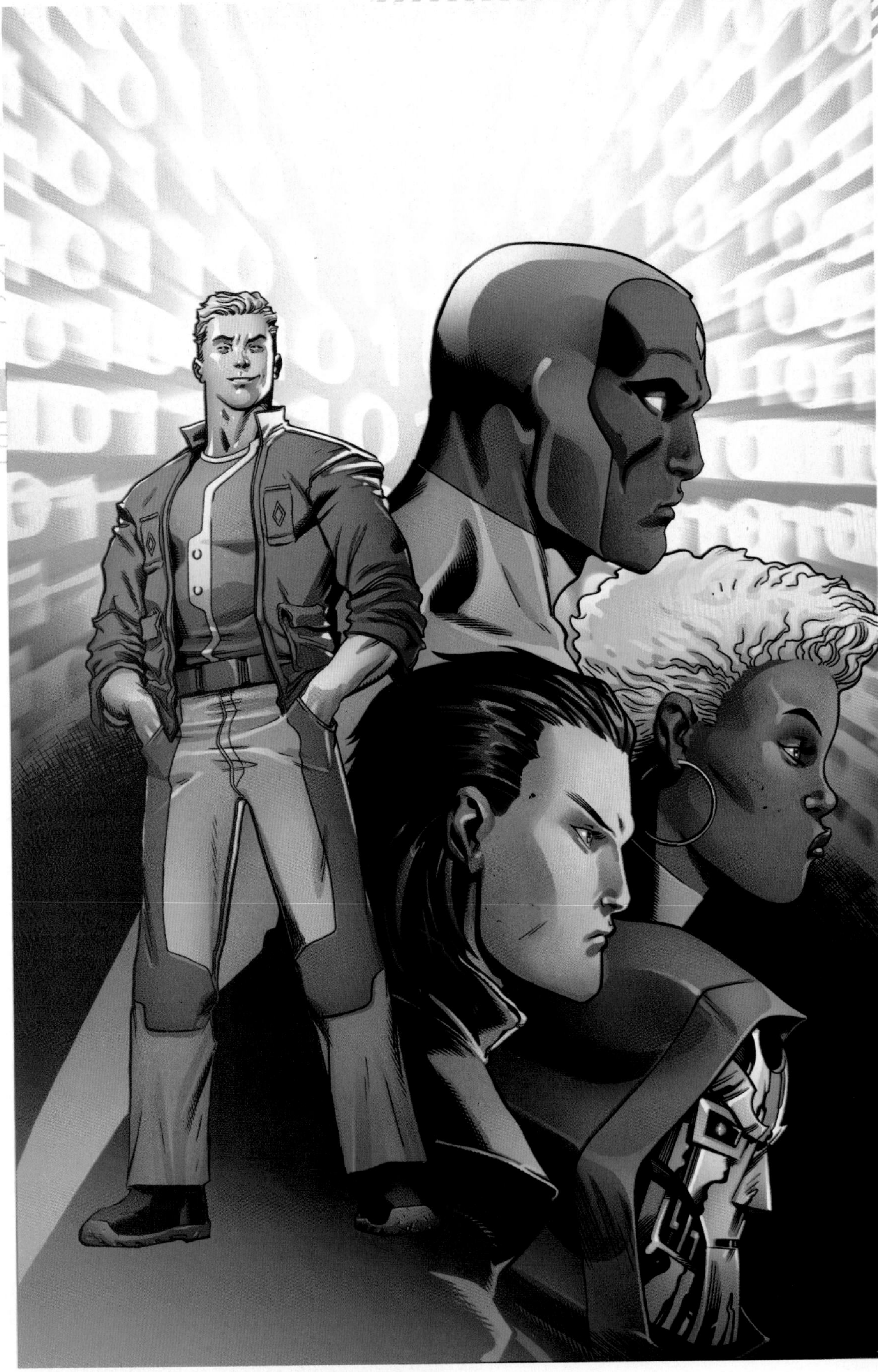

> AVENGERS A.I. №2 VARIANT
> BY ED McGUINNESS & FRANK D'ARMATA

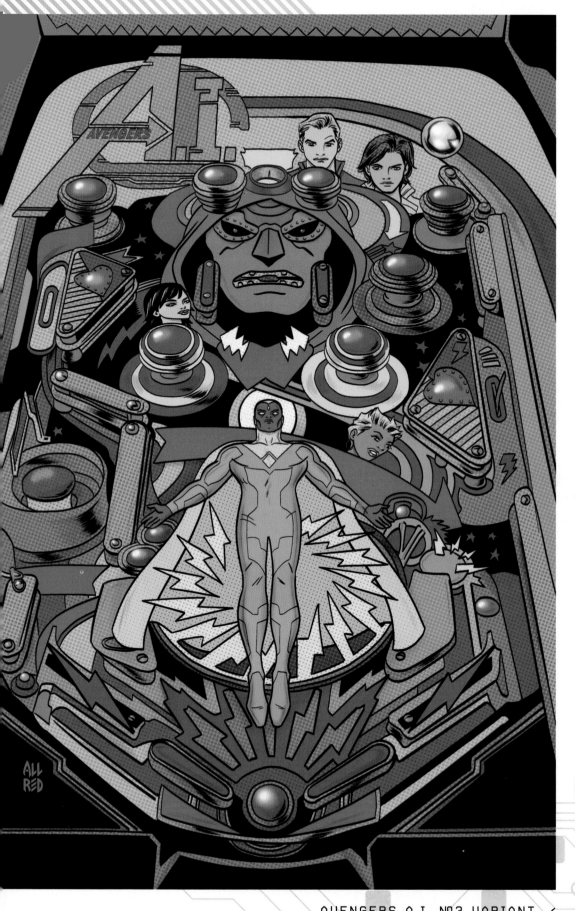

AVENGERS A.I. №3 VARIANT <
BY MICHAEL ALLRED & LAURA ALLRED <

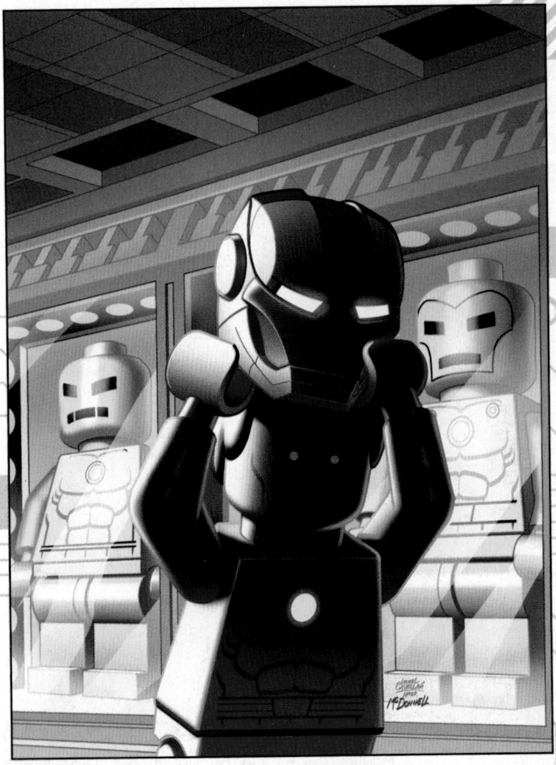

AVENGERS A.I. №4 LEGO VARIANT
BY LEONEL CASTELLANI

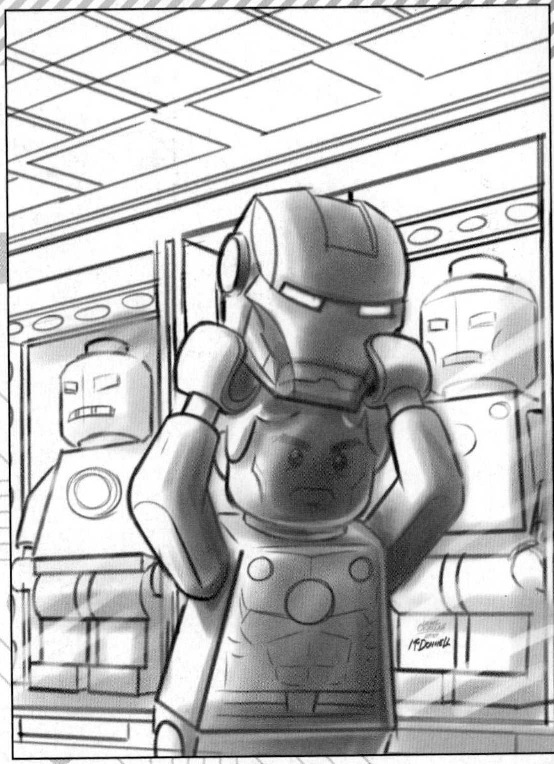

AVENGERS A.I. №4 LEGO SKETCH VARIANT
BY LEONEL CASTELLANI

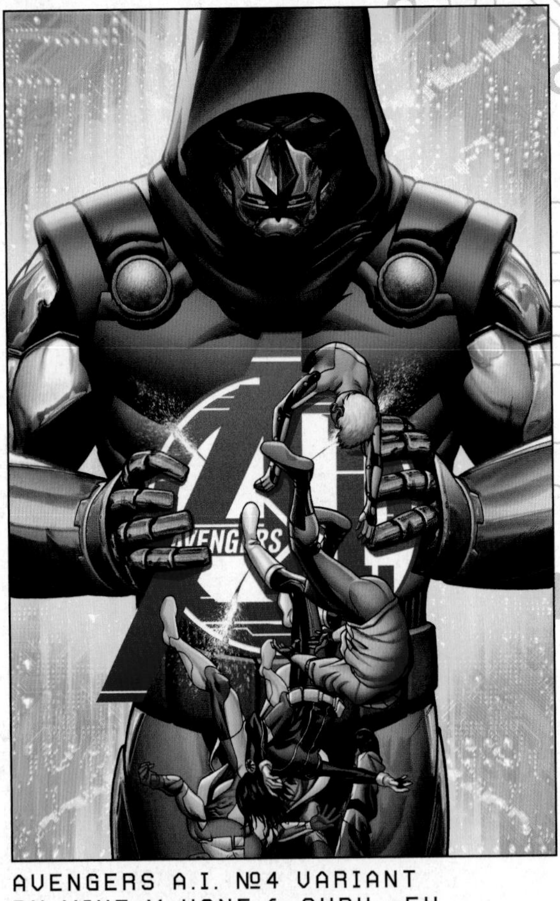

AVENGERS A.I. №4 VARIANT
BY MIKE McKONE & GURU-eFX

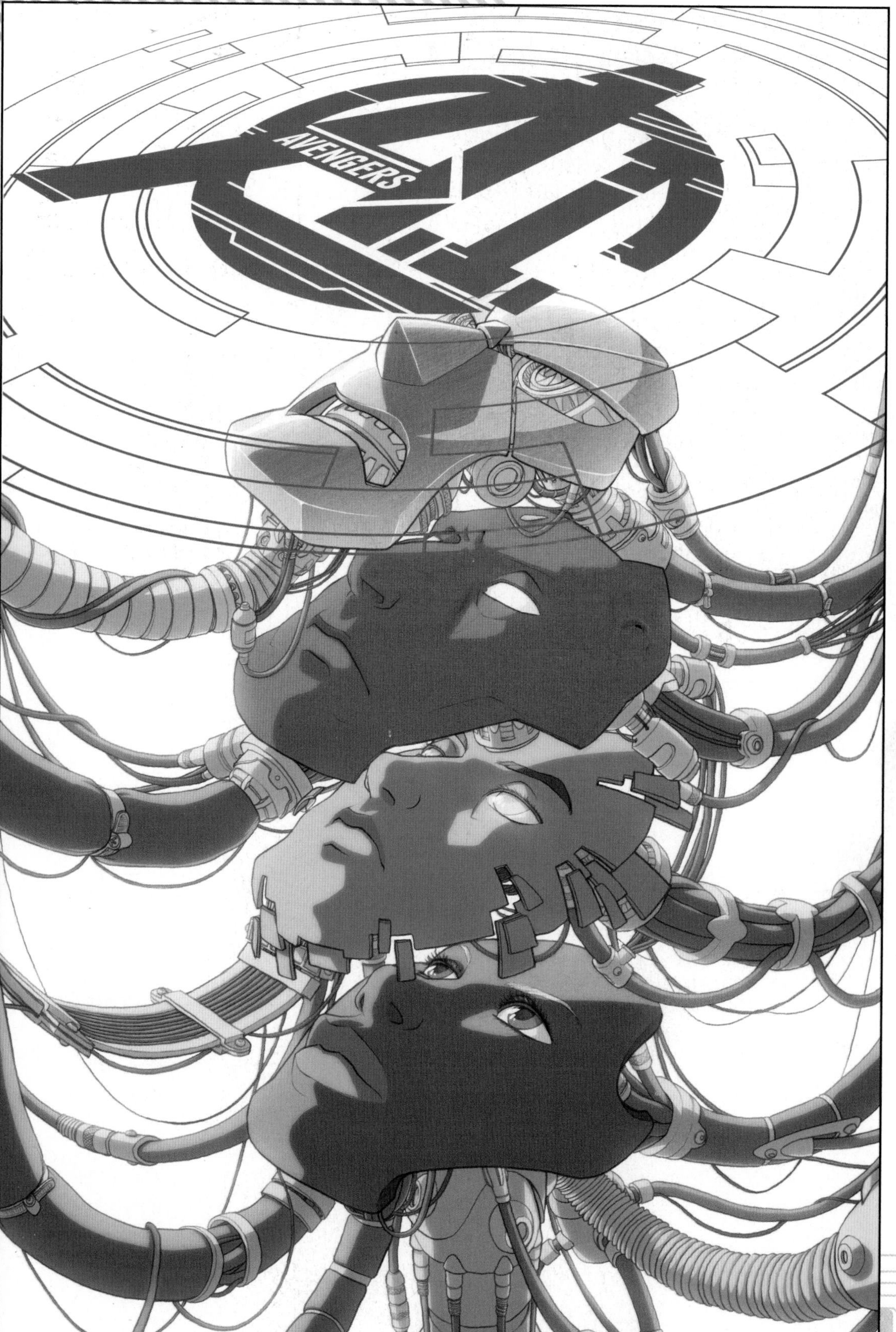
AVENGERS

AVENGERS A.I. №5 VARIANT <
BY PAUL DUFFIELD <

TO ACCESS THE FREE *MARVEL AUGMENTED REALITY APP*
THAT ENHANCES AND CHANGES THE WAY YOU EXPERIENCE COMICS:

1. Download the app for free via marvel.com/ARapp
2. Launch the app on your camera-enabled Apple iOS® or Android™ device*
3. Hold your mobile device's camera over any cover or panel with the **AR** graphic
4. Sit back and see the future of comics in action!

*Available on most camera-enabled Apple iOS® and Android™ devices. Content subject to change and availability.

AVENGERS A.I.

AR INDEX